SHOOTER'S GUIDE to AKs

MARCO VOROBIEV

Published by

Gun Digest® Books, an imprint of F+W Media, Inc.
Krause Publications • 700 East State Street • Iola, WI 54990-0001
715-445-2214 • 888-457-2873
www.krausebooks.com

To order books or other products call toll-free 1-800-258-0929
or visit us online at www.gundigeststore.com

ISBN-13: 978-1-4402-4641-8
ISBN-10: 1-4402-4641-6

Designed by Dane Royer
Edited by Chad Love

Printed in USA

10 9 8 7 6 5 4 3 2 1

RELATED TITLES

Gun Digest Book of Tactical Weapons
Assembly/Disassembly

Gun Digest Book of Centerfire Rifles
Assembly/Disassembly

Gun Digest Shooter's Guide to the AR-15

Standard Catalog of Military Firearms

Gun Digest Book of the AK/SKS

FOR MORE INFORMATION VISIT
GunDigestStore.com

CONTENTS

DEDICATION

To my father

In the life of every person there is someone who has impacted or influenced or even shaped their lives the most. Someone whom one would refer to every time that life demands an answer. What would he or she do?

For me it was my father, Evgenii (Eugene) Vorobiev. I am writing this book two months after his unexpected passing that hit me, and my family, as hard as a ton of bricks with the realization that there is no longer someone who can answer questions or make a suggestion or simply lend an ear. There is only this void that suddenly I have to fill for my kids.

Embarking on this project there was never a question for me who I would dedicate this book to. My father has influenced my life so much that I would say he shaped and molded me into the man I am today.

Growing up in war-torn Russia in a small village, my Dad had to hunt and fish for food at age five. He had to learn many other skills and trades the men of that time possessed. Kids of his generation had to grow up extremely fast, as most of their fathers perished in the war. They had to become the "men of the family" as did my Father.

As a young adolescent kid my Dad worked on the shipyards of the great Siberian rivers. At age 18 he, like all Soviet boys, was drafted into the Soviet Armed Forces and wound up on the Island of Sakhalin, where he served for three years sighting in regimental rifles.

I do not know where my father acquired his love for firearms; in the thick Murom Forests or on the barren rolling hills of Sakhalin, but he carried it through his life and passed it on to me. From age five my dad took me to the local market every free weekend for the purpose of visiting an air rifle range, where my father taught me very basics of marksmanship, and differences between slot and aperture sights. All of these are distant memories now, but I am sure they will last me a lifetime.

All of the adventures that my father and I went on were coupled with life and survival lessons that at the time I though nothing of, because I took my Dad's word for it. If he said we'd catch a fish, we caught it. If he said the storm will last for "X" number of hours, it did. If he built a shelter to keep us dry and warm, dry and warm we were. I took it as an axiom, a postulate of natural being, and if I found myself in the same situation again, I already knew what to do because my father taught me.

Looking back at time spent with my dad, if I had to highlight one thing about him, it would be his readiness, his steadfastness. Presented with a dilemma, he never hesitated. He always knew what to do and how to do it. He was ready and prepared.

Now that I am a dad myself with two rapidly growing boys, I try to pass on to them as much useful knowledge and teach them as many essential skills as I can. My main goal is not to make them into some superhumans, but reliable citizens who in the face of adversity could provide for themselves and their families and lend a helping hand to those in need. If I can teach them half of what my father passed on to me, I will have succeeded.

Thank you, Dad.

ACKNOWLEDGMENTS

In Russia they say, "Don't have 100 rubles, but have 100 friends." Everything we do in life, every path we take, is beset with people who influence the decisions we make. We hope that most if not all of those people are friends. I am lucky, my path took me far and wide where I've met many people whom I call friends. Some of them gave me inspiration that ultimately made this book possible. I want to thank my family, wife Barrie, and sons Brendan and Ian for putting up with me and sharing my hobbies; my deceased parents Tatiana and Evgenii Vorobiev for giving me life and instilling principals and virtues in me that I live by today.

I want to thank my friends who were always ready to lend a helping hand: Irek "Eric" Mustafin, David Fortier, Marc Krebs, Dillard "CJ" Johnson, Patrick Sweeney, Timothy Yan, Bill Alexander, Richard Parker, Anton Vatnitskiy and even James Tarr; and firearms industry professionals who one way or the other provided support and helped me to become a writer: Troy Storch, Bill Geissele, Steve Kehaya, Uli Wiegand, Tim Brandt, Bill Filbert, SGM Kyle Lamb USA (ret.), Jeff Hoffman, Joe Ancona.

Special thanks go out to the companies with innovative products that make it easy to tell a good story: Midwest Industries, Inc., MagPul, Krebs Custom, Inc., IO, Inc., Century Arms, Wolf Performance Ammunition, Hi-Lux, Inc., Elcan Optical Technologies, Black Hills Ammunition, Geissele Automatics, 5.11 Tactical, Hornady Ammunition and BLACKHAWK!.

I also want to thank the American firearm industry at large, without which I wouldn't have a job, and the main Law of the Land, aka the U.S. Constitution, that preserves and guarantees fundamental rights to the American citizens, including the right to have and bear arms.

A very special thanks to the man without whom the very idea for this book would not exist, the man whose wisdom I will cherish for the rest of my life – Mikhail Timofeyevich Kalashnikov.

Images in this book are by Peter Draugalis (www.draugalisphotography.com); Richard King (Richard King Photography); Marco, Brendan and Ian Vorobiev; and/or came from Vorobiev's personal archives and other open public sources.

ABOUT THE AUTHOR

Mark was born in the foothills of the Southern Ural Mountains in the city of Orsk in the Soviet Union, to Evgeniy and Tatiana Vorobiev. In 1973, his family relocated to a regional center city of Orenburg. Mark's father, an avid fisherman and hunter, would take Mark and his brother to the air rifle range every weekend to teach them the basics of marksmanship. At school Mark and his fellow students were introduced to .22 competition rifles and the basics of proper firearm handling. This would be coupled with by annual trips to the school's 50-meter gun range. At age 12 as part of scout games Mark was introduced to the AK rifle. At 15, Mark, as a future conscript, started the mandatory beginner's military preparation class at high school. By the time of graduation, Mark could disassemble an AK in twelve seconds flat and had shot his future service rifle twice.

Mark, like many Soviet boys, played ice hockey, but at age twelve he became interested in SAMBO wrestling and joined one of the premier clubs. At age fifteen, he had won junior national championship, and a year later he placed third in the USSR senior nationals.

After graduating from high school, Mark was accepted on an athletic scholarship to Orenburg Polytechnic Institute School of Mechanical Engineering, where he studied mechanical engineering and continued to wrestle, placing high at junior and senior nationals for both Sambo and Judo, earning him a rank of Master of Sports of USSR in Sambo, and Black Belt in Judo. At the end of his sophomore year at Orenburg Polytechnic Institute Mark transferred to Leningrad Institute of Railway Engineers in today's Saint Petersburg, where he continued to pursue a mechanical engineering degree.

His relationship with firearms continued when in the summer of 1985, Mark was drafted into military service. At the end of basic training at the Airborne training center, Mark was selected and transferred to SpetsNaz mountain training center, where he completed three months of training before being deployed to Afghanistan as a sniper and assaulter. Mark spent the next sixteen months fighting insurgents and interdicting the enemy's re-supply convoys and caravans. In February of 1987, Mark was airlifted out of Afghanistan after sustaining injuries in combat.

Mark spent the last months of his military service, and after recovery, wrestling for the Soviet Armed Forces. After discharge from military service, Mark continued his studies at the School of Mechanical Engineering at Railway Institute in Leningrad. In 1989, Mark moved to the United States and settled in Long Island, New York, where he got married and eventually started a long and successful career in the railroad industry. His sixteen-year-long railroad career took him to Alabama, back to Russia, Arizona, and Michigan, where he finally settled with his family.

In 1994, Mark's affinity for firearms led him to start collecting. His collection started with gathering rifles and handguns that were issued to him in the service and grew to a sizable collection of many variations of Kalashnikov rifles and other guns. At about the same time, Mark started consulting several writers and AK gunsmiths. In 2001 he organized and led a trip to Russia's arsenal city of Izhevsk to visit the famous Izhmash plant, the premier AK manufacturer in Russia. During that visit he met AK creator Mikhail Timofeyevich Kalashnikov.

After "retiring" form railroad work, Mark started his own consulting company that helped American companies to expand their business abroad, and it wasn't too long before the company's activities "spilled" over to the firearm side. In 2005 Mark's company launched a firearms and tactics training division that focuses on Warsaw Pact doctrine for small arms application.

In 2009, in response to calls from his firearm industry friends, Mark started to write. Since then he has written extensively about firearms and tactics. His articles have appeared in Guns & Ammo, Shotgun News, The Book of the AK, The Book of the AR, and Be Ready magazine, among others. Mark has hosted and appeared in many segments of G&A TV. He consulted and appeared in the NBC Discovery Production's "Foreign Special Ops" show on AHC (Military Channel) and the award-winning documentary "The Maidan Massacre".

Today he continues to write for several publications and consult for firearms, firearms accessories, and tactical gear manufacturers.

Mark lives in Ann Arbor Michigan with his wife and two sons.

FOREWORD

The Kalashnikov is not just 'a' rifle; it is one of the most significant rifle designs of the 20th Century. Mated to its stubby 7.62x39mm intermediate cartridge, the Avtomat redrew boundaries around the globe. It toppled old empires and created fresh ones that waved a red banner. In the 1960s and 1970s its distinctive report seemed to scream revolution. A generation of Americans came to know it in the jungles and rice paddies of South East Asia. Decades after the memories of Vietnam had faded their sons and daughters would meet it in the deserts and mountains of other far-off lands. Down through the decades the Kalashnikov earned an enviable reputation for reliability. Specifically designed as a compromise, the Kalashnikov's 'jack of all trades' personality is what makes it so affable. In the pages which follow Mark 'Marco' Vorobiev will introduce you to this fascinating Soviet design.

I have long been intrigued by the Kalashnikov, its development and performance, and this is how I came to meet Marco some 15 years ago. A mechanical engineer by trade, Marco's background includes service in the Soviet Union's elite Spetsnaz. Due to this he has a unique view of the Kalashnikov which is very different than your average American author. He writes as one systematically trained in the care, use, and employment of this design. Yet his knowledge goes far beyond simple theory or instruction. A veteran of the Soviet Union's war in Afghanistan, he has employed it in actual combat and credits the design with saving his life.

Marco's knowledge of the Kalashnikov isn't limited to his military service either. As a professional in the firearms industry Marco has traveled extensively in Russia and the United States to the factories where Kalashnikov rifles, accessories, and ammunition are produced. He has trained civilians, LE and military on operating and employing the Kalashnikov. Plus he has consulted with numerous companies on the development of new products and accessories. He has written extensively on the design and appeared on TV.

In the pages that follow Marco will open up the world of AK rifles and accessories in his unique style. Over the years I've read many books on AKs, most are put to best use stuffed under the leg of a wobbly table. This one is different. It is both a great read and chock-full of truly useful and practical information. I'm sure you will enjoy it as much as I did.

David M. Fortier
Editor Outdoor Sportsman Group's Book of the AK47

INTRODUCTION

I was introduced to the AK at an early age growing up in the Soviet Union. Never had I thought of it as anything but the most effective battle rifle out there. As I went through life I developed a more personal and almost intimate relationship with the Kalashnikov rifle. I got to know it on a closer level than most and I have learned a few things that are not common knowledge to some AK shooters. So, when I started writing this book, my intent was not to recycle same old information, but to write a book based on my personal experience and things I've learned and uncovered over the years. I wanted to share the information I possess with anyone, from someone who owns many AK rifles to those considering getting their first AK to those who just like reading about rifles and firearms in general. Nevertheless, in pages that follow I've attempted to cover most of the important information pertaining to the AK rifles. I may have dropped a detail or two, but if you'd discover at least one interesting thing about an AK rifle that you did not know before reading this book, then I've succeeded..

CHAPTER ONE

THE AK:
RIFLE FOR THE MOTHERLAND

The appearance of the AK Rifle on the world stage was spurred not by the ambition of some government, but by the drive of one soldier to help his Motherland. It was in the hospital while recovering from wounds sustained in combat that Tank Corps Sergeant Mikhail Kalashnikov first had the idea to create an entirely new infantry rifle. After talking to many wounded infantry soldiers, the aspiring designer drew a picture of many shortcomings with Soviet small arms that were carried into combat against well-armed and equipped enemies.

He wanted to create a gun that would give his Motherland an advantage on the battlefield. Unlike many firearms designers, Kalashnikov was driven with only one desire: to make a contribution to his country's victory over Nazi Germany.

He started work on his new gun in 1943 in Kazakhstan, where he was recovering from his wounds. It was there, and not in Tula or

When asked, Lt. General Mikhail Timofeyevich Kalashnikov would always say that he wanted to create a rifle that would help his Motherland win the war.

The Kalashnikov's first working gun was assembled at the railroad depot in Kazakhstan. It looked nothing the AK we know today.

The very first variant of Kalashnikov's rifle was submitted for testing in 1946. It started to resemble the current AK rifles.

Hugo Schmeisser creation the MP43. It was later named the Stumgewehr 44 by Hitler himself and was the first mass produced assault rifle.

Izhevsk Arsenals, where the AK rifle got its roots. Later came years of trial-and-error, configurations and re-configurations, with relocation to the Degtyaryov Machine Plant in the city of Kovrov, before the very first AK sample was presented for testing in 1946.

Meanwhile, the Germans were delivering a new rifle of their own to the battlefields of WWII - The MP 43 (Machinenpistole Model 1943), or later renamed by the Fuhrer himself, Stg .44 (Sturmgewehr Model 1944), the world's first assault rifle.

The new rifle, created by Hugo Schmeisser, did not employ any new technological principals or concepts. After all, the concept of a battle rifle capable of full automatic fire and chambered for a less powerful cartridge compared to the conventional rifle caliber belonged to the Russian designer Vladimir Fyodorov and his automatic rifle.

Adapted for service with the Russian Imperial Army, the Avtomat Fyodorova (Fyodorov Automatic) chambered in the lighter 6.5X50mm Arisaka cartridge, was put into mass production in 1915 and saw service in WWI, the Bolshevik Revolution, the Russian Civil War and the Soviet "Winter" War against Finland.

However, the true breakthrough for the new Stg .44 gun was the design and development of a new intermediate rifle cartridge, the 7.92X33mm Kurtz. This laid the basis for the development of virtually all modern carbine cartridges, including the infamous Soviet 7.62X39mm Model 1943, or as it is known, the M43 round. Another of Schmeisser's achievements was the creation of a reliable rifle that could be built out of stamped steel and supplied to the troops quickly and in large numbers.

The Avtomat Fyodorova truly was the first assault rifle created during WWI by Russian designer Vladimir Fyodorov.

The Fyodorov Automatic Rifle fired the smaller 6.5X5 mm Arisaka rifle cartridge and was capable of full-automatic fire.

The Avtomat Fyodorova saw action in WWI, Bolshevik Revolution, Russian Civil War and the Russo-Finnish Winter War. Troops on both sides used these rifles.

The decision to transition all the main small arms in the Soviet Union to an intermediate cartridge was made while WWII was still raging. Such a cartridge had been created by 1943, and shortly thereafter the development of the entire family of small arms began, including a self-loading carbine (SKS), the automatic assault rifle, and a light machine gun (RPD).

Several designers and designer teams entered the assault rifle development competition, and among them was young sergeant Mikhail Timofeyevich Kalashnikov, who at that time was already working on his new rifle.

In 1946 Kalashnikov and his team, alongside other participants, submitted a sample of his automat (автомат) to the competitive evaluation, where it demonstrated very good results.

One of the revolutionary concepts of the new Sturmgewehr rifle was the intermediate cartridge it fired (Right). Based on this concept, the Soviets developed their own cartridge, the M43 (Left).

For the second stage of the competition that took place in 1947, Kalashnikov reworked his rifle, and in the modified form it was recommended for acceptance by the Armed Forces. After initial army tests in 1949 Kalashnikov's automatic rifle was officially accepted as "7.62mm Kalashnikov's Automatic Rifle model 1947", or more simply, AK (sometimes in addition designate AK-47). In its original form the AK-47 had a combination receiver assembled from stamped and milled parts, however that design proved to be insufficiently rigid, so the AK-47 went into mass production with a fully milled receiver.

One of the myths connected with the AK is that Kalashnikov "copied" the AK from the German WWII assault rifle known as the Stg.44. At first glance, the external configuration of the AK and the Stg.44 is similar, as is the concept of the automatic weapon firing an intermediate cartridge. Similar barrel outlines, front sights and gas tubes are caused by the utilization of similar gas systems invented long before Schmeisser and Kalashnikov.

Other than mere appearance, however, these rifles couldn't be more different. It is quite probable that Mikhail Kalashnikov knew about the Stg.44, however it is also

The milled receiver version of the Kalashnikov rifle is what is commonly known as the AK-47 and was the first variant produced on a truly mass scale.

Although similar at first glance the StG 44 and AK-47 cannot be more different by the way they are configured and how they operate.

obvious that the creation of his rifle was guided by other known samples and systems. Kalashnikov's main achievement (or his team's, to be exact) was optimum configuration of already known and proven solutions into one uniform working machine that met all the requirements.

In fact, the AR-15 has more similarities with StG44, configuration and feature-wise.

Later, the original Kalashnikov design saw several changes. Due to a production expense the milled receiver was ditched in favor of a more economical and lighter stamped one. A muzzle brake compensator was added and the bayonet-knife was redesigned.

EVERYMAN'S RIFLE

The inherent reliability, simplicity of production, and the simplicity of operation saw a huge demand for the new rifle. By the 1950's, the entire 1.5 million-strong Soviet Armed Forces were armed with AKs. After signing the Warsaw Pact that united militaries of all the socialist states in Europe, the need arose to standardize the way combined forces were armed and how they fought.

At the same time, scores of new AK rifles were already being supplied to communist China. Arming the Warsaw Pact allies put a strain on the Soviet firearm industry, so the decision was made to start licensing other countries to build their own AK rifles. This move would ultimately provide the necessary relieve to increase domestic production and grow the import of AKs to the USSR "friendlies" around the world.

This is a prop for Soviet Action movie with "bad" Americans. On order from movie studios, captured StG44s were converted to look similar to M-16 rifles by the Soviet Kovrov Arsenal. It had to fire blank ammunition.

Mikhail Kalashnikov's rifle persevered. Its original design was far ahead of its time and remains the basis for new AK rifles.

China was the first "friendly" country that received a license to manufacture its own AK.

The AK got its widespread "popularity" in the US when it appeared on TV news reports from the battlefields of Vietnam.

Rumor has that US GIs in Vietnam would drop their issued M16s and pick up an AK instead. I seriously doubt that was a widespread practice and in no way would be condoned by the US top brass.

AKs saw a great amount of action in Afghanistan during the Soviet-Afghan Campaign. Here is a Soviet Motorized Infantry company resting on the march.

In Afghanistan AKs were used by all warring parties. Here Akhmat Shah Masood, one of the more successful Mujahedeen commanders, instructs his personnel.

In Africa the AK has become the main battle rifle for every armed group both government and tribal.

Most of the African countries involved in anti-colonial movements received "generous" help in the way of military aid from the Soviets. The aid usually included a healthy helping of Kalashnikovs.

The Northern Africa and Middle Eastern countries were also "assisted" by Soviets with supplies of AK rifles. Egypt however, secured a license to produce its own AKs.

Proliferation of the AK throughout the world was done both ways: in the form of the ready weapon, and in the form of licenses to manufacture with all necessary documentation, tooling, and technical assistance.

AKs were manufactured in Bulgaria, Hungary, East Germany, Egypt, Iraq, China, Romania, North Korea, India, Finland, and Cuba. Even greater numbers were simply "given" to numerous other countries, basically anyone who would, even in passing, mention sympathy to the Marxist-Leninist ideology. The post-Soviet Union era saw the continuation of those licensing practices, with factories built in Venezuela, Libya, and Malaysia.

The spread of this iconic weapon is so wide that it is almost impossible to imagine an armed conflict today without an AK playing first fiddle in it. The rifle had seen service in every conflict in every theatre, from Korea to the present. Every so-called revolutionary

Poland used to manufacture its own AK rifles. Today as a NATO member Poland continues to produce the highly-modernized Beryl AK.

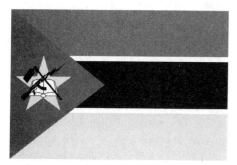

Many view the AK rifle as a symbol of resistance and liberation. Several countries have it on their state emblem or flags.

Many countries' armed forces use the Kalashnikov rifle or one of its variants as their main battle rifle. In fact, more men and women in uniform carry AKs today than any other rifle, bar none. No other rifle even comes close.

Kalashnikov's rifle has, to some extent, served as an example for design and development of such systems as Valmet (Finland), INSAS (India), Galil (Israel) and the SIG SG-550 (Switzerland). Commercial semi-automatic variants of the AK rifle enjoy considerable popularity in Russia and abroad, especially here in the US.

A truly prolific weapon, the AK in one form or another has been and continues to be sold by the millions. It is estimated that over 70 million rifles have been produced and sold worldwide.

group in South America, every anti-colonial movement in Africa in 60's and 70's, every anti-west organization in the Middle East in the 80's, every Balkan conflict in the 90's, Iraq, Afghanistan, Al-Qaida, and ISIS, all are forever associated with AK rifles.

CHAPTER TWO

AK EVOLUTION

The final version of Kalashnikov's rifle was the AK-47. Following the great initial success of the design it was clear that some improvements were needed to make the gun easier and cheaper to produce

Borrowed from the German MP38-40 design, the under-folding stock made it possible to develop the paratrooper variant of the AK-47, called the AKS-47.

By 1959, based on feedback from the field, the AK had been modified, and in that same year the new, modernized AKM rifle - Kalashnikov's Automatic Rifle Modernized - was adopted.

The differences included, first and foremost, a lighter stamped steel receiver. In addition, the buttstock was raised upwards and the trigger group was redesigned to include a hammer retarder (often mistakenly referred to as a rate of fire retarder).

Along with the AKM, a new bayonet knife was adopted. The new knife had a hole in its blade that allowed it to be used together with the scabbard as a wire cutter. One more improvement that appeared on the AKM rifle was the muzzle brake-compensator that screwed on to the threaded tip of the barrel. The threaded barrel also allowed the use of other devices such as the PBC-1 sound suppressor.

In addition the AKM also received a rear sight marked up to 1000 meters instead of the AK-47's 800 meters.

In 1974 the Soviet Armed Forces adopted the 5.45mm small arms system consisting of the AK-74 automatic assault rifle and RP -74 light machine gun.

AK-74 FAMILY OF RIFLES

The 5.45mm AK-74 assault rifle (Avtomat Kalashnikova Obraztsa 1974 goda, Index 6P20) was adopted for service with the Soviet Armed Forces in March of 1974. The new weapons family chambered for the 5.45X39mm low impulse cartridge consisted of four versions of the assault rifles and the same number of light machine guns or squad automatics.

The hard financial situation in Russia in the early 1990s saw Russian small arms manufacturers reaching to their foreign customers with introduction of two new rifles based on successful AK-74M configuration: the 7.62X39 mm AK-103 and 5.56X45 mm (NATO) AK-101.

In 1974 a new family of AKs was adapted by the Soviet Armed Forces. The AK-74 family rifles fired the subcaliber 5.45X39 mm cartridge.

The folding stock variant, the AKS-74, was the main rifle of the Soviet reconnaissance and SpetsNaz units.

The new AK-74 rifle included a total of nine assemblies representing 36 percent of the original design, and 52 individual parts representing 52 percent of the AKM rifle that came directly from the original AK-47 design; this led to the simplification of the manufacturing process and a faster production launch.

Barrels were manufactured using a cold-rotating forging, and the bores were chrome lined utilizing an enhanced technology. A new two-chamber muzzle device performed the dual functions of muzzle brake-compensator and flash suppresser.

The 30-round box-type magazines were curved and originally made of Bakelite. Later versions were made of high-impact plastic and had a staggered cartridge arrangement.

The AKS-74 (6P21) model with a metallic folding (to the left side) triangular skeletonized stock was designated the Paratrooper model. The AK-74N (N-2) and AKS-74N (N-2) modifications featured a universal side-mounted rail designed to accommodate

Replacing the automatic Stechking pistol then in service with tank, APC, and artillery crews, the AKS-74U shorty was a logical choice due to its commonality with the main AK-74 battle rifle.

a night vision scope or optical sights.

The AK-74 family of guns also included 4 variations of squad automatics or light machine guns; the RPK 74, the RPKS 74 Paratrooper model with folding stock as well as both variant equipped with optics rail and designated RPK 74N and RPKS 74N2, respectively.

One more rifle from the same family that is worth mentioning is the famed AK-74 short version AKS-74U.

Here in the States, for some strange reason it's called the "Krinkov". As a Russian speaker I do not know what this word means or how it came to be.

Designed as a personal defense weapon for tankers, APC drivers, artillery crews and helicopter pilots, it was to replace the Stechkin Automatic Pistol (APS). It packed far more serious firepower than a pistol, even an automatic pistol.

However, it did not get the intended respect among the troops, especially the Spetsnaz. It did not offer any advantages over the regular AKS rifles and was always discarded in favor of its full-length siblings. However, the AKSU or "Suchka", "Ksyuha" or "Okurok" ("little bitch", women's name "Kseniya", and "cigarette butt" respectively) had a "cool" appearance and was often used as a prop for picture taking.

AKS IN AFGHANISTAN

The 5.45-caliber AK-74 and its folding model AKS-74 assault rifles were the most widely issued main battle rifle to the Soviet Armed Forces in Afghanistan. It was issued with a bayonet that had to be numbered to the gun, a belt pouch that had to be identified to the individual with hand-made wooden tag (later in the war use of belt pouches was all but abandoned in favor of captured or hand-made chest pouches and post-'85 Soviet-made chest pouches called "Lifchik"), cleaning kit, oil bottle, four 30-round magazines, 4 stripper clips with loading spoon, and a drop case that no one ever used.

The Spetsnaz units were mainly armed, among other weapons, with the AKS-74 (folder) and AKS-74N (with optics rail).

The AK-74 was the main battle rifle that the Soviets used entering their Afghan campaign in 1979. It performed extremely well in the extreme environment conditions present in Afghanistan.

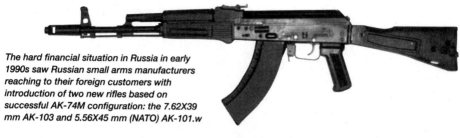

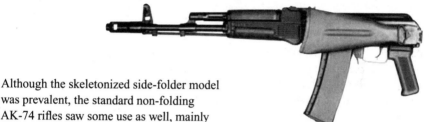

The hard financial situation in Russia in early 1990s saw Russian small arms manufacturers reaching to their foreign customers with introduction of two new rifles based on successful AK-74M configuration: the 7.62X39 mm AK-103 and 5.56X45 mm (NATO) AK-101.w

Although the skeletonized side-folder model was prevalent, the standard non-folding AK-74 rifles saw some use as well, mainly because these rifles had a side rail installed for use with optics and had a designation "N" for night vision.

Many would argue that some Spetsnaz soldiers preferred the 7.62mm-chambered AKM to the 5.45mm AK-74 due to its better stopping power. As valid as this argument may be, other reasons may have had more weight. The main rifle of the opposition was a Chinese clone of the AK-47 chambered in 7.62X39, and the ability to "refill" magazines with captured ammo on long-range patrols was by far a more valid reason than stopping power to prefer the AKM.

The other reason for widespread use of the older AKM rifles was due to a lack of silenced devices for AK-74 guns. However, the proven PBS-1 silencer that was designed for 7.62X39 AKM rifles was widely utilized, with good effect, when used to engage sentries or point guards.

CONTINUED EVOLUTION

Even today, a significant number of AKM 7.62mm rifles still remain in service with various branches of the Russian military, as well as the Russian Interior Ministry and police units.

The advantages of the AK rifle are well

known. Its exceptional reliability even in the most adverse operating conditions, its simplicity in use and service, and its ease and low cost of production are legendary.

However, by Western standards the rifle does have a few "kinks". First of all, the less-than-perfect ergonomics of the weapon - especially its safety/rate of fire lever that when operated is rather awkward and makes a loud and distinct click. The standard "U" slotted rear sight may be considered less than convenient, especially for an American shooter. Personally I think it is an advantage in a dynamic firefight.

Other "western" complaints included a shorter so-called aiming or sight radius, representing a distance between the rear and front sights in comparison to an AR. Supposedly making a rifle with a longer sight radius makes it more accurate. However, the ability of the shooter is not taken into the consideration in this argument, and this point became moot with the introduction of the M4 carbine as the US Armed Forces main infantry weapon. A side-by-side comparison reveals that the standard M4 carbine's sight radius is one inch shorter than that of the AK.

Many would also argue that Kalashnikov's rifle is outdated, but results speak for themselves, and after more that 60 years of service with first the Soviet and later Russian Armed Forces, as well as many other countries, the AK rifle continues to be a main battle rifle for militaries around the world.

After the dissolution of the Soviet Union in 1991 the newly-democratic Russia saw tough economic times coupled with no political obstacles to explore newly-opened arms markets. The main Russian AK arsenal, the Izhevskiy Machine Building Plant, "Izhmash" for short, introduced its first "black rifle," the newly updated AK-74M featuring black polyamide plastic furniture, including a folding stock and standard optics rail.

At the same time the Russian Armed Forces launched a cautious re-armament program with the newly-adopted main battle rifle.

The initial success and expansion of NATO into the Eastern European countries inspired Izhmash to introduce several models in all three main carbine calibers: 7.62X39mm, 5.45X39mm, and 5.56X45mm NATO (.223 Remington). These models were based on the successful AK-74M in hopes of appealing to those new Warsaw Pact-to-NATO converts.

The new family of rifles was called the 100 Series and included - apart from the above

The short "sighting radius" as a distance between front and rear sight argument as one of the AK shortcomings impacting its accuracy is no longer valid with adaption by the U.S. Armed Forces of an M4 carbine.

mentioned AK-74M, the AK-101 in 5.56 NATO and AK-103 in 7.62X39mm calibers. All three new rifles were full-length carbines and featured the very effective AK-74-style muzzle brake, a side rail for mounting optics, and new black plastic furniture with now-standard side-folding solid plastic buttstock.

In an effort to appeal to the anti-terrorism and police SWAT units, shortened or mid length rifles were also released: the AK-102, AK-104 and AK-105, in 5.56 NATO, 5.45X39mm and 7.62X39mm calibers, respectively.

The advent of the US Afghan and Iraq campaigns saw a huge leap in the development of rifle accessories and other rifle-mounted combat implements. Naturally, the AR rifles issued to the US forces got updated with modular systems for mounting those accessories utilizing a 1913 rail, or as it is frequently referred to, the "Picatinny" rail. Removing a carrying handle from the top of the AR receiver and replacing it with mounting rails together with replacing a large hand guard with a quad rail mounting system gives the AR the desired modularity and a huge advantage over the AK rifle.

Although at that time the modern AK rifle was equipped with a side rail mounting system, it was unique to the AK and offered limited space for mounting optics or collimator-type sights only. This led to Izhmash's desperate attempt to catch up with its American competition, and the result was a prototype named AK-200 (for 2000's) representing a "modernized" version of the good 'ol AK-74M.

The facelift included a modified lower hand guard that now had short "Picatinny" rails, a redesigned ergonomic pistol grip and hinged top cover with an eight-inch rail. The rifle was submitted to the Russian Armed Forces for

The real and deep modernization of the AK-74 design was embodied in the newest Concern Kalashnikov release, the AK-12.

an evaluation, where it was respectfully rejected, with the Russian military citing as its reason an inadequate modernization that did not offer a significant benefit over its predecessor.

In spite of the rejection from the Russian Armed Forces, Izhmash arsenal continued to work on developing a new battle rifle. Using the principal of "if not broken, do not fix" the basis for the new development was still the old, many-times-proven AK-74.

However this time the designers group got really deep into a complete overhaul of the old system, concentrating on modularity and shooter ergonomics while at the same time retaining the AK's legendary reliability and user-friendliness.

The result was the introduction of a new rifle in 2010. The new rifle was designated the AK-12 and represented a departure from the conventional Russian battle rifles of the past.

The gun had completely redesigned furniture with an ample number of mounting rails allowing it to be accessorized to Western standards. The new telescopic folding buttstock could be folded to the left or the right side based on the shooter's preference, and is equipped with an adjustable cheek piece.

The rifle's controls are now ambidextrous, allowing reloading to be completed with one hand. The gun's charging handle can now be swapped from right to left and back by the operator in the field. The conventional AK-74-style muzzle brake was also redesigned and now had two chambers further reducing a muzzle climb by "leveling" the recoil and thus reducing it.

This, together with small but potent changes within the gun's gas system positively impacted the accuracy of the new AK-12 in full auto mode. In comparison to the AK-74M the accuracy enjoyed a fifty percent improvement. The hinged top cover also equipped with full-length Picatinny rail offered additional mounting options for various sights. The new gun impressed the top Russian brass and today it is being field-tested with all branches of the Russian Armed Forces.

Attempts were made to replace the AK with more advanced and technologically superior designs, such as the AN 94 (Abakan), AEK 971 or even another AK - the AK 107.

Despite the clear initial advantage of these new weapon systems, the AK rifle in its original configuration and design perseveres, so much so that the entire series of new rifles in various calibers was developed utilizing many features of this gun. No doubt there will be future attempts to replace this well-respected weapon. However, many years will pass before the AK is retired from the service to the Motherland.

CHAPTER THREE

SIMPLER IS BETTER: THE AK'S DESIGN

The design of an AK is pretty simple and as I've mentioned earlier, does not represent a huge technological breakthrough in firearm technology. All of the systems and mechanical principals had already been invented and employed prior to its introduction.

But how they worked together to produce the desired result is what really mattered in the creation of Mikhail Kalashnikov's masterpiece. Everything came together beautifully to produce an extremely reliable rifle that was cheap and easy to produce, and easy to master even by the non-educated, peasant conscripted soldier.

This inherent reliability was achieved by the spacing of the components, with a receiver allowing the contaminants to "fall" though the gun or accumulate for some time before they started to impede the normal operation of the gun. Utter simplicity of operation was also a main goal, and it was achieved by mimicking a conventional rifle configuration, which made it easy to re-train existing soldiers and train new recruits on a rifle that can be mastered within days.

As a side note, most Soviet youth were trained on the operation and maintenance of the AK by the time they graduated from high school. Most of them could take a gun apart

The Kalashnikov's design was not a clear technological breakthrough, but rather an ingenious way to make existing systems work together in one well-functioning and reliable machine.

Most of the major systems of the AK rifle have been invented and tried before. It is a simple long-stroke gas-operated system.

Firing Pin
Hammer
Return Spring
Bolt
Trigger
Rear Sight
Gas Piston
Gas Block
Front Sight
Stock
Hand Guard
Barrel
Cleaning Rod
Chamber
Gas Port
Rear Sling Attachment
Magazine
Cleaning Kit
Feeding Spring
Trigger Guard
Pistol Grip
Hammer Spring

and re-assemble it under 20 seconds.

The AK operating system is based on a long-stroke gas piston driven back by the powder gases compressing the main recoil spring that in turn feeds the round out of a box-type magazine, chambering it and locking a two-lug bolt.

The AK bolt locking is achieved by rotation, unlike in the Stg .44, which used tilting. The guide rails on the inside of the receiver enable the rotation of the bolt within a bolt carrier.

The trigger group is fully housed in the receiver and consists of trigger, sear for automatic rate of fire, disconnector, hammer and hammer spring. All of the components rotate on three pins that are installed through the receiver. For commercial hunting or sporting models the auto sear is removed, reducing the number of axle pins to two. The fire rate selector lever also serves as a safety lever.

The selector lever on military models with select-fire capabilities have three positions: Safe, Full Auto, and Single Shot (Semiautomatic). Due to the removal of the auto sear, the commercial models have only two positions: Safe and Fire (Semiautomatic). The feeding of the gun is done out of a box-type magazine with a checkered pattern arrangement for rounds.

The magazine is inserted into the magazine well opening in the bottom of the receiver and secured along the longitudinal axis with a notch in the magazine itself and

Many believe the AK's reliability is due to its "loose" tolerances. The tolerances are as good as they should be on a firearm of this type. The loose fitment of the moving components is where the dog lies.

The fire control group of the AK, though not a new invention in principal, is well executed with the return spring partially concealed in a bolt carrier and not protruding past the gun's receiver.

spring-loaded latch in front of the trigger guard.

The hammer-forged barrel with four right-hand grooves at a 240mm or 1-in-9.45 inch *rifling* twist *rate* and chrome-lined bore is pressed into the front trunnion block. Most of the commercial models that are imported into the US from Russia have chrome-lined military-spec barrels. The same could be said for European models, depending on the country of origin.

Most of the US-made AK barrels are not chrome-lined, however other forms of corrosion prevention are employed. The barrel has a gas port drilled in the top to align with a gas block that is pressed on and pinned in place. The original design had a 45-degrees port to vent powder gases to cycle the rifle.

Later models like AL-74 and 100 series had the gas port bored at a 90-degree angle. The front sight is also pressed on and pinned to the barrel. The front sight is a post type with protective hood. The sight post is threaded and screws into a floating cylinder that is used for windage adjustments during sighting. The protective hood over the front sight post is an integrated part of the front sight block.

Originally, on the first model of the AK-47 the hood had a tube shape to enclose the sight post entirely, with an opening on top to allow for elevation adjustment. The same design feature can be seen on Chinese

Type 56 models that were imported into the United States in the 90's. Later models up to this day have a "U" shaped hood that was first employed by the Soviets in the 50's as part of modernizing the AK rifle. This move made casting simpler and eliminated two milling steps to make the process cheaper.

The end or muzzle of the barrel is threaded for the installation of muzzle brake/compensators or flash hiders for use with night optics or the PBS-1 Suppressor. The AK-47 or AKM type rifles have 14X1 left-hand threads, the AK-74 and 100 Series have 24X1.5 right-hand threads.

The sighting system for the AK was borrowed from the standard military two-sight alignment system where the elevation-adjustable "U" shaped rear sight is aligned around the "fixed" front sight. The leaf spring-tensioned rear sight is hinged on the top of the "rear sight" block and it has graduations from 1-10 in single-digit increments representing 100 meters. i.e. 1-100 meters and 10-1000 meters.

The sight also has an additional setting marked as " " or "P". This setting is called "Permanent" and used as a battle setting and is recommended after a rifle was properly sighted in. The earlier model AK-47 had graduations from 8 to 800 meters only. This type of rear sight can be seen on the early Chinese imports.

The AK furniture consisting of a fixed

or folding (for airborne and reconnaissance troops) buttstock, pistol grip and upper and lower hand guards.

Just like the rifle itself the furniture has also gone through several upgrades and face lifts. When the AK-47 was first adapted for service with the Soviet Armed Forces it had furniture made of hardwood, but cost-cutting measures switched that to birch laminate. This move achieved a double benefit: It was much cheaper because the material was plentiful, and it was much more rigid and could withstand more abuse. Advances in plywood production allowed for an infinite supply of components, as it did not require a careful selection for the wood used.

Later attempts were made to replace all of the rifle's wood furniture with composite parts. Early Bakelite technology was widely employed throughout the firearms industry, and the Soviets jumped on the Bakelite bandwagon as well. However, Bakelite proved to be an excellent heat conductor and was abandoned in favor of laminate wood, with the exception of the pistol grip and bayonet handles and scabbard.

Finally, in the early 80's, the first AK-74 had its furniture replaced with "plum" colored glass-filled plastic, and not before 1990 would the first all-black plastic-clad AKs appear, and in the process giving the AK more of a modern look. The majority of the Kalashnikovs built in the US now have some sort of black polymer furniture.

The overall configuration of the AK rifle is patterned after all of the main battle rifles in service at the time of its inception. As such, it has the basic traits of a conventional infantry weapon. The AK receiver is set between the stock and hand guard, with a pistol grip under the back end of the receiver replacing and mimicking the neck of the buttstock on a conventional battle rifle.

The magazine is inserted at the bottom of the receiver and in front of the trigger guard,

just like the other rifles of the day. The front sight is located at the end of the barrel with a rear sight at the point of barrel and receiver merger, just like any other rifle on the battle fields of the WWII, with the exception of the British Lee-Enfield rifle, which employed a dioptrical or aperture sight, or as it is now widely known a "peephole" rear sight.

The AK's charging handle, along with the safety/selector level, are on the right of the gun, following a traditional layout for a battle rifle suited for right-handed operator and not so much for the lefties. In this configuration, the shooter would take his/her right hand off the fire controls and proceed to conduct all of the reloading manipulations with that hand.

This is a particular point of contention with modern shooters, especially American shooters, who are constantly comparing the AK to the AR. Most of the Close Quarter Combat Courses teach their students to never take their "operating" hand off a pistol grip and do all the reloads with the support hand. They forget that before the arrival of the AR rifles on the battlefield, all of the military guns - with a rare exception for weird European rifles here and there - and including all of the American guns of that time, had their bolt and charging handles on the right.

Nevertheless, considering the US CQB dogmas, the AK rifle is uniquely suited for a left-handed shooter.

One idiosyncrasy of the AK design and configuration is that the rifle is front-end heavy. This has a positive effect on results and accuracy during rapid fire of the rifle by reducing muzzle climb. However, at the same time it makes it harder for a person who is accustomed to the American style of carbine shooting to maintain positive shouldering of the gun during reloading. The effect is exacerbated by the addition of accessories such as a flashlight or laser designator.

CHAPTER FOUR

AK OPERATION AND MAINTENANCE

The AK's basic operation is just as simple as its design. Once again, all of the main principals by which the Kalashnikov Automatic Rifle operates had already been invented and employed before making this rifle a collection of proven system designs and additional innovative solutions.

At the time of the shot, while the bullet is traveling through the bore, a part of the powder gases are vented through the gas port on the top of the barrel and into the rifle's gasblock. There, the gases push back a long-stroke piston that is affixed to the bolt carrier containing the bolt itself, compressing the main (return or recoil depending on various descriptions) spring and resetting a hammer.

After the main spring's tension reverses to movement, pushing the bolt-bolt carrier assembly forward, the bolt grabs the next round out of the magazine and feeds it into the chamber. The grooves machined into the front trunnion block then force the bolt to rotate and lock the chamber, at which time the hammer strikes a floating firing pin that ignites the primer and the process is repeated.

The extraction of the spent casing is performed by the extractor on the bolt and the deflector on the right-side guide rail of the receiver.

DISASSEMBLY AND MAINTENANCE

The maintenance of the AK is rather simple and falls squarely in line with the idea of the rifle itself. The AK was designed to be cleaned and maintained in the field quickly and efficiently, by simple conscripted soldiers. Most of the military-configured rifles come with a standard cleaning rod that is inserted into a specially-designed place under the barrel, and that is where it resides when it isn't being used for cleaning.

The AK battle rifle, no matter what model or where it was made, was also issued with an oil bottle and standard cleaning kit. The cleaning kit consisted of a bore brush, the slotted tip or punch that screwed onto the cleaning rod for patch swabbing of the bore, screw driver/front sight adjustment combination tool and gas port cleaning pin.

All of the Soviet, Russian, Chinese, and most of the European models come with a cylindrical container that contains all of the cleaning tools and is stored within a wood or plastic buttstock, with the exception being the rifles equipped for the airborne troops with metal fold stocks.

Although these rifles were also issued with the cleaning kits, they had to be carried in the magazine pouches issued with the gun.

An interesting detail about the cleaning kit is that the standard Soviet Army AK Marksman Manual in the "Cleaning and Maintenance" section specifically mentions "small wooden sticks". The instructions on how to clean the surface of the bolt would have been something like this: "...

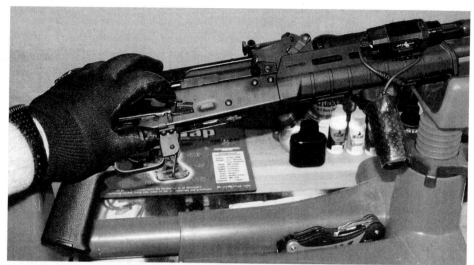

The first step in the AK disassembly process is to take the rifle off safety by pushing the safety lever down to its "Fire" position. This is critical because the safety lever in its "Safe" position would block the disassembly.

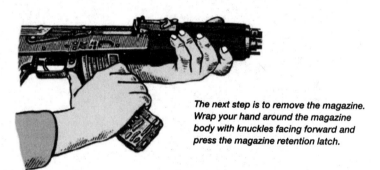

The next step is to remove the magazine. Wrap your hand around the magazine body with knuckles facing forward and press the magazine retention latch.

The magazine is disengaged by pressing the magazine retention latch and rocking the magazine forward.

to properly clean the surface of the bolt face from residue, use small wooden sticks." The "small wooden sticks" were not issued with the gun, but soldiers were expected to have them by whittling them out of any piece of wood that is available to them at the time and place and have those on their person at all times.

To disassemble the AK one must make sure it is unloaded and safe by disengaging the magazine, sliding the selector lever/safety to the fire position, and pulling the bolt handle back. After releasing the bolt handle with the muzzle of the gun pointed in a safe direction, one pulls the trigger to release the hammer.

With magazine removed, make sure the rifle is unloaded by pulling back on the charging handle, inspecting the chamber, and releasing the handle. At this point it is recommended to release the hammer.

The cleaning kit resides behind a trap door in the buttplate of the AK's fixed stock. To remove it one needs to push the trap door with a finger until the spring tensioned kit pushes past the open trap door. Then the kit "springs" out and can be removed.

Next, the cleaning rod is removed and the cleaning kit is released from the stock by pressing the retaining plate with a finger into the stock until it passes the kit. By removing the finger from the cleaning kit hole the embedded spring would push the kit out.

The cleaning rod is removed from under the rifle's barrel next. Both the kit and the rod are needed for a variety of cleaning and maintenance operations.

After that is done, the muzzle brake/compensator is removed by depressing a spring-loaded retaining pin at the base of the front sight block and unscrewing the brake clockwise or counterclockwise, depending on the model of the rifle, until it is free.

To remove the cleaning rod from its place under the rifle's barrel is relatively easy; just grab and pull it out of its "nest" behind the muzzle attachment, then pull it forward.

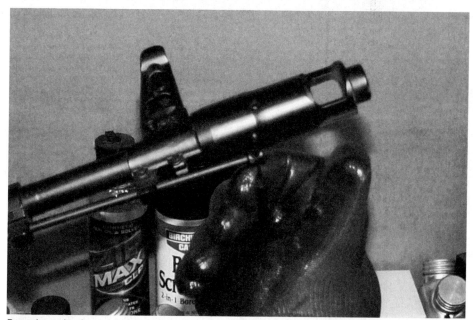

Removing a cleaning rod from the AK-74 style rifle may present a challenge. Soldiers in the field would often thread a grenade pin ring into the cleaning rod hole and use it to pull the rod out. You can also use a gas port cleaning pin tool that comes in the rifle's kit.

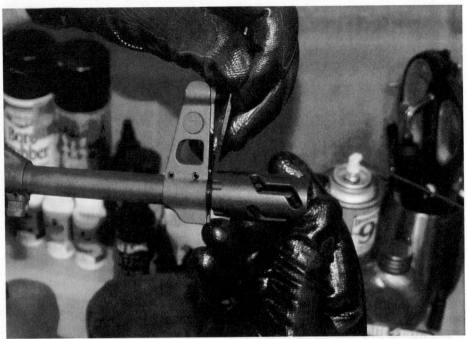

No matter what type of thread is on the rifle, all of the AK muzzle devices are secured in place by the detent spring-loaded pin. One can use a tip of a finger, screwdriver or a screwdriver/sight adjustment tool that comes with the rifle's cleaning kit.

After the muzzle device passes the detent pin's reach it can be simply screwed off.

Remember, the muzzle thread on AK-47 and AKM-style rifles is a left-hand thread and on the AK-74 and 100 Series it is right-hand.

Next, the receiver top cover is removed from the top of the rifle by pressing the button protruding through the top cover recoil spring retainer, while at the same time pulling the top cover itself up and away from the gun.

With the internal components exposed, the mainspring assembly is removed by sliding the spring retainer forward toward the front of the rifle from its slot. Reversing the direction, the spring then pulled out of the bolt carrier.

The AK top cover is removed by pressing in the return spring retainer tab and pulling up on the cover.

Once free of the spring the top cover is removed from the slot in the front sight block and completely detached from the gun.

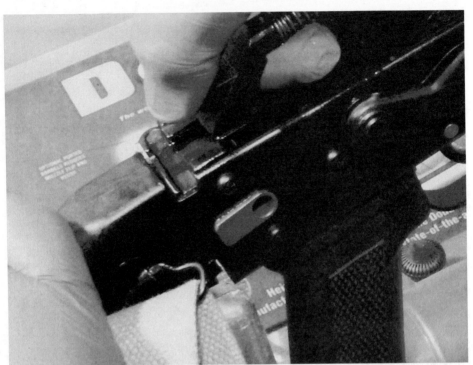

The AK return spring is resting with its retainer block in the slots in the rifle's rear trunnion block. To release the spring retainer block push it forward until loose.

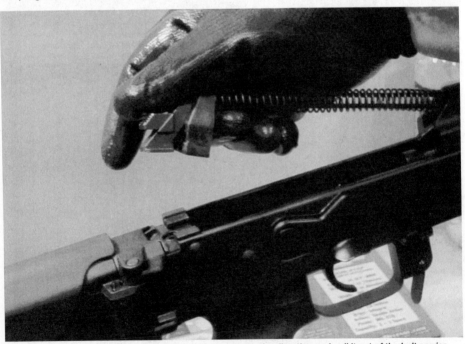

Once the spring is out and free of the trunnion block, reverse the direction and pull it out of the bolt carrier.

With the spring removed, the bolt carrier assembly is removed by sliding it back and lifting it from the receiver.

The bolt itself is contained within the bolt carrier and slides with rotation freely within the assembly. The bolt then is removed by rotating it clockwise and sliding it forward.

The next step is to remove the gas tube which is done by sliding a retaining block lever, located on the right side of the rear sight block, straight up and pulling on the tube itself up. Note that the gas tube may not slide freely out of its place and one may have to use a little effort to remove it, but

The bolt carrier assembly is removed by sliding it back in the receiver to the most rear position and lifting it out of the gun.

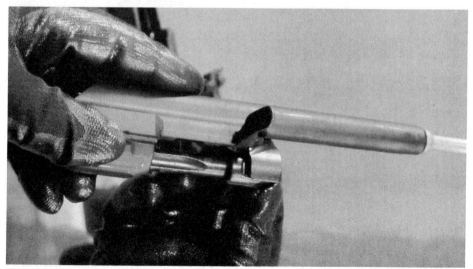

The bolt is removed from the bolt carrier assembly by pushing it back and rotating it counterclockwise at the same time. Once the rotation guide log rotates loose off the carrier, reverse the direction and pull the bolt forward until free.

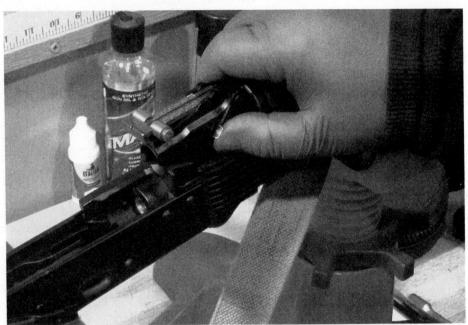

The gas tube is nestled in between the gas block and the rear sight block and secure in place by rotation wedge. The release lever is on the right side of the front sight block and has to be rotated upward to release the gas tube.

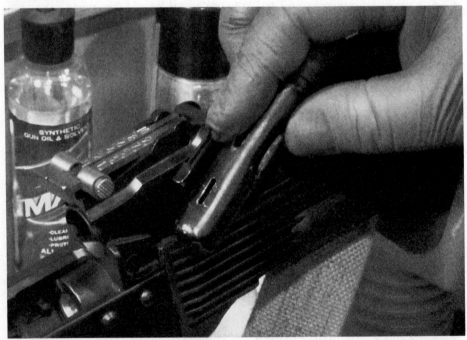

Sometimes the gas tube retaining wedge is a tight fit and it is difficult to release the lever. Once again the AK cleaning kit comes to the rescue. The kit container has several slots in it. One of them can be used to operate a stubborn gas tube release lever.

By placing a release lever tang into a cleaning kit container slot, one gains enough leverage to move the tightly-fitted lever.

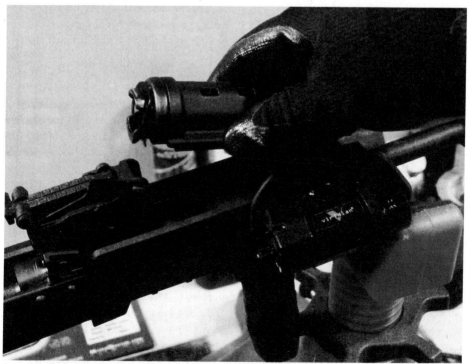

Once the lever is up and retaining wedge is out of the way the gas tube is simply lifted away from the gun.

Once the AK is field stripped it can be properly cleaned and maintained.

very little effort. If it has to be forced out, it means the retainer block did not rotate out of the way.

With the gas tube removed, the inner chamber of the gas block is exposed and ready for cleaning.

This concludes the field-stripping of the AK rifle that is necessary for its proper cleaning and maintenance; however, the gun can be further disassembled by removing the trigger group and furniture. I describe this later in this book.

Now back to the cleaning and maintenance. Of course, everyone has heard some fantastic story of an AK being buried in the dirt and after it was dug up and the rusted-shut bolt carrier kicked open, it fired.

I would not doubt this story for a second because the extremely reliable AK can take a lot of abuse and would continue to shoot, most likely better than any gun out there in the dust, water, dirt, grime and other thinkable and unthinkable contaminants and debris. But would it function as intended and for how long and will it be safe for a shooter? That is where the cleaning and maintenance come in.

As any mechanism or machine, the AK - or any gun for that matter - requires maintenance and regular cleaning. The lack of that care can, obviously, cause the gun

to malfunction. Yes, the AK by design is extremely reliable, but even the most reliable implement has its limits, more so when it comes down to the guns that are supposed to protect your life.

Soldiers have to keep their guns clean at all times and perform regular maintenance every time permitting, even if the gun has already been cleaned. This is just a good habit to have that will in turn pay off by prolonging the life and proper functionality of your rifle.

Luckily, when it comes to the AK, the cleaning is easy and can be performed relatively quick and without the use of any special tool. All one would need are two hands and the tool kit that came with the gun or any other commercially available gun cleaning kit.

Apart from the cleaning kit and rod one would need a solvent and gun oil.

In the early days the AK rifle were issued with a double container for an alkaline solvent and oil. Later, the Soviets did away with solvent and issued an oil container only for cleaning the gun in the field. However, every military unit had large containers of solvent and gun oil in the barracks inside the company's armory. So there is a field cleaning, and then there is a proper cleaning. Both have a place, but one is just a bit more thorough.

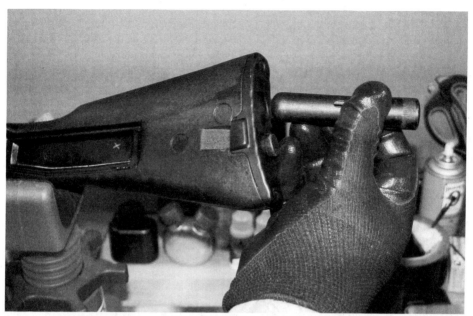

A cleaning kit containing all the essential tools for the AK's field maintenance. The kit was either stored in the butt stock or in the magazine pouch.

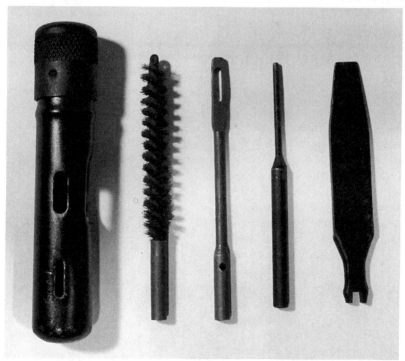

The AK standard cleaning kit contains the bore brush attachment, the bore swabbing attachment (slotted as pictured or punch type), gas port pin tool and universal screwdriver and front sight adjustment tool. The container itself is an integral part of the kit.

One starts the cleaning of the AK with the field stripping of the rifle as I have described above. Once the gun has been stripped one needs to inspect the gun and its components for any damage or wear to make sure that all of the gun's parts are in good order, intact, and undamaged. Since some parts of the various AK models have an anti-corrosion finish, either enamel, paint, phos-phate, bluing, or others, it is OK to see some wear of the finish on the surfaces, especially where the moving parts come in contact with others such as bolt and bolt carrier, receiver rails, the inside of a gas block and gas tube, magazine well, and latch.

There can be some surface finish wear on the outside of the rifle as well from rubbing against something like the inside of a car-

Every AK was issued with an oil bottle. Earlier AK rifles were issued with a double container for solver and oil (my personal favorite). Later the single oil only bottle replaced the double containers.

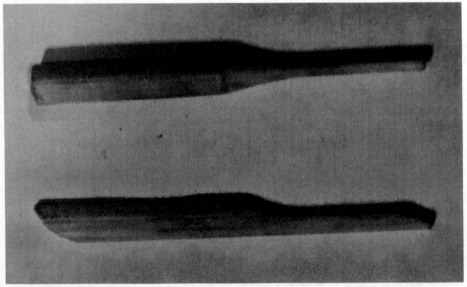

Though not a part of the AK kit, the small wooden sticks were assumed to be a part of its maintenance. Soldiers were expected to wittle these out of piece of wood and use them.

rying case, clothing, or from frequent and rigorous cleaning. During the Soviet-Afghan Campaign, some of the rifles that Soviet soldiers carried looked like they have been sandblasted to an almost polished chrome finish. In no way did this affect the actual intended performance of the guns as long as they were properly maintained.

With use the rifle should display some wear, but with prescribed maintenance it will continue to function as intended. At no time, however, should the rifle have any rust or any other corrosion on itself and its components. If a newly-purchased used rifle has been neglected by a previous owner and corrosion has settled in and cannot be cleaned out, the components need to be replaced and the gun itself needs to refinished by a gunsmith to insure its proper function. However, most of the corrosion and rust with the exception of rare cases of extreme neglect can be removed from the AK rifle with a good amount of elbow grease.

If everything is in its right place and in good working order following the visual inspection, one should start with the bore of the gun. Unlike the Western sporting hunting gun cleaning practice of cleaning the bore of the gun from the breech or chamber end, the AK manual instructs shooters in the opposite method, using the issued with the gun cleaning rod and kit.

First, the cleaning kit is opened and all the tools are taken out of the case. All of the cleaning kit contents including the case itself are used in cleaning and maintaining the rifle.

Next, one has to thread the cleaning rod through the neck of the cleaning kit case and into an oval side hole, effectively creating a "T" handle.

With the cleaning rod threaded through the case, the cap of the cleaning kit is "skewered" by the rod from the top. This serves as a muzzle cap to protect the barrel crown and threads.

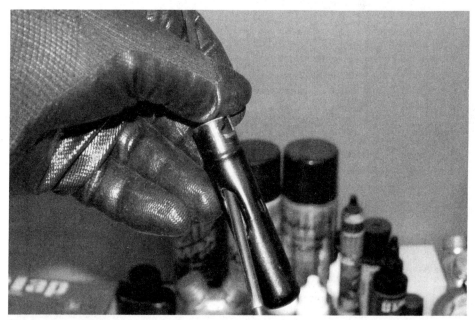

To assemble an AK cleaning rod one must thread the cleaning rod through the neck of the cleaning kit container and on through the side hole, making a "T" handle.

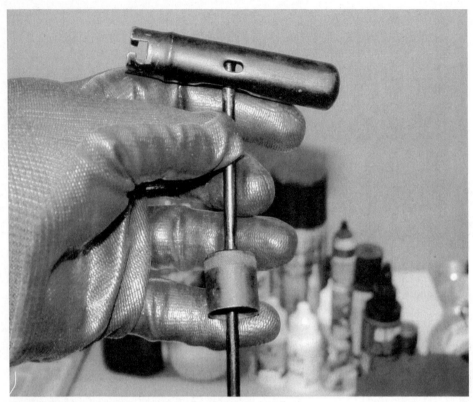
Next the rod is threaded through the top of the cleaning kit container cap.

After the cleaning rod is fully assembled the bore brush is attached to the rod's threaded end and the brush is inserted into the muzzle of the gun with the cleaning kit case cap placed on and over the muzzle.

Next, the rifle is placed between one's knees in the field or on the gun rest in the shop. While the cap is held in place, the cleaning rod is moved back and forth down the length of the bore with the brush scrubbing and loosening any carbon built up.

Modern times allow us to get any solvent from our friendly neighborhood sporting goods store, and solvent will loosen any contamination in the bore, but it will not replace a good scrubbing. If one chooses to use a solvent for bore cleaning it must be used in combination with a brush.

After the bore is properly brushed it must be swabbed with a clean soft fabric or patch threaded through a slotted tip or wrapped around a punch that replaces the brush on the end of the cleaning rod. Swabbing the bore with a patch or piece of fabric would remove debris and loose contaminants. The swabbing should continue until patch or fabric comes clean.

Next, the patch or piece of fabric gets a drop of gun oil on it and the bore swabbed again to insure that a thin layer of oil covers the surface of the bore. One should avoid an excessive amount of oil. The "wet" bore will attract dust and grime. It also creates smoke when the barrel gets hot.

With the bore cleaned and oiled, it is now the receiver's turn. The AK receiver collects most of the contaminants such as unburned powder, carbon built up, sand, dust, paint

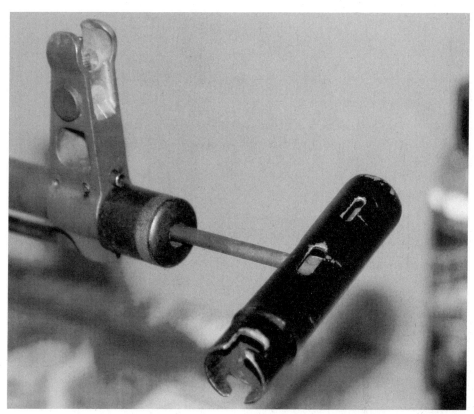

The cleaning kit container cap is placed over the AK muzzle and would serve as a guide.

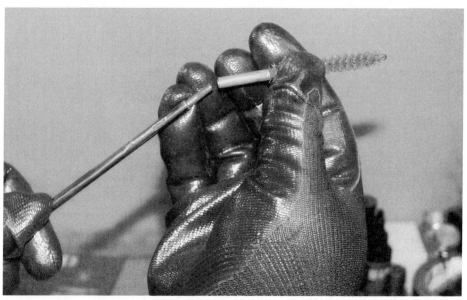

To begin a bore cleaning the brush attachment is screwed on the cleaning rod.

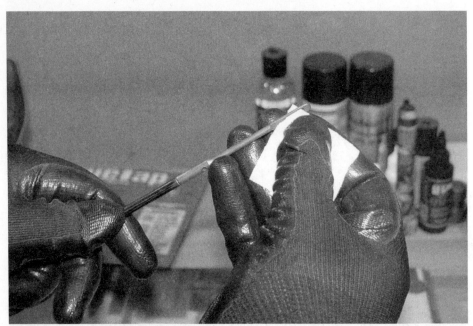

After the brushing the bore is then swabbed with rag or paper patches using a slotted swabbing attachment.

Using a cleaning kit container as a "T" handle, the bore is cleaned until the patches come out clean.

or enamel chips, metal shavings, and other undesirable grime.

Many people here in the States look for an easy way out when it comes to the cleaning of their guns, and the AK is not an exception. I've heard all kinds of ridiculous methods described - with no authority on the subject, from dipping a rifle into a 50-gallon drum of diesel fuel to submerging an AK into a bathtub full of window cleaner. I am not going to laugh out loud at those suggestions, but simply state that all of them are wrong and detrimental to the proper operation of the AK rifle.

Anyway you view it, one has to actually use his or her hands and prescribed tools to clean an AK. One has to set a little time aside and put forth the effort to do so. The AK receiver will require most of the time during cleaning, as it has moving and fixed components inside.

Using a rag or oiled paper, the visible grime and debris must be removed using a flat part of the front sight-adjusting tool and

The "Small Wooden Sticks" are often used to get into small creases inside the AK receiver.

The use of the "Small Wooden Sticks" for cleaning a bolt face makes the process much easier.

a pick for removing contaminants from hard to get places and creases.

Remember those "small wooden sticks" that Soviet soldiers were expected to whittle out of wood and have on them at all times? Those "sticks" are very handy for cleaning a receiver and reaching into all those hard-to-get places. Even without these handy implements one can do a very good job using just the tools that came with the gun. Special attention should be paid to any surfaces where friction occurs, especially inner rails. On the AK-type rifles grime likes to collect in the creases where rails are attached to the receiver.

After cleaning, decontaminating and degreasing a receiver one must wipe it down. Using oil-saturated cloth, evenly oil the receiver and all of the inner components. With oiling complete, now the receiver must be wiped dry with a clean cloth to remove all of the excess oil. Though the metal surfaces will feel dry to the touch, rest assured a thin layer of oil is still there.

The removal of excess oil is a must as it acts as a "magnet" for dust, sand and other dirt. The outside of the receiver should now be cleaned with clean rag, oiled, and wiped dry. Particular attention should be given to the pins and rivets. Rust and sulfate corrosion has a tendency to accumulate there.

Now it is time to clean the components that have been taken off the rifle during the disassembly. The easiest is the gas tube, and it should be cleaned first using a cleaning rod and brush for thorough inside cleaning. Then it should be swabbed with clean cloth or a shotgun patch and slightly oiled, just like the bore.

Moving on to the bolt, using a clean cloth you should wipe it down until dry and free of visible residue and debris. Then, using the bore brush that came in the cleaning kit with the gun, scrub all the surfaces of the bolt where the "stubborn" residue remains. Now, using the same flat part of the front

sight adjustment too and pick that are part of the gun's cleaning kit, the face of the bolt is cleaned and decontaminated. Again, the Soviet soldiers would use those "small wooden sticks" to do the same.

After the bolt is cleaned, it is oiled and wiped dry. The next step is to clean the bolt carrier. Other than wiping it down and removing most of the powder residue, special attention should be paid to the gas piston. The surface of the piston is susceptible to a carbon build up. Most of the AK rifles have gas pistons with round grooves similar to that of internal combustion engine pistons.

Although it is a good practice to keep the piston surfaces free of any carbon residue, sometimes it is impossible in under in-the-field conditions. The rule of thumb would be to keep the friction surfaces clean and take care of the grooves and face of the piston later at home or on-base.

Although the AK is usually delivered with a cleaning kit, one can use any commercially available generic rifle cleaning kit. I often use the small OTIS cleaning kit in the field. During a class I have their expanded T-Mod cleaning system kit. Just in case.

Once again the "Small Wooden Sticks" come in handy when cleaning the AK's gas piston.

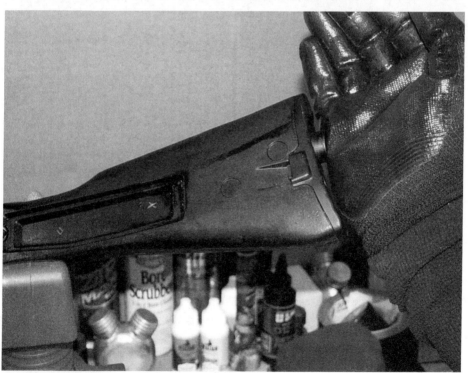

The trick to putting away an AK cleaning kit with an injury to the finger is to slide it partially into its storage compartment and then hitting it firmly with the palm of your hand.

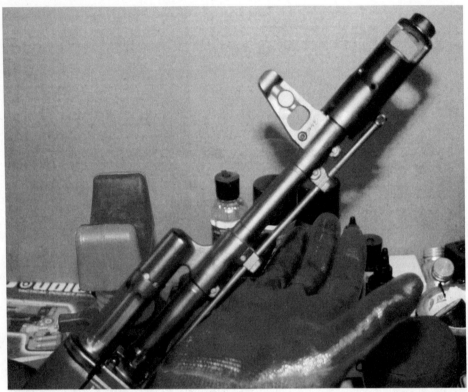

There is also a trick to stowing away an AK-74 cleaning rod. When the cleaning rod seems stuck and does not want to go any further, one should strike it with the palm of his or her hand firmly downward at an angle at the spot between the hand guard retainer and gas block. The rod will snap into place as proscribed.

Apart from mechanical removal of the carbon residue in the field, one can use solvents it finish the job at home. Once the bolt carrier is clean, it has to be oiled the same way as other parts and wiped down dry. Particular attention should be paid to the surfaces and slots where the bolt slides and rotates.

Next, the main return or recoil spring is swabbed clean with a cloth and oiled. The top cover should also be wiped clean, oiled and wiped dry the same way the other parts were. The wooden furniture should not be oiled or treated with solvents. Good cleaning with a clean cloth will do the job nicely.

The cleaning of the AK rifle is now complete. It is reassembled in the reverse order from the disassembly process. i.e. first, the gas tube is installed and secured with the rotating retainer. Next, the bolt is placed in the bolt carrier and the bolt carrier is installed piston-first into the gas tube with the body of the carrier resting on the top of the receiver in the far back position.

Pushing on the top of the bolt carrier, slide it forward to the chamber. The return spring is then installed into the bolt carrier and its retainer base is slid into the slot in the rear trunnion block. The top cover then is fitted into the round slot in the rear sight block, leveled over the top of the gun and pushed down and forward until the tab on the main spring retainer snaps through the top cover, signaling the cover's proper installation.

At this point, the rifle should be cycled

Next the hammer has to be released by pulling the trigger.

The last thing is to do is to safety your AK rifle by sliding the safety lever into its upmost position on "Safe".

several time to check proper installation of all its components, then the hammer should be released and safety lever placed in safe condition.

The final two steps include stowing away the cleaning rod by placing it in its place under the barrel and reassembling the cleaning kit and storing it in the buttstock (for fixed stocks or later 100 Series rifles).

Putting away an AK cleaning kit may prove to be a challenge if you don't know how. The kit is placed into the hole in the stock plate bottom first so that about one inch of it sticks out, then with the palm of the hand one should hit it firmly. The kit case should compress the spring momentary, clearing a space for a trap door to close.

Now the AK rifle is ready for normal operation.

Keeping your AK clean will insure its legendary reliability and prolong its operational life. One should take care of his or her gun and keep it in working order at all times. Simple cleaning will insure that. In fact, the Soviet Military Manual instructs a soldier to perform regular cleaning of an AK in the field while resting on the march or during a lull in a firefight.

MALFUNCTIONS

The AK is an awesome machine with unmatched reliability, but a machine nevertheless. As such, it is susceptible to malfunctions. Most of the malfunctions are similar to those that other guns experience, although not as often.

Due to the AK's robust design, with liberal spacing between its components, some of the typical malfunctions and breakages are eliminated. However, some classic and unavoidable malfunctions do remain, relating mostly to the condition of the gun (clean/dirty), the quality of the ammunition,

and condition (damage) of the magazine.

However, unlike any other gun, the AK can be cleared and rendered operational with either no tools or use of the ones that are on the gun (cleaning rod, etc.).

Here are some typical AK malfunctions, the reasons for them, and ways to clear them:

- Failure to feed a round into the chamber. Usually caused by a "dirty" or damaged magazine or faulty magazine latch. Cleared by recharging (rechambering) the rifle or by replacing a magazine.

- Mis-feeding when the round has failed to chamber and instead become stuck with bullet tip jammed against the barrel. Usually caused by the damage to the feeding lips of the magazine. Cleared by the removal of the round from the receiver and recharging the gun. If the problem persists, swap the magazine.

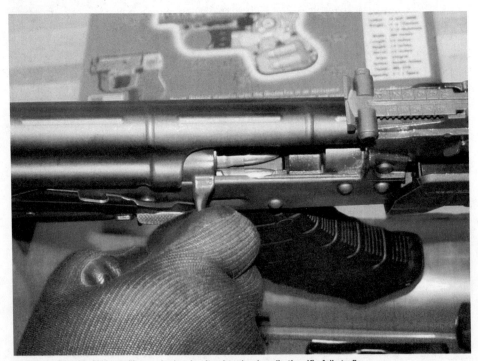

If after cycling the AK by pulling and releasing its charging handle the rifle fails to fire, it is most likely a failure to feed.

- Failure to extract with double feeding. Usually caused by "dirty" ammunition or "dirty" chamber or rarely by faulty extractor or the extractor spring. Cleared by detaching the magazine, removing the round from the gun with the cleaning rod, and knocking the spent casing out. If problem persists, clean the chamber.
- Misfire when the gun is locked and loaded, but there is no shot when trigger is pulled. Caused by faulty round, dirty rifle, frozen lubricant, or faulty trigger group. Cleared by recharging the rifle. If the problem persists, clean the firing pin channel and, if needed, trigger group. If these steps do not help take it back to the armory.
- Failure to eject when the spent casing remains attached to the bolt held by the extractor. Caused by the excessive fouling of the friction surfaces of the gas return mechanism or chamber or by fouled extractor. Cleared by recharging the rifle. If problem persists, clean the gas system, friction surfaces, bolt face, and chamber. If these steps do not help take it back to the armory.

That is it. This is taken right out of the Soviet/Russian AK Operator Manual. Basically, all of the typical AK malfunctions can be cleared by cycling a bolt handle or by cleaning. From my experience in the field, I would add one more common hiccup related to the AK-74 only, which is an occasional spent shell making its way back behind the bolt carrier and smashed against the rear trunnion block.

If after releasing the AK charging handle the bolt fails to close and the bolt carrier assembly gets stuck open it is because the round failed to camber and is now stuck between the bolt and the edge of the barrel.

Double feed is when the spent casing fails to extract and is still partially in the chamber of the gun, but the next round has been already been released by the magazine.

The spent casing would be still attached to the bolt face, preventing proper cycling of the rifle.

AK malfunction clearing procedure step one: Remove magazine.

AK malfunction clearing procedure step two: With magazine out, cycle the rifle a few times by pulling on its charging handle.

AK malfunction clearing procedure step three: Insert different magazine.

Though it may sound serious, it most likely will not stop the gun from firing and would reveal itself during an inspection and/or cleaning. Again, it is cleared by shaking the casing out of the gun with the top cover off, which is another AK-specific feature or ability. The typical AK rifle will fire and operate normally with a top cover even in full auto mode.

Sometimes AK maintenance requires more serious maintenance, repair, or part replacement. In this case the owner should seek a help of a qualified gunsmith, or if he or she is mechanically inclined they can do it themselves.

Usually no gunsmithing shop or special tools are needed even for a "deeper" maintenance of the AK rifle. The "deeper" maintenance is typically associated with damaged or faulty part replacement or an upgrade. The easiest and the most popular is furniture replacement.

The AK rifle furniture was originally designed with the practical ergonomic requirements for an average Soviet soldier of 5'10" and 170 lbs. Based on the biometric parameters of an average Soviet conscript the length, circumference, width and height of the furniture components was set. Today, especially in the commercial market, AK shooters often choose to individualize their rifles, hence, the frequent furniture swap.

The fixed stocks are frequently removed in favor of either folding stocks or longer ones. The original AK stock is notorious among American shooters for being short. I personally find it extremely comfortable and perfectly suited for a fighting carbine, especially for CQB. However, as they say in Russia: "There are no friends when it comes down to color and taste," and as such, many prefer a longer length of pull. In both instances the original fixed stock is replaced to achieve a desired level of ergonomics.

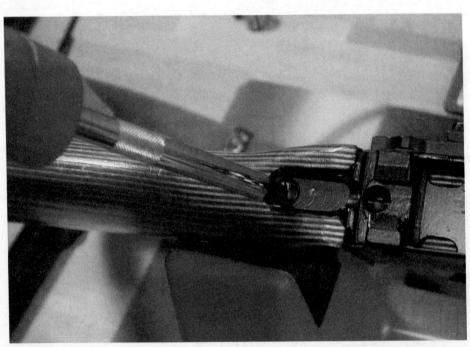

There are two slot screws holding the AK stock in place. Using a flathead screwdriver remove the screws. The stock can be removed with screws out.

To remove a fixed stock off the AK, wood or polymer, one would follow same procedure for the most modern AK rifle on the market today, since most of the AKs sold today are either copies of the Soviet AKM rifle or models that are based on it.

After the rifle is disassembled or field-stripped, two stock retaining screws are located. One is screwed into the stock through the rear trunnion block and the other through the rear trunnion tang that protrudes past the receiver and rests on the top of the stock. With both screws out the stock can be removed from the rifle. Some stocks can have a tighter fit and might require a little "encouragement" with a rubber mallet. The new stock is then placed in the same spot and secured with the original or new screws to the trunnion block of the gun.

The next component that is often replaced for ergonomic reasons is the AK pistol grip. The AK pistol grip is secured to the gun's receiver by means of the long bolt that runs the length on the pistol grip, and the "T" nut that protrudes through a square-shaped hole at the bottom of the receiver.

Using a flathead screwdriver, the bolts are unscrewed and pistol grip is removed. Using the same "T" nut, the new pistol grip is installed and secured with same bolt or the one provided with a particular grip.

The AK forehand or hand guard is usually removed to replace a broken or faulty part or to gain additional ergonomics and modularity. It consists of an upper guard that is installed on the gas tube and a lower that is inserted into the front of the receiver and retained with a hand guard retainer.

To remove an upper guard off the AK gas tube one needs to rotate the hand guard along its horizontal axis 180 degrees and separate it from the tube.

To install a new hand guard one has to repeat the process in reverse by placing in into the retaining brackets and twisting it 180 degrees. Some upper guards' fitments are tight, and require use of pliers or even a vise.

The lower guard is loosened by flipping a

The "T" nut that is holding the AK rifle's pistol grip can be located toward the rear of the receiver behind the safety lever axis.

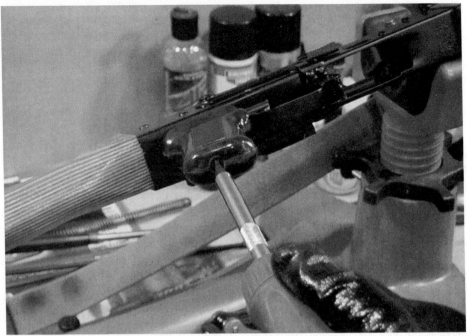

The slot head bolt goes through the pistol grip and screws into the "T" nut securing the grip in place. Using a flathead screwdriver unscrew the bolt to remove the pistol grip.

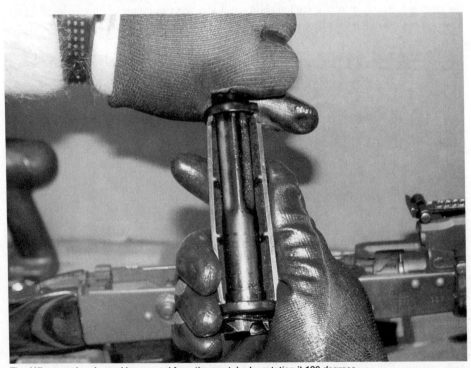

The AK's upper hand guard is removed from the gas tube by rotating it 180 degrees.

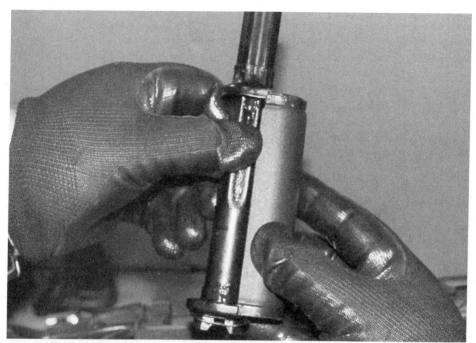

When the upper guard is rotated 180 degrees it slide out of its brackets.

If the upper guard is seated tightly in its brackets, use of a vise is sometimes necessary.

small lever on the top of the right side of the hand guard retainer to the opposite position and sliding the retainer forward or toward the muzzle of the rifle.

Next, the lower hand guard is removed by pulling it forward out of the receiver and away from the gun. Again, some lowers are tighter than others and some rubber mallet encouragement may be required.

The new guard is installed by following the steps in reverse. Some of the modern hand guards that feature mounting rails may come from a manufacturer with different mounting instruction. All the furniture replacements can be done by an average person with little or no experience, with a couple of screwdrivers.

To replace or repair the trigger group is

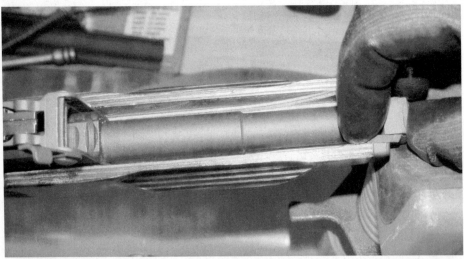

The AK's lower hand guard is retained in place by the hand guard retaining bracket. There is a small release lever in the retaining bracket itself.

Simply flip the release lever up and away with your hand or a small tool.

Once the release lever is loose slide the retainer off the hand guard. Sometimes a small amount of a rubber mallet "encouragement" is required to get the bracket loose.

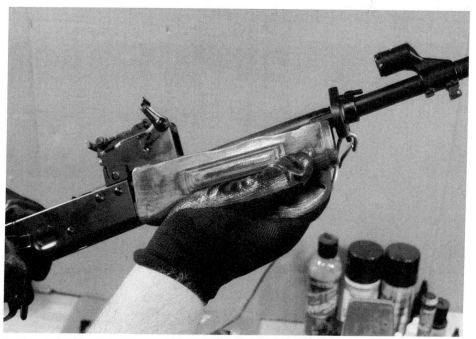

With the retaining bracket off, the hand guard should slide out of the receiver and can be removed.

where some mechanical ability is a big plus. As far as tools are concerned, no specialty tools are necessary. However, the gunsmithing hook or needle nose pliers will make the job easier.

Before starting on disassembling an AK trigger group for the first time, one should familiarize him or herself with the precise locations and positions of all internal components. The AK trigger group consists of three main components: trigger, a hammer and disconnector that rotate on two axle pins, one hammer spring, and a pin retaining clip for commercially available semi-automatic rifles.

Full-auto or military model AKs with select-fire capabilities have additional parts associated with full automatic rate of fire. Since the military manuals already explain the full auto rifle operation, repair and maintenance, I will concentrate on the semi-automatic AK's that are commercially available to a wide range of shooters.

To remove the AK trigger group one must remove the safety/selector lever by rotating it straight up or 90 degrees from its "Safe" position and sliding it out of the gun.

Next, using a hook or needle-nose pliers, the hammer spring tension is relieved off the trigger by removing the spring tangs off the trigger on both sides and placing them on the hammer head.

Now the tension of the hammer spring is relieved and the axle pins can be punched out of receiver.

The safety lever is rotated up for removal as a first step in the AK's internal component disassembly.

In the up position the AK safety lever is removed.

To do that one needs to remove a pin-retaining clip using a hook or pliers. Once the clip is removed from the grooves in the pins the trigger pin can be removed, followed by the hammer pin releasing the rest of the inner components from the receiver.

To reassemble the trigger group within the receiver just follow the same steps, but in reverse starting with hammer installation.

Knowing the proper steps to field strip an AK, to further disassemble it, clean it and regularly maintain it will prolong the rifle's life and insure its proper operation for years to come.

Though not entirely necessary for maintenance of the AK rifle, it helps to use proper tools like this hook.

Using the hook, place the hammer spring leads on to the hammer head to relieve the tension before removing axle pins.

CHAPTER FIVE

MAGAZINES

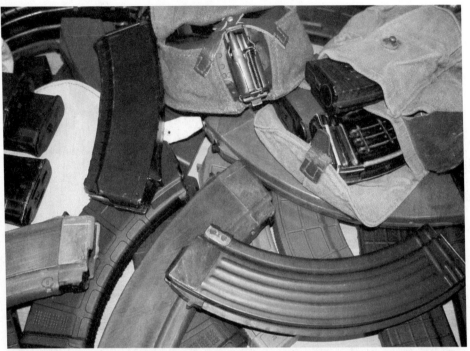

There is certainly no shortage of AK magazines on the US market today. One can find anything from the US made to imported in variety of calibers.

One of the main features of the AK that has a tremendous positive effect on its reliability is the rifle's magazine.

Among its peers it is probably the closest thing to a perfect magazine. The box-type magazine with 30-round capacity, originally made of steel, has influenced the development of 30-round AR magazines, according to Mr. Eugene Stoner himself. Prior to encountering Kalashnikov rifles in the jungles of Vietnam, the American GI fed his M16 out of 20-round mag.

The three main characteristics of the AK magazine that make it an extremely reliable feed device and set it apart from similar magazines are: the robust design that allows the magazine to sustain rigor of combat, thicker feeding lips to insure a positive round retention, and magazine retention system in the rifle.

Looking at the AK magazine it's hard to miss its massive feeding lips compared to other types of magazines. It is the heaviest part of the mag to insure positive round retention. Even in the polymer or composite magazines the feeding lips are made of steel.

From the beginning the AK magazine was designed to be robust to be able to withstand the rigors of combat. Left is the original "slab-sided" AK-47 steel magazine. Right is the most popular and widely proliferated "ribbed" steel AK magazine.

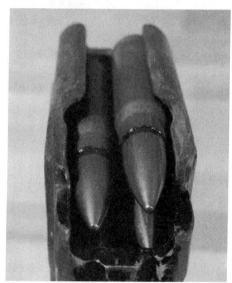

The AK magazine is a box-type mag with checkered pattern rounds. arrangement.

To get a round out of an AK magazine one has to slide it forward. The ammo simply would not come out of the top on the magazine unlike with other weapon systems.

From the get-go the parameters were set for how robust the AK magazine had to be. A series of tests were devised to determine the lever of magazine toughness.

One of the tests involved drops from various heights, including the most demanding drop while inserted in the rifle, from the height of five feet on to concrete. The rifle is expected to fire without a change of magazine. None of the Western-designed magazines would pass this test.

The other advantage of the AK magazine design is how it is inserted and retained in the rifle. The magazine is hooked into the slot in between the bottom of the front trunnion block and the receiver and latched in place by the spring-loaded magazine latch located in front of the trigger guard.

This system creates a positive magazine retention along the longitudinal axis of the gun and would not allow any lateral deviations. This is unlike other weapon systems, where, when the magazine is secured in place within a magazine well with side latch, applying pressure to one side of the magazine torques it and causes a deviation from the bore centerline. This can potentially have a negative effect on the feeding system of the gun, resulting in frequent misfeeds and other malfunctions.

During my service we would often perform push-ups while balancing on the AK

The AK magazine was designed with a two-part longitudinal retention system as opposed to the single side latch of the AR.

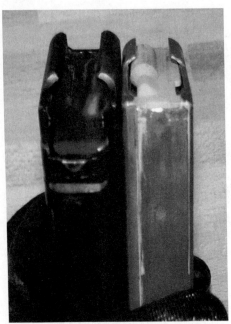
The round retention lips are by far more robust in comparison to that of AR magazines.

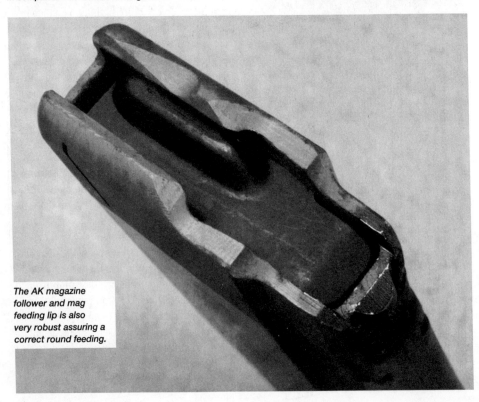
The AK magazine follower and mag feeding lip is also very robust assuring a correct round feeding.

Both parts of the original AK that are responsible for positive magazine retention in the gun: the front and rear tabs are made of steel and heavily re-enforced.

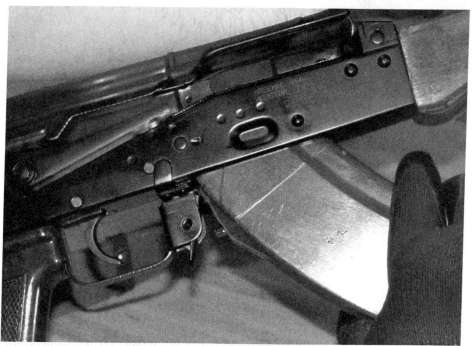

Once inserted the front tab catches on front trunnion block of the rifle.

Next the AK magazine is "rocked" back where the spring-loaded magazine latch catches magazine's rear tab.

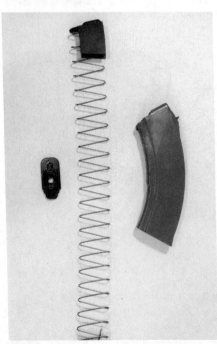

The AK's box-type magazine is very simple in design and follows other box-type magazines. It consists only of 5 parts: the body, spring, follower, spring floor plate and magazine floor plate.

magazine. We did that just because we could.

The AK magazine itself is not a major technological breakthrough and represents a collection of elements that have been employed in the box-type magazines years before the AK rifle was introduced.

It is simple in design and only has five parts: the body, floor plate, spring, spring floor plate and feed ramp.

The magazine can be taken apart for cleaning and maintenance, something many gun owners and shooters often neglect. However, regular magazine maintenance is just as important as the gun's.

In fact, most firearm malfunctions are usually attributed to feeding problems. i.e. the magazine. As I've described above, most AK problems are related to a faulty magazine. Therefore the shooter must regularly inspect and clean the magazines he or she uses in the AK rifle.

Most of the AK magazines on the market today are imported and as such follow the same pattern, no matter from what material

Taking an AK magazine apart is very easy. First using a finger or small tool you need to push is the spring floor plate tab protruding though the magazine's floor plate.

Next step is while pushing a spring floor plate down, remove the mag's floor plate by sliding it off to back of the magazine. Be very careful and keep the mag spring compressed through this procedure. The spring is under tension and can cause injury if sprung out.

they are made or what country they've come from. Some of the domestically produced AK magazines follow the original configuration and can be disassembled the same way. But there are some that cannot be taken apart and have to be maintained from the outside through access holes.

To take the AK magazine apart one needs to flip the magazine bottom up and depress the spring plate that is protruding through the magazine floor plate. With the spring plate pressed, the floor plate is slowly slid toward the back of the magazine.

It is important to do it slow and keep a finger covering the spring plate as the magazine's floor plate slides out of the way.

The magazine spring is always under tension and would spring out with force po-

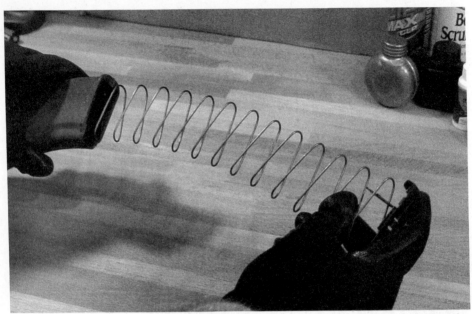

All that's left is to remove the magazine spring along with all other components from the body of the magazine.

tentially causing injuries or damages. With the floor plate out of the way the magazine spring is removed.

The spring plate and feed ramp are attached to the spring itself and are removed with it. The disassembly is complete. The magazine and all its parts need to be degreased and decontaminated with a rag or even under running water, then wiped dry, oiled and reassembled. Again, there should be no excess oil, but all the parts should have a thin layer of gun oil on them.

From the start, all AK magazines were made of steel. Slab-sided thick steel magazines were introduced with the AK-47 and adapted for service. However, almost immediately the Soviets put the new rifle on a weight-loss program that saw the introduction of "ribbed" steel magazines that were made of thinner metal.

The main advantage of the ribbed stamped steel mag is that it is essentially indestructible.

Though it is heavy, it has its advantages. The steel AK mag can be used in a variety of tasks, such as a weapon, hammer or beer bottle opener. This type of AK magazine was manufactured in several countries with license and without, and today remains the most common AK magazine in the World and the most-sold AK magazine in the US.

However, the weight reduction program continued. This effort saw the introduction of a stamped aluminum-ribbed magazine that was significantly lighter than its steel brother. However, the manufacturing process was so expensive that aluminum magazines have been produced in very low numbers and were only issued with the under-folding AKM rifles designated strictly for the airborne troops.

Even though this mag offered a significant weight reduction in the combat load, its size and shape did not fit well with the combat gear of the day. Today some such magazines are "floating" around on the

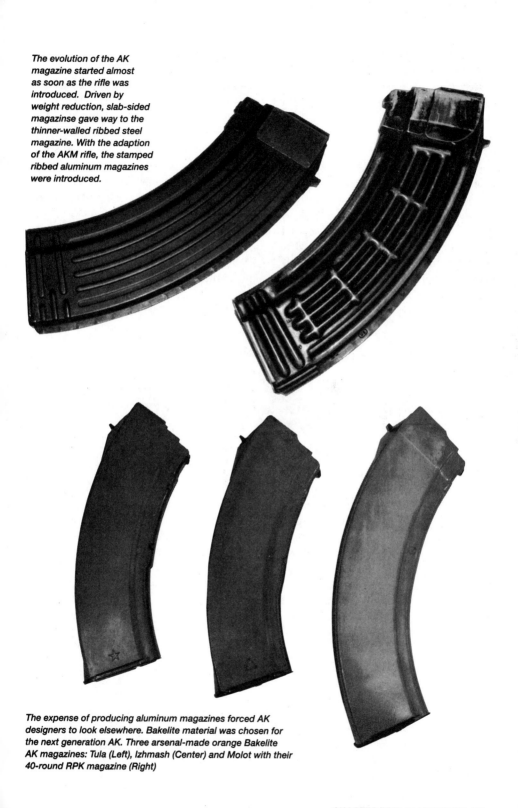

The evolution of the AK magazine started almost as soon as the rifle was introduced. Driven by weight reduction, slab-sided magazinse gave way to the thinner-walled ribbed steel magazine. With the adaption of the AKM rifle, the stamped ribbed aluminum magazines were introduced.

The expense of producing aluminum magazines forced AK designers to look elsewhere. Bakelite material was chosen for the next generation AK. Three arsenal-made orange Bakelite AK magazines: Tula (Left), Izhmash (Center) and Molot with their 40-round RPK magazine (Right)

secondary market here in the US. The aluminum AK magazines are fully functional and represent a certain page in the AK magazine development history, they should remain as a collectors or museum items.

The aluminum magazines were soon replaced by the newer, steel-reinforced composite AK magazines. The Soviets came up with a resin bonding process that would bond materials with different molecule structure such as steel and composite materials, hence the infamous orange Bakelite AK magazine.

The new composite magazine solved both AK magazine riddles: the excessive weight and cost. Apart from being much lighter than its predecessors and just as robust, it was cheap and easy to produce. Moreover, it fit perfectly for any standard-issue combat gear.

Of course, one may be surprised by the magazine's bright color and question the sanity behind the decision of the designers. Surely, the Soviets could come up with darker shade of Bakelite or simply paint it, right?

The truth is revealed as soon as one enters the woods during daytime (at night everything is dark anyway). The bright orange magazine, along with the reddish-brown AK wood furniture, simply disappears.

The new magazine very quickly replaced steel and aluminum mags in the Soviet Armed Forces. By the 60's the steel AK magazines were a rarity and most were relegated to the generous assistance packages to the "friendly" countries. The Soviets con-

Apart from the Bakelite surplus magazines, one can encounter black polymer imported magazines like these Polish ones: all plastic commercial magazine (Left) and steel re-enforced surplus (Right).

tinued to produce these magazine for their AKs into the late 80's and for RPK machine guns into the mid 90's.

Today the orange Bakelite magazine remains the most reliable, desirable, and affordable AK magazine on the market. Though some of the retailers and distributors carry these mags, the best place to find them is the secondary market.

The US market contains a plethora of AK magazines. AK owners can literally pick and choose between imported from different countries and domestically-produced magazines, depending on the caliber.

The magazines for 7.62X39mm-chambered AKs are widely available and can be slab-sided steel Russian or ribbed steel from Romania, Russia, Poland, China, or even North Korea, with occasional Serbian or Bosnian mags here and there.

Most of the steel AK mags have a 30-round capacity, however there are RPK Russian or Romanian 40-round and some 20-round Hun-

Though both of these are made by Radom they are totally different. The surplus magazine is steel reinforced and can take more abuse that its all-plastic sibling.

garian magazines that are sold today on the secondary market. One can also find Chinese five and 10-rounders imported with Chinese sporting/hunting models years ago.

The orange Bakelite magazines come from two places: Russia and China. Though not imported any longer, the Chinese Bakelite magazines are still around and can be purchased on the secondary market. The Chinese mags are darker in color and appear slightly wider. The Norinco logo can also be found on the side of the mag. However, there are Chinese magazine with the Norinco logo removed.

The Russian orange Bakelite AK magazines come with a 30-round capacity and - much more rare - with 40 rounds. The 30-round magazines vary in shades of orange depending on place and year of manufacture. The 30-round Bakelite magazines were produced by two Soviet arsenals: the Tula Arms Works located in Tula, and Izhevsk Machine-building Plant (Izhmash) in Izhevsk.

One can tell them apart by the arsenals' logos; a star for Tula and triangle with arrow for Izhevsk. The rare and much-coveted 40-round magazine has only been produced by the Molot Arsenal in Vyatskiye Polyany, Russia, and was originally designed for the Squad Machine gun, an RPK. These magazines are rare and as such demand a higher price. One can identify them by the Molot "Shield" logo on the side.

The introduction of the 100 Series AK in the 90's also saw production of black polymer 7.62X39mm magazines. The black polymer 7.62X39 AK magazines on the market today are Polish-made surplus and commercial mags, and the much more rare and desirable Russian military and Saiga magazines.

Again, most of the black polymer 7.62X39 magazines have a 30-round capacity, however there are plenty that were imported with sporting and hunting Saiga rifles from Russia with five or 10-round capacity.

Perhaps the best black polymer imported magazines are the original Russian Saiga (Left) and AK-103 (Right) mags built by Izhmash. Both are steel reinforced and can be distinguished by the lack of strengthening ribs on the commercial Saiga magazine.

The Polish surplus magazines are of a decent quality and very functional, as they are steel reinforced. Poland, as a new NATO member, switched to the NATO standard 5.56X45mm cartridge, making the 7.62X39 AKs and magazines obsolete. As a result, good numbers of black polymer surplus AK magazines were imported from Poland years ago.

Poland still imports their new-production black plastic magazine to the US for hunting and sporting rifles. Although both surplus and newly-imported magazines look very similar, the difference is in the construction and quality. The newly-imported Polish commercial magazines are not steel-reinforced and therefore only useful at the range, in my opinion.

Another import worth mentioning are the black plastic "Waffle" pattern magazines from Bulgaria that come with thirty and 40-round capacity. The lower-capacity mags of five, ten, and 20 rounds are also imported.

Bulgarian-made Arsenal AK mags are excellent-quality mags with great rigidity. They are imported by Arsenal USA, and while they are not the cheapest, they take abuse and last for years.

Separately, I would also like to mention another Russian import: the Izhmash-manufactured black plastic 30-round magazines, one for the commercially-sold Saiga carbines and the other for the 7.62X39mm-chambered true military AK-103 and AK-105. Both have been imported to the US in small numbers and as such demand a premium. Both magazines are fully steel-reinforced, however the military model has

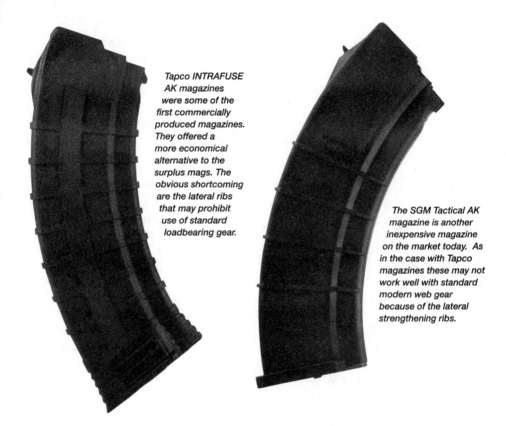

Tapco INTRAFUSE AK magazines were some of the first commercially produced magazines. They offered a more economical alternative to the surplus mags. The obvious shortcoming are the lateral ribs that may prohibit use of standard loadbearing gear.

The SGM Tactical AK magazine is another inexpensive magazine on the market today. As in the case with Tapco magazines these may not work well with standard modern web gear because of the lateral strengthening ribs.

more pronounced "ribs" along its sides.

The huge rise in AK popularity in the States saw great demand for rifles, and therefore magazines. So-called high-capacity magazines have fallen victim to numerous import bans, assault weapon bans, and any other kind of bans in the anti-gun States. Therefore, the gun market has periodically gone through shortages of AK magazines. Apart from the import shortages, the event that most spurred domestic AK magazine development is the infamous BATFE Regulation 922r, where the import of sporting guns in military configuration was restricted.

To allow a conversion of the imported rifle to the "military" configuration, manufacturers or gunsmiths had to incorporate six domestically-produced components.

The magazine could account for three of those components, saving some original features of the gun. Many domestic companies have jumped into the void and started making polymer AK mags, for better or worse.

When talking about domestically-produced AK magazines, there are two clear categories: the ones I would not hesitate to take with me into the fight, and the ones only suited for the range.

The first category includes products produced by companies that want to match their magazine to the gun in the qualities of robustness and reliability. The second category includes companies that want to match the gun's reputation of being an inexpensive gun to produce and shoot.

Either way, magazines in both categories would work just fine with any AK at the range; the difference comes in prolonged use of the magazine in the field. But let's face it: how many of us are still fighting our gun battles? Therefore, for the occasional shooter, the cheaper mags work just as well as the more robust mags.

One of the first companies to offer US-made AK magazines was Tapco, with their line of INTRAFUSE AK magazines. Made entirely of glass fiber-filled black polymer, they come in both a "waffle" pattern that may not work well with original AK combat load gear, and smooth sides that would work in any gear, as they are very similar to the commercial magazine imported from Poland.

It usually works well with any AK, and any fitment problems can fixed with light filing of the magazine feeding ramp or latch tang. At a cost of around ten dollars, it is an attractive addition to anyone's AK package.

Another inexpensive AK magazine is made by ProMag Industries of Phoenix, AZ. Made entirely from polymer with a "Waffle" pattern for additional strength, the ProMag AK magazine is sold for about $15 and comes

in a variety of "military" colors including semi-transparent smoke. This mag is also functional in any AK and very inexpensive. However, because ProMag chose to replace the stamped steel floor plate of the magazine with a plastic one, it made their magazine wide at the bottom that would not fit well in any loadbearing gear designed for an AK.

The "robust and reliable" AK magazine category is represented by US Palm and MagPul. The US Palm AK magazine was the first introduced to market. Fully reinforced, the mag was a departure from the norm. It did not have a removable floor plate and therefore could not be disassembled. US Palm foresaw a potential problem and re-released their AK mag with flush holes in the feeding ramp.

According to the company, this feature will allow a shooter to flush a magazine with soapy water to remove any debris and let it drain. It was a little unconventional, but

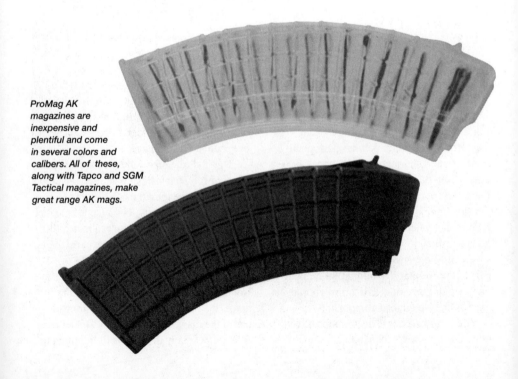

ProMag AK magazines are inexpensive and plentiful and come in several colors and calibers. All of these, along with Tapco and SGM Tactical magazines, make great range AK mags.

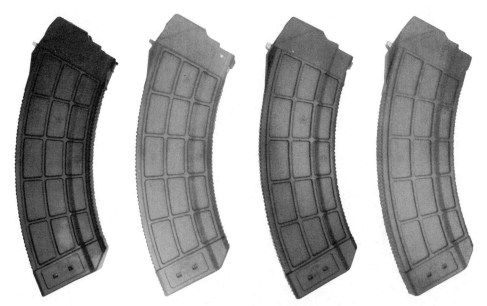

US Palm AK magazines were one of the first US made magazines that were actually designed with ruggedness in mind. These come in several popular AK mag colors.

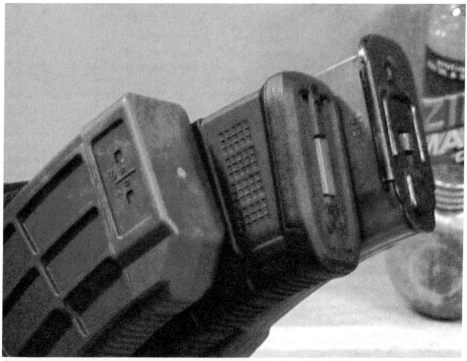

One of the differences of the US Palm AK magazine is that unlike other AK mags that can be disassembled for maintenance, the US Palm mag is a sealed box and cannot be taken apart.

The US Palm AK magazine has holes drilled into the follower. Per US Palm Company the magazine can be flushed clean through these holes.

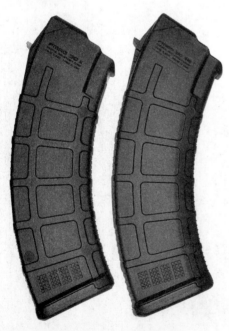

The newest AK magazine market entry is the MagPul's AK/AKM MOE PMAG 30 (Right) and its more robust sibling the AK/AKM MOE PMAG 30 GEN M3 (Left)

the five-sided box design adds rigidity and increased the ability of the magazine to take more abuse and be less affected by drops.

The outside of the US Palm AK magazine is also unconventional, and appears more rectangular in its cross section, with sharper corners. This creates an illusion of the magazine being thicker than a standard AK mag. However, the "Waffle" pattern of the US Palm magazine is "pressed" in rather than protruding like the rest of the field, thus making this magazine easier to slide in and out of the pouch.

The lack of the floor plate also helps the combat load-carrying ability of the US Palm AK magazines when carried side-by-side in the double pouch. The US Palm AK magazines are also reasonably priced and offered in a variety of colors.

The latest entries into the AK magazine market are the PMAG MOE and PMAG M3 mags from MagPul.

MagPul needs no introduction. The

company has been in the market for a long time, and earned a reputation as a high quality manufacturer of all thing AR, especially their legendary PMAG AR magazines. The calling card of MagPul are well-designed, high-quality magazines and accessories at more than reasonable prices.

As of 2014, MagPul became a player in the AK market with the introduction of their new AK magazine. Building on their AR PMAG success, the folks at MagPul have come up with the AK MOE version. Made out of the same proven tough composite material and following the conventional AK pattern, the MOE magazine came out lightweight and tough.

The sides of the magazine are "waffle" patterned like the rest, but the pattern itself is wide and has a low profile, making this mag easy to fit into any field gear designed for an AK. The only departure from the norm is the new magazine's floor plate.

MagPul utilized a similar design to that of the AR PMAG that works great. I always say, "If it ain't broke, don't fix it" so the MagPul MOE floorplate works like a charm and makes the mag disassembly for maintenance very easy.

At a price point of less than $15, this magazine is a steal and a great addition to anyone's AK package.

Along with the whole new line of AK accessories that I will describe later, came the new and improved PMAG M3 AK magazine. The improvements in the new version of the AK magazine from MagPul were geared toward improving the magazine's structural toughness. The steel reinforcement elements were now embedded into the magazine's composite body, bringing it closer to the original AK military specifications. The $10 price increase over the MOE model is still a great value for a robust and reliable magazine that will serve its owner for many years to come.

The main difference between the standard AK PMAG and GEN M3 version is the steel reinforcement rendering the GEN M3 sturdier and more durable.

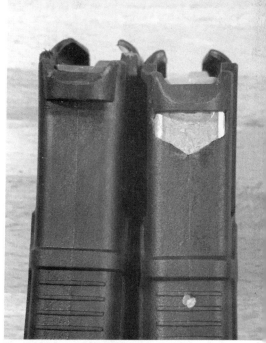

The steel reinforcement of MagPul's AK/AKM MOE PMAG 30 GEN M3 (Right) runs down the entire length of the magazine.

One of the more exotic AK magazines on the market today is the 75-round drum.

A couple other odd AK magazines for 7.62X39-chambered rifles that the AK owner may come in contact with here in the US are the two types of 75-round drum magazines.

All of the metal drum magazines are imported from either Russia, Romania, or China. Obviously, these magazines are not imported anymore from Russia or China. However, some of the US importers were able to import some drums recently from Romania. ProMag Industries is making their version of the Chinese wind up-type drum in a polymer body. It is available from several distributers today.

The 75-round drum magazine was created for the RPK squad machine gun at a time when the Soviet Armed Forced switched from the older, much heavier belt-fed 7.62X39mm Degtyarev RPD machine-gun in favor of the RPK, which was unified with the Kalashnikov family of guns.

Since the RPD was fed out of a 100-round belt housed in the steel drum, but the RPK was a magazine-fed weapon, the decision was made to design and built a high capacity drum magazine.

The Soviet type of the RPK drum magazine was made from steel and had a "ratchet" type loading system. Unlike the box-type magazine where each round is simply placed into the neck of the magazine and pressed in, compressing the magazine's feeding spring, on the drum magazine the feeding spring had to be compressed with a special lever each time the round was being loaded.

Obviously, the loading of the 75-round drum is a long process made longer by the large capacity. The reason for this type of loading is the spiral arrangement of the feeding spring, but the Chinese have come up with their own wind-up design based on

Originally designed for the RPK Light Machinegun, the drum magazine fits perfectly into any AK rifle capable of accepting high-capacity magazines.

The ratchet type drum magazine must be loaded through its neck juke like any standard AK magazine. However the ratchet lever has to be used to load every round.

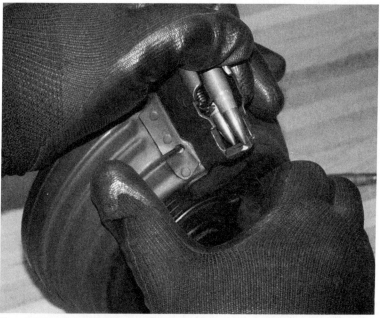

The ratchet mechanism lever is pushed up to create a space where the next round is placed. With practice the loading process goes smoothly and should not take much time.

Unlike the original Soviet drum magazine, this drum is a wound-up type. Its feeding spring has to be wound up using the "butterfly" key on the back.

The other "Chinese" type of 75-round AK drum magazine can be encountered on the market today.

Loading of the "wound-up" type drum magazine is different from the ratchet type. To load it you have to remove the back cover and place rounds is available slots. After the magazine is full, the back cover is replaced and spring is wound.

WWII machine pistol drums.

For loading, the rear plate of the Chinese AK drum magazine is removed and rounds placed into the slots arranged in the spiral (nautilus) pattern. After all the slots are filled and the rear plate is closed, the magazine's flat spiral feeding spring then has to be wound up.

Romanian arsenals have produced both types of the drums, and both types of the drum magazine could fit into and be used with any 7.62 AKM-type rifle. From the get-go these magazines were somewhat finicky and required special maintenance. However, if properly fitted and maintained, both of these types of drum magazine will serve any AK shooter well. The only negatives are the long time it takes to load them and the size and weight of the drum, which is not

friendly with any load-bearing gear.

Today both types of Romanian AK drum magazines are available to AK shooters in the US at reasonable prices. However, the original Chines and Russian drums demand a pretty penny.

The situation with the magazines for AKs chambered in 5.45X39mm is very similar to that of 7.62X39mm magazines. Since the AK-74 chambered in 5.45X39 mm caliber was introduced in 1974, by the time the Soviets were producing AK magazines in Bakelite only, it was only natural to manufacture the first AK-74 magazines from Bakelite material.

It is believed that other Warsaw Pact countries that swapped their .30-caliber AKs for their smaller sub-caliber cousins, including East Germany, Poland and Romania, have also produced 5.45 magazines.

Back in the early 90's the Sterol Bakelite 5.45 AK magazines believed to be East German but almost identical to the Soviet ones, were sold everywhere rather cheaply.

The new version AK magazine appeared after the adoption of the AK-74 family of rifles by the Soviet in 1974.

Since the new AKs were chambered for the high-intensity, but smaller 5.45X39 mm round, an entirely new, slimmer, lighter straighter magazine had to developed.

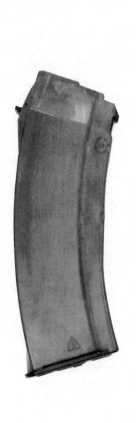
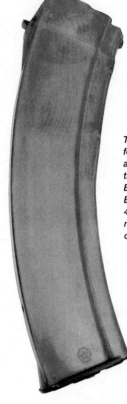

The orange Bakelite magazines for the new AK-74 rifle was a natural progression since the Soviets have been making Bakelite magazines for years. Both the 30-round (Left) and 45-round capacity (Right) magazines can be encountered on the US market.

Romanian 5.45 magazines were made from stamped steel. They are quite rare, but do not demand a higher price.

In appearance the AK-74 magazines are similar to the AKM 7.62X39mm magazines except for less curvature. The 30-round capacity AK-74 magazines imported from Russia have been manufactured by two arsenals: the Tula Arms Works in Tula for their version of the AKS-74U (shortened version of the AK-74) and Izhevsk Machine Building Plant or Izhmash in Izhevsk, the main AK manufacturing plant.

One can be distinguished from the other by the arsenal logo, either a star or a triangle with arrow on the side of the magazine.

In addition, the 45-round magazines for the squad automatic RPK machinegun were being produced by the Molot arsenal in Vytskiye Polyany, Russia. Similar in appearance but longer to accommodate for the extra capacity, these magazines were made for the Soviet Armed Forces with Molot's Shield logo, but without logo for supply to "friendly" regimes around the world.

With the onset of the modern era in the 80's, the Soviets introduced a new "dress" for their AK-74 family guns. The newly-developed glass-filled polyamide furniture had a distinct dark plum color. The socialist allies, however, were still playing with good 'ol Bakelite, or simply preferred wood as a good heat insulator.

All three Soviet arsenals started making their magazines out of the same composite material that was merged with bonding tech-

Plum-colored Soviet polyamide 5.45X39mm magazines have been produced by all three main Soviet arsenals: Tula (left), Izhmash (Center) and Molot (right). While both Tula and Izhmash plum magazines are quite common, the 45-round capacity Molot RPK-74 magazine is rare and as such demands higher price.

niques to incorporate the steel reinforcement for the new AK-74 magazines, hence the appearance of the "Plum" magazines in the US.

All of magazines I have mentioned have been imported into the States at one time or the other. There are some distributers who offer these for sale, but the secondary market is where one finds a variety, and the best deals. These magazines can be had for as little as $20 for sterol or poor condition 30-round mags, and as high as $200 plus for the Molot "Plum" 45-rounders.

Similar to the black polymer 7.62 magazine, the new black plastic 5.45 magazines were introduced in the early 90's by the Izhmash arsenal and the Arsenal company in Bulgaria. The magazines are identical and can only be identified by the arsenal logo:

the triangle with arrow for Izhmash and double circled "10" for Bulgarian.

Though the Izhmash black 5.45 AK-74 magazines have been imported in very small numbers, which makes them more coveted and thus more expensive, the Bulgarian magazines are still being imported and can be purchased relatively cheaply from the distributers and on the secondary market.

The RPK machine gun manufacturer Molot also tried to make their 45-rounders more black. They have succeeded to a point, making their new mags a really dark plum color instead of true black. These are truly rare and highly coveted by AK collectors and shooters alike.

All the 5.45X39 AK-74 magazines I've covered here are of impeccable quality, a

The latest development in 5.45X39mm AK magazines saw the introduction of black polymer mags in Russia and Bulgaria. While the Bulgarian black AK-74 magazines were imported in significant number, very few of the Izhevsk ones made it stat side.

true military grade implement. I wouldn't hesitate to make any of then a part of my loadout.

I must say a few words about the domestically produced 5.45X39 magazines. Two companies offer them at very reasonable price and as such sell a fair amount of them to AK-74 enthusiasts. One is Tapco with their INTRAFUSE AK-74 magazine and the other is the ProMag AK-74 magazine. Both are made of black polymer and both display the same traits as their 7.62 brethren I've described earlier. For only around $16, both are decently functioning range magazines.

For magazines chambered in 5.56X45 or .223 Remington caliber, things are a bit different, because the .223 or 5.56X45 NATO are not traditional AK calibers.

The first AK variants in .223 or 5.56 NATO caliber that started to arrive stateside were the Israeli Galil rifles, followed closely by Chinese AKs imported by two separate arsenals, Polytec and Norinco.

These rifles accepted stamped steel 30-round magazine that were not interchangeable. Even the two Chinese guns would have fitment problems with each other's magazines. Both the Galil and Chines .223 AK magazines are still sold on the secondary market in the US. Very tough, high quality Israeli or Chinese .223 magazines may or may not fit into more modern AKs chambered in this caliber. Some filing and/or a little welding may be required to make them fit.

The undisputed leader in .223 AK magazines are the imported and domestic polymer mags. Numerous sources for these make it literally look like plastic fruit salad. Such is the color spectrum of .223 AK mags that can be purchased today.

The import segment is represented

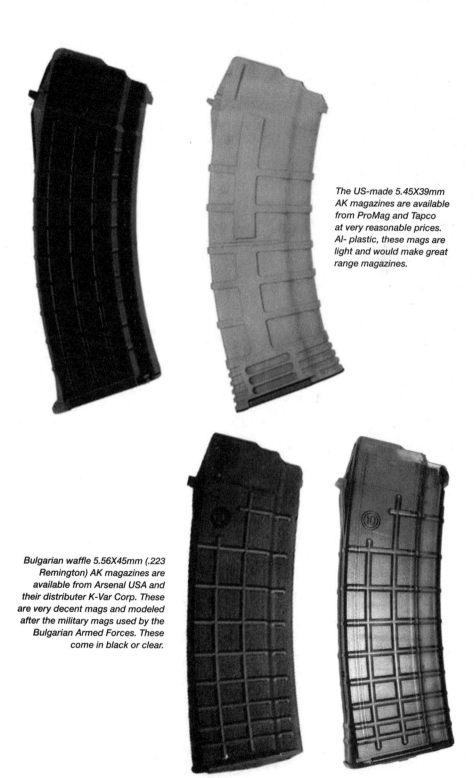

The US-made 5.45X39mm AK magazines are available from ProMag and Tapco at very reasonable prices. Al- plastic, these mags are light and would make great range magazines.

Bulgarian waffle 5.56X45mm (.223 Remington) AK magazines are available from Arsenal USA and their distributer K-Var Corp. These are very decent mags and modeled after the military mags used by the Bulgarian Armed Forces. These come in black or clear.

Aside from the standard 30-round capacity, the Bulgarian 5.56X45 mm AK magazines also come in reduced capacity configuration, like these 20-rounders.

mainly by Poland and Bulgaria. In both cases the Polish and Bulgarian AK magazines for the .223 Remington or 5.56 NATO ammo are product for these new NATO countries' efforts to convert to the NATO military standards.

The Bulgarian .223 AK magazines are produced by Arsenal and imported into the US by Arsenal USA in Las Vegas, NV. They have the typical commercial "Waffle" pattern just like their 7.62 and 5.45 siblings, and just like other commercial mags, are made entirely out of plastic without reinforcement. They come in black or clear and 30 or 20-round capacity.

The other import is made by Lucznik Arms Factory in Radom, Poland, and brought into the States by IO, Inc. in Palm Bay, FL. The Polish 5.56 NATO (.223) magazine is made from semi-transparent or black plastic. The shade of the transparent magazines varies. Most of Polish magazines that are imported are 30-round capacity.

Both of these imported .223 Remington or 5.56 NATO AK magazines are of good

Polish Beryl rifle magazines fit any AK in 5.56X45mm (NATO) caliber. These are copies of Polish Military mags and are being imported.

One of the most coveted 5.45X39mm AK magazines is the Molot 45-round RPK-74 mag.

Also around are various .223 steel AK magazines of different origin. Most widely available are the East German Weiger magazines.

quality and work well with any AK chambered in this caliber. They are reasonably priced at $30-$40 and can be purchased from the importer or distributer and on the secondary market.

Two more imported 5.56 (.223) AK magazines stand above all, and have only been imported in very small numbers. One is the original black polymer steel reinforced 30-round AK-101/102 Russian magazine from Izhmash. The second is the dark "plum" ribbed 45-round RPK magazine from Russia's Molot arsenal. Both of these are outstanding military-grade magazines that exceed any other .5.56 (.223) AK magazine in quality and functionality. Because they are rare, they demand a premium price.

Various hunting five and 10-round 5.56 (.223) AK magazines are also available to the AK shooters here in the US. Anything from steel Chinese to polymer Russian or Bulgarian short mags can be had relatively cheaply.

If there is a void, there will be a domestic company that will try to fill it, and the .223 AK magazines are not an exception. Since the numbers of magazines imported into the States from other countries has always been low, and demand remains high, several American companies have released their own version of the 5.56 NATO or .223 Remington AK magazines.

ProMag Industries makes and sells their

Domestically produced 5.56X45mm or .223 Remington magazines are represented by all plastic ProMag (Left) and SGM Tactical (Right) mags. Both are excellent range magazines.

AK-223 black polymer AK magazine for less than $20. It is very similar to the 7.62 and 5.45 magazine the company produces and displays the same traits. The other company that makes their own design black polymer 5.56 or .223 AK magazine is SGM Tactical out of Knoxville, TN.

The SGM magazine appears well made out of black composite material. It is not steel or aluminum reinforced. However, the SGM mag has lateral strengthening "ribs" for shape integrity so that the magazine, made by the injection molding process, will not "collapse".

Just like the ProMag magazine, the floor plate is also made of plastic and therefore makes this magazine slightly wide at the bottom. As I've mentioned before, this feature and the strengthening ribs would cause a problem when this magazine is used in standard AK gear. Nevertheless, the SGM 5.56/.223 AK magazine is a fine functioning magazine. It is readily available from the manufacturer or distributes for under $35, which makes it a good range mag. SGM Tactical also makes .223 AK mags with five and 15-round capacity.

Since the need for high quality, military-grade AK magazines in .223 Remington or 5.56 NATO calibers remains high, many, myself included, have tried to improvise with the materials at hand. Just like they say,

The 5.45X39mm AK magazine will insert into the .223 rifle and can be loaded with .223 ammunition. But the capacity of this magazine will be reduced for the rifle to function properly.

the bolt will not be able to "grab" the next round out of the magazine. So, any practical use of 30-round 5.45 magazines in the .223 AK is limited to about 10 rounds.

A much better method is to replace the 5.45 magazine follower with a 5.56 or .223 one. Luckily they are several on the market today. In this case one can increase a magazine's practical capacity to about 20 rounds. Further loading would meet obstructions from the curvature radius of the 5.45 AK magazine. As a good measure, only proper magazines should be used in any rifle, and AK is not an exception.

The lack of the military-grade magazines and subsequent high prices of the 5.56X45 AK magazines can lead to some innovative ways to adapt an AR magazines for use with the 5.56 (.223) AK rifles. The AR GI magazines are plentiful and cheap and they would allow shooters to use any AR load-bearing gear. Note, however, that to convert an AK to be able to accept AR magazines would require a permanent modification to the gun. It would not be possible to convert it back due to permanent modifications to the receiver.

In any case, there is no shortage of magazines in the US in all the major calibers AKs are chambered in. An AK enthusiast can easily pick and choose what magazine to get for his or her rifle based on practicality, functionality, reliability, etc. But whatever AK magazine is chosen, the important thing to remember is that a magazine is a part of the machine, has moving parts, and as such has to be maintained and cared for. Keep it clean, keep it oiled, and it will last for a long, long time.

"Life gives lemons, make lemonade," except in this case, some of the AK enthusiasts tried to make Coke or Pepsi out those lemons.

Since the radius of the curvature of the 5.45 AK magazine is similar to that of the 5.56, and the length of the cartridge itself is very similar, some owners of .223 AKs have tried to simply load 5.56X45mm ammo into a high-capacity 5.45X39 mm magazine and use it in their 5.56 (.223) AK rifles.

The 5.45X39 magazine will take 30 rounds of 5.56 ammo and will insert and retain in the .223 AK properly. However, due to a difference in diameter of the bottom end of the casing, at about the 11-12 round count, the rounds will start to mis-align and

CHAPTER SIX

AK BAYONETS

This chapter will appeal to collectors and serious AK enthusiasts. If they are like me then it is a short series of steps from the AK shooter to the AK enthusiast to the AK collector. What often started as just a weekend at the range with an inexpensive gun shortly turns into full-blown collecting.

Since the AK rifle was designed as a military fighting battle rifle at the end of WWII when bayonet charges were a regular occurrence, the AK had a bayonet as a standard issue from the beginning. Today's modern warfare doctrine has all but forgotten the bayonet, although the occasional use of a bayonet charge in combat is still recorded as recently as 2011.

Bayonet charges were used by the British during the Falklands War in 1982, and the Soviets used bayonets during hand-to-hand combat with the Mujahedeen in Afghanistan in several documented instances in the 80's. In 2004 a British Army sergeant led his squad in a bayonet charge after his unit was ambushed near Basra Iraq. In 2011 in Afghanistan another British sergeant led his small group of soldiers in the bayonet charge against the Taliban.

All who served in the Soviet Armed Forces most likely pulled sentry duty where the attached bayonet to your AK was a must.

When writing about
an AK rifle it is hard
to imagine it without
its iconic bayonet.

Today's modern Russian military continues to train with bayonets.

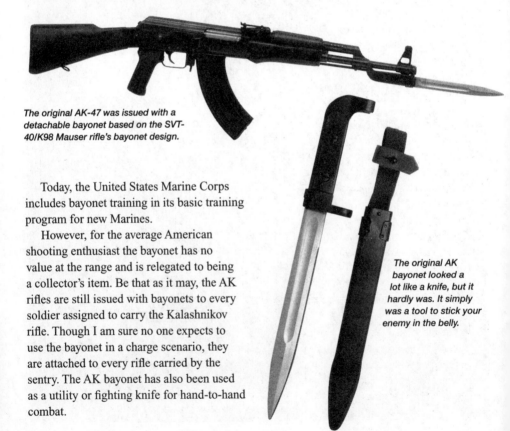

The original AK-47 was issued with a detachable bayonet based on the SVT-40/K98 Mauser rifle's bayonet design.

Today, the United States Marine Corps includes bayonet training in its basic training program for new Marines.

However, for the average American shooting enthusiast the bayonet has no value at the range and is relegated to being a collector's item. Be that as it may, the AK rifles are still issued with bayonets to every soldier assigned to carry the Kalashnikov rifle. Though I am sure no one expects to use the bayonet in a charge scenario, they are attached to every rifle carried by the sentry. The AK bayonet has also been used as a utility or fighting knife for hand-to-hand combat.

The original AK bayonet looked a lot like a knife, but it hardly was. It simply was a tool to stick your enemy in the belly.

In 1959 when the new lighter version of AK was introduced, apart from many improvements to the rifle the modernized AKM gun also came with a new bayonet.

Most of the AK rifles that are configured to the military specification come with a bayonet lug, a feature that has been deemed as "evil" by the federal government and widely identifiable with so-called assault rifles. As such, during federal or state assault rifle bans, the bayonet lug is one of the evil features that must be removed from the gun. That means there are many post-ban rifles that may not have the lug for a bayonet. That, however, is neither here or there for an average AK shooter, as one can date the rifle by the presence or lack of this feature.

Just like the AK rifle itself, its bayonet has gone through several modifications, from a longer double-edged and narrow-bladed bayonet suitable only for the charges across a no-man's land, to more of a multi-functional field tool.

There have been three major stages in the AK bayonet evolution, each one making it more practical and adding more universal functions. The first was in the early 50's when the AK "pig sticker" bayonet was replaced with a single-edge Bowie-type knife bayonet that could also be used apart from the gun. The blade also featured a saw.

Although the original AK-47 bayonet came with a steel scabbard, where it was carried when not attached to the rifle, the scabbard itself wasn't meant to be used as anything else. However, the newer steel AK bayonet scabbard had an added feature: when coupled with the blade of the bayonet it became a nifty wire cutter.

To be able to remove the scabbard from the belt, the new leather frog had a karabiner. An additional rubber insulating handle-sleeve was slid over the steel scabbard for soldier protection if the wire was electrified.

Interestingly, some of the Soviet satellite countries chose not to further modify their

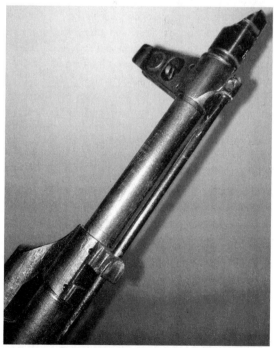

The new AKM rifle now had an accessory lug that served as an attachment for a newly redesigned bayonet and underbarrel grenade launcher.

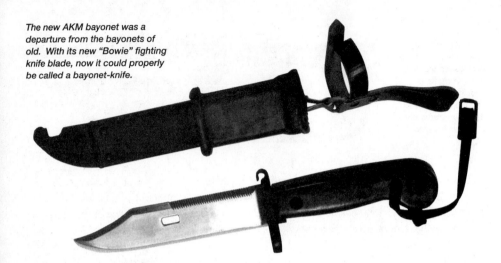

The new AKM bayonet was a departure from the bayonets of old. With its new "Bowie" fighting knife blade, now it could properly be called a bayonet-knife.

AK bayonets and kept the original model as the standard issue bayonet for their Armed Forces. However, the others chose to follow the Soviets in development of the newer, more functional AK bayonet.

With the introduction of the Bakelite-to-steel bonding process and its use in the firearm production, the Soviets modified the AK bayonet further. The new model had a ridged Bakelite scabbard that was lighter and did not require a rubber insulation sleeve.

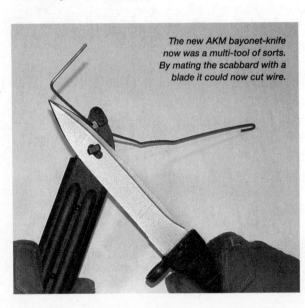

The new AKM bayonet-knife now was a multi-tool of sorts. By mating the scabbard with a blade it could now cut wire.

The bayonet's Bakelite handle was redesigned and given several new features. Besides being a wire cutter, the new bayonet could be used as a hammer and a pick. To do so one needed to press the muzzle ring/hand guard into the opening of the scabbard, then the steel butt of the bayonet's handle became a hammer and blade a pick, with the scabbard being the handle.

A final modification was made when the "Plum" AK-74 was adapted for service. The new bayonet had a spear type double-edged blade with handle and scabbard made from the dark plum-colored, glass-filled polyamide as the new rifle's furniture.

Like the rifles, the bayonets have been produced in all the countries where AK production was established. Whereas strict adherence to the original AK design was a must, the bayonet configuration was left up to the individual country so the AK bayonets could be configured to fit that particular country's military's field gear.

As a result there were a fair

A handy tool for scouts and reconnaissance troops to breach enemy defenses.

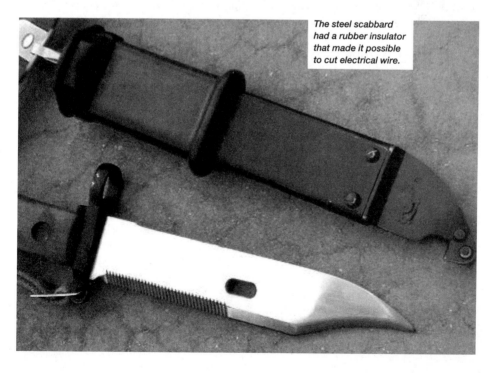

The steel scabbard had a rubber insulator that made it possible to cut electrical wire.

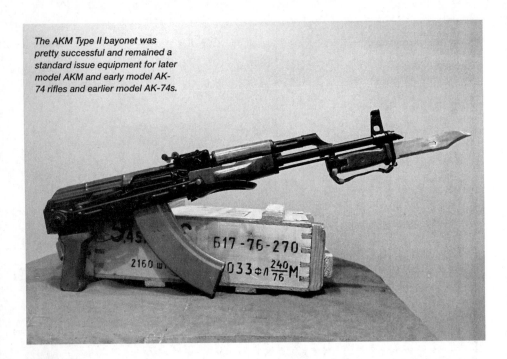

The AKM Type II bayonet was pretty successful and remained a standard issue equipment for later model AKM and early model AK-74 rifles and earlier model AK-74s.

number of AK bayonet models and modifications based on the country of origin. Just about every type of the AK bayonet has been imported into the US at one time or another. What one can buy on the secondary market today range from the original Russian bayonets from the earliest AK-47 'WWII' pattern to the most recent AK-100 Series.

The Chinese, Yugoslavian, Polish, East German, Bulgarian, and Romanian bayonets can be purchased for reasonable prices today. These versions of the AK bayonet lost the hammer and saw functions, but retained the wire-cutting ability. In the 90's the same model bayonet was produced dressed in black plastic to match AK 100 Series rifles. Only Bulgaria, out of all the foreign AK manufacturers, adopted the new double-edged bayonet.

Final modifications to the AK bayonet were made when the "Plum" AK-74 was adapted for service. The new bayonet had a spear-type double-edged blade with handle and scabbard made from the same dark

"plum" color glass-filled polyamide as the new rifle's furniture. This version of the bayonet lost its hammer and saw functions, but retained the wire cutting ability. In the 90's the same model bayonet was produced dressed in black plastic to match AK 100 Series rifles and still is the current model for all new Russian AK-74M that are issued Russian soldiers today.

What can be bought on the secondary market today are the original Russian bayonets from the earliest AK-47 'WWII' pattern once to the most recent AK-100 Series.

The Chinese, Yugoslavian, Polish, East German, Bulgarian and Romanian bayonets can purchased for reasonable price today. Only one out of foreign AK manufacturers only Bulgaria adapted the new AK-100 series double edged bayonet dressed in black plastic.

All of the AK bayonet models from the earliest to the latest and from different countries of origin are easily obtainable here in the US on the secondary market.

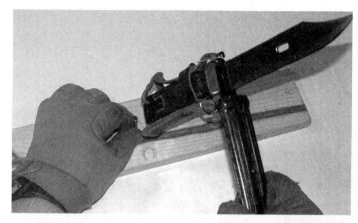

The new Type II bayonet also gained a couple more functions. By placing a muzzle ring into the scabbard's neck it can be used as a hammer.

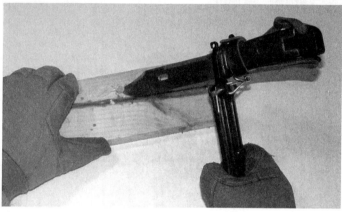

If you turn the bayonet around it becomes a pick. The usefulness of this tool always escaped me as I'd rather grip the bayonet by its handle if I need a pick.

The mid -80's saw the introduction of new polyamide furniture on Soviet AK-74 rifles. New "plum" color furniture was coupled with a completely redesigned AK bayonet dressed in the same color polyamide.

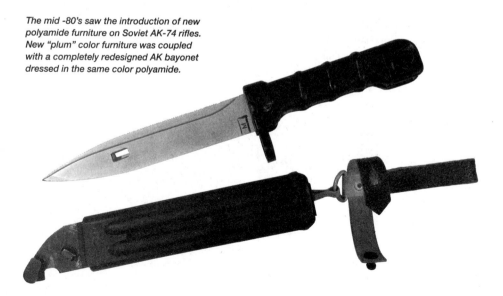

The "spear" double-edged AK bayonet dressed in black polyamide remains a current issued bayonet for all Russian AK-74M and 100 Series rifles today.

Not all AK bayonets were detachable. Some of the Chinese Type 56 AK variants came with non-detachable folding bayonets.

Romanian AK bayonets followed an early Soviet AKM pattern, but in combination with a different suspension system instead of the traditional karabiner leather frog. Several other countries adapted the same system for their AK bayonets.

CHAPTER SEVEN

AMMUNITION

When we say "AK" we almost automatically mean an AK rifle chambered in 7.62X39 mm. This would not be too far from reality, as most of the AKs that are involved in various wars and conflicts around the world are in fact chambered to fire the original AK-47 cartridge, the 7.62X39mm Model 1943, or M43 for short. The same can be said about the commercial civilian market here and abroad.

However, even though the original caliber prevails, AKs have been made in a variety of calibers. The most famous non-.30-caliber AK rifle is the AK-74, introduced by the So-

viets in 1974 and chambered in 5.45X39mm in response to the American 5.56X45mm round that was use in the M16 during the Vietnam War. An entire family of weapons was developed to fire the new cartridge, designated as 7N6. Even some Warsaw Pact countries produced their own AK rifles for the newly adapted sub-caliber ammunition.

The fall of the Soviet Union and adoption of a free market economy saw Russians and former socialist camp satellites modifying their AKs to accept Western caliber ammunition, hence the introduction of several models capable of firing a 5.56 NATO round.

Many things have changed since the inception of the AK-47 battle rifle. Calibers in which the modern AKs are chambered are no exception. These are most of the cartridges that you'll find AK rifles chambered in today.

Other Kalashnikov action-based sniper rifles were produced earlier by a couple of Soviet allies for the heavier 7.62X54R round, such as the Yugoslavian M76 and Romanian ROMAK III, aka PSL. The 1990's saw Russian arsenals enter the hunting/sporting commercial market with Saiga and Vepr rifles chambered in other calibers in addition to the traditional AK calibers, including .223, .308, and the 6.5 Grendel.

Nevertheless, the two main calibers for an AK on the Market today still remain the original 7.62X39 and very potent 5.45X39.

7.62X39MM M43 CARTRIDGE

Work on this intermediate cartridge began in the USSR in 1939, although the idea had been discussed much earlier. To study the effects of the intermediate cartridge concept, a special 5.45 mm round was developed. To further explore the potential of this cartridge an order was issued to design an automatic rifle capable of firing it. However, with the beginning of WWII all of the development work was suspended and diverted elsewhere to help with the war effort.

In 1943 the development of an intermediate cartridge started again in response to the advent of the German intermediate cartridge

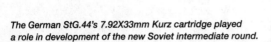

The German StG.44's 7.92X33mm Kurz cartridge played a role in development of the new Soviet intermediate round.

that had been used in their new assault rifle, the Stg .44. Once the captured German Stg .44 rifles started arriving in the hands of the Soviet designers, the rifles and ammunition were carefully studied, analyzed, and compared to the American-made .30-caliber M1 Carbines which were being supplied to the Soviets under the Lend-Lease program.

It was decided that the new intermediate cartridge had to replace all calibers in semi-automatic rifles, machine guns and other small arms. As it turned out, the introduction of the new intermediate cartridge made it easier to develop a whole new series of

Though the idea and concept may have been partially borrowed from the German 7.92X33mm Kurtz cartridge (left), the new Soviet 7.62X39mm Model 1943 (right) was far superior in every aspect and became one of the most prolific cartridges of all times.

weapons, including a completely new individual automatic rifle with greater range of effective fire than the sub-machine gun.

To determine the optimal characteristics of the cartridge, three calibers were proposed based on wide use: the 5.6mm, 6.5mm, and 7.62mm. After testing, the latter was determined as an optimum caliber for the new intermediate cartridge. At the same time the new parameters for the casing were laid out. It was to be rimless, as was most of the modern cartridges. The new cartridge was intended for use with semi-automatic rifle, machine-gun and automatic carbine, so the energy of the cartridge had to be significant to allow a reduction of barrel length.

The specified trajectory of the projectile and other ballistics of the 7.62 intermediate cartridge had to exceed that of the German 7.92X33mm round.

On September 3, 1943 the new intermediate cartridge was adapted by the Soviet Chief Armament Counsel and named the 7.62mm cartridge model 1943 (M43).

In December of the same year the first batch of the new ammunition was delivered to the test range for field testing. The tests and further modifications to the M43 cartridge continued and the final version with bi-metal core was finally adapted and began to be supplied to Soviet troops alongside the new AK-47 rifles. In service for close to 70 years, the 7.62X39mm M43 cartridge continues to be a main AK cartridge and will remain so for years to come.

5.45X39MM 7N6 CARTRIDGE

The introduction of the AK-74 rifle by the Soviets in 1974 was coupled with the arrival of a totally new high-velocity, low-impulse 5.45X39mm cartridge. The round the AK-74 fired was drastically different from the original 1943 7.62X39 intermediate round and had a designation of 7N6.

The flatter trajectory of the 5.45mm round

The Soviets introduced a new family of guns in 1974 chambered for an entirely different cartridge, the 5.45X39mm 7N6. The high energy and low impulse sub-caliber round improved accuracy and combat effectiveness of the AK and offered 30% reduction in weight for a soldier's loadout.

increased the range of point-blank fire against a running target from 526 meters to 625 meters; however the range of terminal effect decreased from 1500 meters to 1350 meters.

The decrease in the diameter and size of the bullet delivered the inevitable increase in the muzzle velocity accompanied by the decreased recoil impulse.

It was different not only in the bullet diameter and muzzle velocity but also in the construction of the bullet itself. The 7N6 cartridge's bullet had a full metal jacket and steel core surrounded by lead. It also had an "air pocket" at the very tip, causing its jacket to deform on the impact.

The higher bullet speed flattened the trajectory, decreased wind deflection, and light-

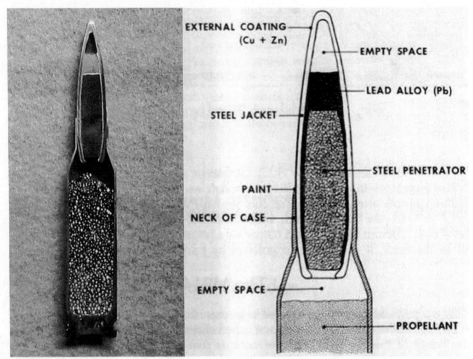

EXTERNAL COATING (Cu + Zn)

EMPTY SPACE

LEAD ALLOY (Pb)

STEEL JACKET

STEEL PENETRATOR

PAINT

NECK OF CASE

EMPTY SPACE

PROPELLANT

The biggest and most drastic departure from the original 7.62X399mm round lies with the 7N6 bullet. Due to a hollow space and core shift the trajectory of the round once it strikes the target radically changes, causing significant destruction.

There is a plethora of commercial 7.62X39 mm ammunition on the market today, of both imported and domestic origin. Domestic 7.62X39 mm ammo is non-corrosive, but it varies in quality. One can find regular steel jacketed ball and suitable for hunting HP ammo along with some copper jacketed rounds.

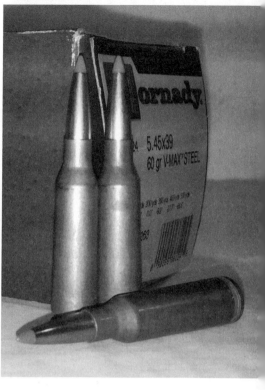

Hornady Ammunition has developed their own domestically produced steel case V-Max 5.45X39 mm round.

These are the most popular 5.45X39 mm ammo on the market today. Though banned from further importation, 7N6 (left) is still obtainable. Also shown here, Wolf (center) and domestically produced Hornady ammo (right).

Wolf is bringing in considerable quantities of 5.45 ammo, all non-corrosive and good to go.

ened ammunition load. All this addressed the problem of enhancing combat efficiency of the "cartridge-weapon" complex. However, due to its light weight in comparison to its 7.62 mm predecessor, it got a bum wrap for its lack of stopping power. In my opinion, it stopped everything and everyone just fine. On impact the 5.45mm projectile is deformed and loses its stability. It then starts to tumble and changes its original trajectory. Bullets with such flight characteristics cause extensive damage to the soft tissue, internal organs and bones.

Many would argue that Soviet soldiers in Afghanistan preferred the 7.62mm-chambered AKM to the 5.45mm AK-74 due to its better stopping power. As valid as this argument may be, other reasons (stated earlier in the book) of easier ammo accessibility and silencer performance may have had more weight than stopping power.

Nevertheless, the new high-velocity and low-impulse 5.45X39mm 7N6 cartridge offered a far superior controllability on full auto and more importantly, thirty percent reduction in weight in a full ammo load.

There are many anecdotal stories about the 5.45X39mm cartridge and its bullet. One involved how the bullet with its offset center of gravity causing horrible wounds. That one is partially true, unlike the one that due to its light weight the 5.45mm bullet would easily be deflected and would not penetrate as good as its heavier .30 Caliber sibling. That one is actually totally opposite reality.

My favorite came from the Afghan Mujahedeen, who called it a "wasp" and "poisoned bullet". The names have some merit because of the 7N6 bullet's drastic and unpredictable pattern. Once it enters a soft tissue it leaves a nasty wound channel and two cavitation cavities, making it hard to treat wounds in the field.

In 2001 when I met the Man himself, Mikhail Kalashnikov, he told me that he was against the adoption of the 5.45-caliber cartridge. He though that 7.62X39mm had more unexplored potential.

However, later in our discussion Mr. Kalashnikov mentioned that he was a huge fan of the AKS-74U rifle, the shortened version of the AK-74 that was, like all AK-74 family guns, chambered in 5.45X39mm. He then described how the gun and cartridge exceeded expectations during tests on year-old hogs at 350 meters.

Personally, I love the 5.45X39mm round. I think that it is pretty close to being a perfect carbine cartridge that has low recoil impulse and at the same time carries its energy way past any other modern carbine round. But, that is my opinion that may not reflect the opinion of other AK shooters.

Although the 7.62X39mm and 5.45X39mm are the two main AK calibers, there are many AK or AK-based rifles that were made in other calibers. A distant third to the AK-47/AKM and AK-74 type rifles are the rifles chambered in 5.56X45 NATO or .223 Remington, followed by hunting rifles in .308 and 7.62X54R calibers, as well as the 6.5 Grendel from Molot Arsenal.

Just like with AK magazines, we in the US have a "smorgasbord" of ammunition for our AK rifles. There is hard-to-get ammo available only on the secondary market for surplus ammunition. There is new manufacturer-imported ammo, and there is US-produced ammunition in all of the AK calibers.

The accessibility and affordability of ammunition caused a rapid rise of the AK popularity in the US. Years ago, the surplus ammo in both calibers was flowing stateside from China, Russia, and the newly independent East European countries. So much ammo was coming in that it made owning an AK a very attractive option from an economical point of view.

The bliss lasted until someone made an AK pistol chambered in 7.62X39mm, thus qualifying the surplus ammunition in this caliber as pistol ammo. The ban on steel-core pistol ammo was instituted years earlier. Since all of the surplus AK ammo had a steel or bi-metal core, this event put an end to any further imports of 7.62X39 mm ammunition into the US no matter of country of origin. With the import of 7.62X39 mm surplus ammo banned and prices starting to climb, AK shooters and enthusiasts were still able to enjoy the awesomely low-priced 5.45X39mm surplus ammo in their AK-74's. The supply of the imported surplus ammunition in this caliber seemed to be plentiful indefinitely. Prices at one point got to less than 10 cents per round.

Again, this lasted until someone built an AK-74-based pistol. In 2014, the 5.45X39mm ammunition was also classified as pistol ammo, and as such, any further importation of bi-metal core surplus ammunition was prohibited.

I should also mention that most of the Russian, Chinese, Romanian, and Ukrainian surplus ammo in both calibers came not only with steel or bi-metal core, but also with steel casing and corrosive Berdan-type primers. Since all AK surplus ammunition was made with steel casing and steel jacketed bullets, anti-corrosion coatings had to be devised by the manufacturers.

Ammunition produced in the 40's through 70's was a copper wash coating to prevent the steel casing and jacket from rusting. Later the green lacquer coating was introduced and is still in use today for both main AK calibers in military and commercial ammunition alike.

The myth that the coating lacquer would melt and built up in the chamber is just that - a myth. None of my rifles or the rifles I have been issued ever had any problems with any lacquer-coated ammunition. In fact, according to some specialist the green lacquer serves as a better sealant and lubricant (when hot) than any other coating.

However, all the steel-core ammo importation bans did was drive up prices for such ammo. The sheer amount of ammo imported would insure that it would still be available on the secondary market for year to come.

Even when cheap surplus ammo was freely imported, many companies foreign and domestic developed sporting/hunting lead-core ammunition in these calibers. Considering the surplus ammo pricing, the price of this ammo had to be kept low as well. Most of the domestic ammo manufacturers went even further to improve on the quality of the AK ammunition by making it with brass casing and non-corrosive "Boxer" primers. All of the surplus ammo imported from Russia had highly corrosive Berdan primers that would cause rust and sulfate build-up corrosion if the rifle is not cleaned immediately.

Today there is no shortage of ammunition for the AK rifles in both main AK calibers. The prices are still low, making the prospect of owning an AK rifle an attractive proposition. Even most demanding and picky AK owners can choose ammunition for their rifle based on quality, manufacturer's reputation, material, and ballistics without worrying about corrosion or any damage – mystical or real - to their guns. The less expensive imported ammo has its own positive draw, as it usually mimics the ballistic characteristics of its military cousins.

One of the biggest importers of recently produced AK ammunition is Wolf Performance Ammunition (WPA) out of California. WPA brings in ammo produced in the biggest ammunition plant in Russia, the Barnaul Cartridge Works, which also produces steel cased ammo in .223 Remington, .308 Winchester, 6.5 Grendel, and other popular calibers here in the States.

In 2013, I had a chance to visit the Barnaul plant and observe the R&D and

One of the largest importers of 7.62X39mm ammunition is Wolf Performance Ammunition. Wolf imports a variety of loads. The latest is the Barnaul Cartridge Plant's polymer-coated polyformance ammo.

manufacturing processes and inspect the quality control stations and procedures. Wolf also works with other Russian and European ammo manufacturers, offering a variety of calibers and loads for many rifles and handguns. I have been shooting Wolf ammo for years and never had a problem.

Today Wolf offers several loads of sporting and hunting ammo for AKs. The Wolf Military Classic loads mimic performance of the military load. The newer line of Polyformance Ammunition uses polymer coating instead of conventional green lacquer and offers better cycling performance, and their Gold line ammo offers the better quality loads that today's shooters expect.

The other well-known name in the AK game is the leading importer of firearms and ammunition, Century Arms, with offices in Florida and Vermont.

A couple of years back Century introduced their "Red Army" line of Romanian commercial ammunition. I shot a fair amount of the Red Army ammunition in 7.62X39mm and 7.62X54R calibers. Every time I've ever pulled the trigger I've heard a loud "Bang!" This ammo has produced the expected result every time I've shot it. Reasonably priced, this ammunition stacks up well against any other AK ammo on the market today.

Almost all Russian ammo manufacturers import their ammo into the United States. The biggest is the Tula Ammunition Plant in Tula, Russia. Rather than partner with an importer, Tula has chosen to import their product directly though their offices in Texas. Again, TulAmmo ammunition closely matches the original military AK ammo and when fired produces the desirable result. Their pricing is in line with other Russian imported ammunition.

Other Russian manufacturers also sporadically import their products to the US. American AK shooters can encounter ammunition sold under Golden Bear, Silver

Century Arms is the other well-known importer of AK ammunition. Their lates offering is their Romanian "Red Army" steel-cased and Bosnian "Red Army Elite" brass-cased ammo.

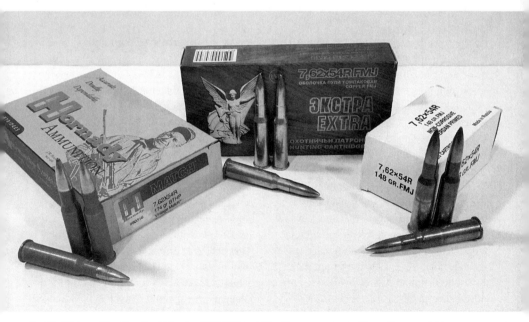

For the AK-type rifles chambered for the 7.62X54R cartridge there are many options. One can choose between inexpensive surplus or Wolf's highly accurate Russian "Extra" competition load (center) or new Hornady Match, or anything in between.

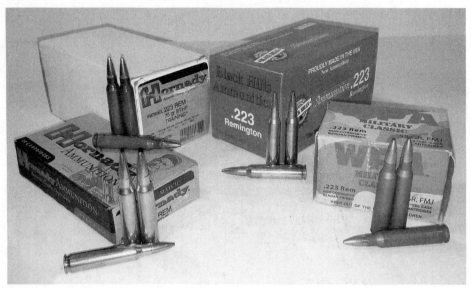

There is an ocean of 5.56X45 mm NATO (.223 Remington) ammunition available for an AK. Anything the AR shoots, the AK will eat up. Anything from economically-priced Wolf ammo to more of the precise Black Hills or Hornady loads can be fed to the AK.

Bear, Brown Bear, and Golden Tiger. All of the abovementioned ammunition is Russian made and good-to-go for use in any AK rifle.

Several importers and distributers such as Sellier & Bellot, Cheaper than Dirt, and Sportsman's Guide offer a vast variety of imported and domestic ammo for the AK. Although the ammo comes from different sources, it is all reasonably priced.

The highest quality AK ammunition in 7.62X39mm comes out Finland and is manufactured by Lapua. This ammo is a far departure from surplus-based commercial ammo from Russia. It would match even the most demanding AK shooter's requirements for modern ammunition. However, the price reflects the quality.

Domestic companies started to produce 7.62X39 mm ammunition years ago, spurred on by the original steel core ammo ban. Today all the largest ammo manufacturers produce ammo for AKs. Though generally higher-priced than the commercial imported steel-case ammo, the domestically-produced AK ammunition offers higher quality, brass re-loadable cases, and a wide selection of loads and projectiles.

Federal Premium Ammunition offers three different loads in 7.62x39mm, Winchester has two, and Remington manufactures several loads to choose from. Hornady is the only American ammo manufacturer that makes AK ammunition in both AK calibers and with steel cases. I have shot most of these loads at one time or the other. Some perform better than others, but they all performed well within the accuracy parameters for AK-type rifles.

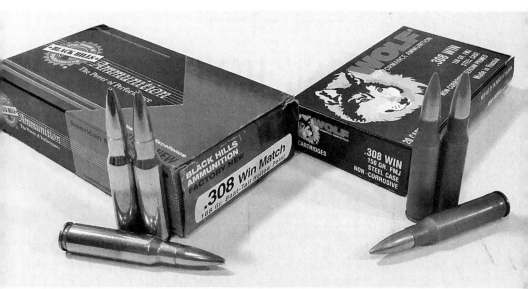

Similar to the .223 Remington ammunition, the 7.62 X51 mm NATO, or as commonly .308, is plentiful from number of manufacturers, including Wolf 's steel case loads or variety of more precise loads from Black Hills like this HP boat-tail round.

The latest development in ammunition is the steel case 6.5 mm Grendel load imported by Wolf from Russia. Recently Molot arsenal launched production of Vepr sporting rifles chambered in this caliber.

CHAPTER EIGHT

AK BASIC HANDLING, LOADING, AND RELOADING

As I've mentioned before, the AK was designed with the conscripted soldier in mind. It had to be simple enough for students, peasants, or factory workers to master in a very short time.

Mr. Kalashnikov achieved this feat rather beautifully. The AK rifle is laid out like many other semi-automatic rifles, i.e. to follow in line with bolt-action rifles with bolt or charging handle on the right. I am afraid that I will be assaulted by more experienced shooters for how I am about to describe the basic handling and shooting of the AK, but there are many techniques that one can learn while mastering his or her rifle. I will touch on some of the advanced handling techniques later, but I wanted to start with basics and build on them.

Mr. Kalashnikov achieved this feat rather beautifully. The AK rifle is laid out like many other semi-automatic rifles, i.e. to follow in line with bolt-action rifles with bolt

The AK was designed to be simple and easy to master by any conscript within two weeks.

As with most rifles of the day, automatic or bolt operated, the AK was designed to be run by the shooter's right hand

or charging handle on the right. I am afraid that I will be assaulted by more experienced shooters for how I am about to describe the basic handling and shooting of the AK, but there are many techniques that one can learn while mastering his or her rifle. I will touch on some of the advanced handling techniques later, but I wanted to start with basics and build on them.

LOADING

To prepare an AK for shooting one must first load its magazine with proper ammunition. The AK magazine is a box-type with rounds arranged inside in the checkered pattern. Although there are loading devices on the market today, most of the do not work and offer marginal advantage over regular hand loading.

Loading of the AK magazine is done by gripping the magazine with the non-dominant hand (for right-handed people it is left and for lefties it is right) at its top (neck)

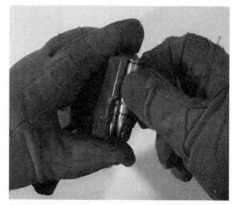

There are so called speed-loading devises for loading an AK magazine. None works as well and as reliably as your own two hands, especially under stress.

and with the front facing toward the shooter/loader.

The grip should be high enough in such a manner that it does not obstruct the opening of the mag, and thumb resting in front of the feeding lips. The round is inserted from the top with bullet facing the loader. It is then

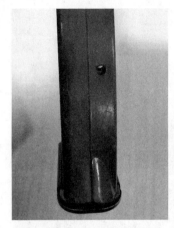

It is important not to overload the magazine. Check a window at the back of the magazine for magazine fullness. You should only see the first round partially from the top.

While the magazine is not inserted and clearly visible, pull the bolt carrier handle back to expose the chamber. Visually insure that the chamber is empty and the gun is not loaded.

pressed into the magazine and, once it is in, slightly pushed toward the back of the mag. Having the thumb in front of the feeding lips makes sure that the tip of the bullet does not extend past the lips and prevent the next round from being loaded into the magazine.

The loading continues until the known magazine capacity is reached. It is important to remember not to exceed the specified capacity even when the magazine would allow additional round to be loaded into it. Do not force rounds into the magazine, either. This will cause misfeeding and general malfunction of the magazine and/or gun.

Once the magazine is loaded it can be inserted into the AK. To do so, one has to make sure the rifle is unloaded and cleared by pointing the muzzle in a safe direction toward the target or down and away, taking it off safety and pulling the charging bolt handle back until it stops.

Next, the bolt handle is released and the trigger is pulled to release the hammer. The rifle's safety lever is then placed on safe.

To insert a magazine into the AK rifle, hold the rifle (while the muzzle is pointed in the safe direction) with the left hand by the gun's front hand guards for righties, and by pistol grip for lefties, then slightly turn counterclockwise to expose the rifle's mag well.

Holding the loaded magazine with bullets pointed away toward the muzzle of the gun, with the right hand the front of the magazine is inserted into the front of the mag well until it catches on the receiver.

The magazine is inserted by inserting its front into the mag receptacle. The front tang should catch the front trunnion block. Then the mag is simply "rocked" back until the magazine release latch clicks.

There are those who tell you to charge your AK "underarm." The underarm reloading can be done in standing position ONLY. The proper way to recharge an AK is with a right hand. If you have to use your left hand, over the top of the rifle is another method that can be performed in any position.

The magazine is then rocked back until it is secured by the magazine latch. A distinct click should be heard once the magazine is secured. The gun is now loaded.

To reload the AK or swap the empty magazine for a full one, one must first disengage the empty magazine by wrapping the right hand around it and at the same time pressing the magazine retention latch tang.

With a firm hold on the magazine and tang pressed, the mag is then rocked forward and away from the shooter. At this point the magazine should become loose and come out of the rifle. The full magazine is inserted in its place as described above.

One important thing to know about the AK is that it does not have a "bolt hold open" mechanism where the bolt is held back in the open position when the last round is fired and the magazine is empty. Most of the modern rifles of other design

To provide for adequate stability for accuracy, shouldering of the rifle is the most important element. There has to be a solid weld between a properly placed buttstock and shooter's shoulder.

have that feature. When the last round is fired the gun simply stops firing and pulling on the trigger does nothing.

When that happens with the AK the shooter pulls the trigger and hears the distinct snap of the hammer striking the firing pin with no shot. Most other rifles would have a bolt release mechanism that would re-chamber a gun after a new full magazine is inserted. The AK has to be re-charged by the bolt handle every time the magazine is replaced.

Some of the experienced AK shooters would argue and suggest their own way to perform an AK reloading. All of their arguments are valid and have a place in the way the AK is run by advanced shooters. I will touch on that and may even have a few of

my own suggestions later in this book.

As with any rifle, the AK is subject to the principles of basic marksmanship that any shooter, whether he or she is a novice or expert, should remember and follow; things like posture, gun placement, shoulder-buttstock weld, breathing, sight visibility and placement, clear target picture, and trigger discipline.

All these must be practiced and exercised by all shooters. Basic shooting positions are standing, kneeling, and lying down or prone positions. Modern ranges with their conveniences have added one more position that is used by the vast majority of the shooters today – sitting at the gun bench.

This position offers similar gun retention

There are three main basic shooting positions: standing, kneeling, and prone.

to that of the prone position. No matter what shooting position is chosen, the proper rifle placement is essential.

The AK is shouldered very much like any other rifle. Holding it by the front hand guards with the non-dominant or support hand and by the rifle's pistol grip with the dominant hand, bring the buttstock to the shoulder and set it firmly into the soft tissue about two inches in from the shoulder joint and right under the collar bone.

After the stock is in position level the rifle with muzzle pointed downrange. The next step is to "lean" into the rifle and place the cheek on the comb of the stock in such a manner that the head remains perfectly vertical and the neck is slightly extended forward so that the eye closest to the rifle sees right over the center line of the gun.

By leaning into the gun, positive and firm contact with the gun is ensured. While holding the AK rifle in place using the right hand (for righties or lefties) the shooter slides the safety/selector lever to the lowest position and pulls the charging handle all the way back. Then the bolt-charging handle is released and the bolt grabs a live round out of the magazine and places it into the gun's chamber, locking the chamber. The gun is now locked and loaded.

It is very important to remember not to push or force the charging handle forward in any way. Just pull back and release. The main spring will do the rest. If the shooter is a righty, he or she returns the right hand back on the pistol grip of the gun; if shooter is left-handed he or she returns their right hand on the front hand guard.

Just like with magazine changes there are other, more advanced ways to run the recharging manipulation on the AK, and I will certainly will cover them later.

SHOOTING

Now that the rifle is 'hot and ready" it time is to pull the trigger. The index finger of the control hand (the hand on the pistol grip) is gently placed on the trigger. Smoothly and slowly, any play or slack should be taken up until the trigger offers a stiff resistance. The shooter then applies even pressure on the trigger with the pad of the index finger until the hammer is released and the shot commenced. Note that every shot should be an anticipated surprise.

The semi-automatic system of the AK rifle will cycle the gun automatically, loading and locking it and resetting the hammer and the trigger. It is hot and loaded with a round in the chamber and will commence firing every time the trigger is pulled. The rifle will discharge a round as fast as the shooter pulls the trigger until the magazine is empty.

If the shooter decides to stop shooting his or her AK rifle they must remove their finger from the rifle's trigger.

Then with the loaded gun still pointed downrange, the shooter must disengage the magazine as described above and pull the bolt charging handle, ejecting the live round from the gun. After this, the safety lever is placed in the uppermost position.

SIGHTING

Shooting an AK, or any gun for that matter, is only fun if you hit your targets. And to hit intended targets one must know how to properly aim the gun. The AK aiming system contains an adjustable front sight and a non-adjustable rear sight that has a provision for range adjustment.

If one takes a look at the front sight of an AK it appears like a straightforward post sight with protective hood. The post is screwed into the cylinder that is pressed into the front sight block. Both the threads on the sight post and the cylinder will come into play a bit later.

The rear AK sight is a conventional "U" slot type and made out of a solid piece of steel. It is hinged on the rear sight block of the rifle and has gradations representing 100-meter range adjustments. A spring-loaded cylinder slides on the rear sight leaf and can be positioned at any of the pre-set marks, elevating the sight to adjust for the desired range.

For example, if the target is set at 400 meters, the rear sight cylinder is moved to the position marked "4". The is also a setting marked "Π" or "P" for some of the European AK models or "D" for some Chinese. This represents the "Permanent" or "Battle" setting that falls somewhere between 300-400 meters, which is considered to be an average engagement range.

To aim an AK rifle one simply shoulders it as described above and sights the aiming eye over the top of the gun. The shooter can close or squint the other eye. Most advanced shooters keep both eyes open during firing. I shall cover it later. In the case of novice shooters, the idle eye should be taken out of action by closing it or squinting.

Using a small and smooth movement with cheek firmly resting on the gun's stock and the stock itself firmly pressed into the shooter's shoulder, the front and rear sight have to be positioned in such a way that the front sight post is even with the rear sight's upper edge and is centered in the middle of the "U" slot.

The front sight of the AK is simple and that is where all the sighting and adjustments are done.

The rear sight of the AK is a "U" slot type with 100-meter increments.

I use both sights in such a way that the front sight post is even with upper edge of the rear sight. Then superimpose both sights over target. At 100 meters the POA should be at lower edge of the target.

Target

POA

Front Sight

Upper edge of rear sight

Rear sight "U" slot

◄ *Focus on your sights while lining them up. Once the sights are over target, switch your focus to the target.*

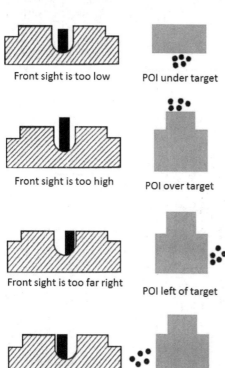

Front sight is too low

POI under target

Front sight is too high

POI over target

Front sight is too far right

POI left of target

Front sight is too far left

POI right of target

Incorrect aim can cause negative results, with impacts deviating from POA and/or missing target.

All that's left to do is position the aligned sights over a clearly visible target. The proper way to aim with the AK is to position the sights or point of aim (POA) at the lower edge of the 12" round target set at 100 meters. This should produce hits or point of impact (POI) at the center of target. If the deviation between POA and POI is more then 6" vertically, i.e., it is less or more than 6" or any distance away from the vertical centerline, the AK rifle needs to be sighted in.

All of the sighting-in procedures are performed on the front sight only. Elevation or vertical adjustment is done by screwing the front post in or out using a sight adjustment tool provided in the gun's tool kit.

The windage, or horizontal adjustment, is done by shifting the cylinder into which the front sight post is screwed. Note that all of the front sight adjustments for the purpose of sighting in a rifle are done in the direction of deviations. i.e., if the gun shoots low the front sight needs to be lowered or screwed in and raised or unscrewed if the POI is high.

It is the same with the windage adjust-

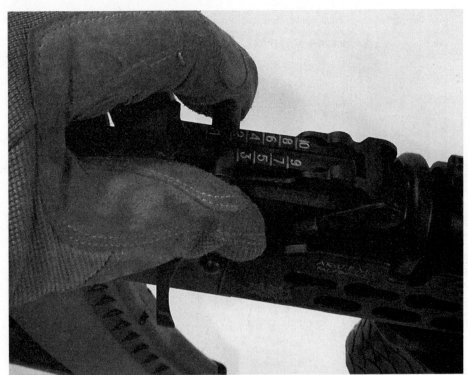

The elevation cylinder in the rear sight leaf is for adjusting ranges on the fly. Simply squeeze the spring-loaded cylinder and move it to desired setting.

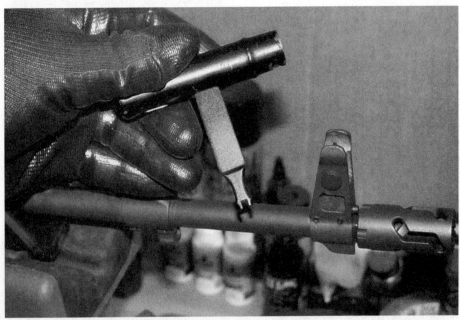

The screwdriver tool can be inserted into the cleaning kit container making a "T" handle sight adjustment tool.

The adjustment tool is placed over the front sight post and can be used to change the elevation settings.

ments. If all of the hits impact too far left the post must be moved left to bring POI to the center. The sighting of the AK can be done without any special tool except those provided with the gun.

First, the elevation is adjusted by installing a target at the 100-meter range and moving the rear sight elevation adjustment cylinder to the setting "1". After a series of shots the vertical POI deviation from POA is established. If it is outside of prescribed parameters, the adjustment is made by screwing in or lowering the front sight post for low impacts, and unscrewing or lifting the post for high impacts.

All the adjustments should be made in very small increments and remembering the geometrical progression effect. Each time the adjustment is made it has to be verified by a series of shots to check the proper adjustment.

With elevation set, it is now time to adjust the windage, or make horizontal correc-

The windage can be adjusted in the field using a spent casing and anything heavy for a hammer.

tions. This is achieved by moving a cylinder side-to-side, depending on the desired result. The cylinder is press-fitted into the front sight block and does move freely. There are special AK front sight adjustment tools that can be purchased relatively cheaply.

However the front sight windage adjustment can be done in the field using a spent casing as a ramrod and heavy object (rock, piece of wood) as a hammer.

For that, the rifle is laid on a flat and hard surface in such a way that the tip of the muzzle and hood of the front sight are resting on the surface. With the bottom (primer side) of the spent casing placed on the side of the adjustment cylinder, the casing is tapped with a hammer (rock or wood) until the cylinder moves.

All of the windage adjustments should be done in very small increments. After each adjustment, the accuracy of the rifle should be checked. Most AK rifles have scale markings in the front side (muzzle side) of the front sight block and windage cylinder. The front sight block is marked with centerline and the cylinder with a series of vertical lines. After the sighting is complete, the position of the cylinder markings in relation to the block centerline is noted and should be memorized.

Now the AK rifle is ready for regular operation as described in its Military Training Manual.

SHOOTING POSITION AND MOVEMENT

As a military weapon of war the AK rifle was designed for firing from two main positions: standing in the foxhole/trench, or lying down in prone position. Both of the positions require the gun to secured in the shooter's hands and supported by his or her elbows. Today it is hard to find a full profile foxhole on a modern rifle range. Instead, shooting benches are prevalent. Either way, both prone and sitting positions are similar in the way the AK is deployed and operated.

In the AK training manual, it is described in great detail how to take each position. For the purpose of saving paper, from here on I will describe AK handling and operation for the right-handed operator. All of you lefties just mirror the description.

Prone is one of the main shooting positions for the AK taught by the Soviets/Russians.

There are, however, some nuances that are unique to the left-handed shooters, which I will highlight. For prone position, a shooter must approach his or her spot on the firing line with rifle held in their left hand by the front hand guard. The right hand acts as a support and determines where the shooter winds up sitting him down. At the same time, the right hand and right knee are lowered to the ground. The left arm, with hand holding the rifle, is advanced forward and placed on its elbow. This move is done simultaneously with left leg extending straight back.

Next, the right leg is also extended straight back and hips are dropped flat on the ground. At this point, the body of the shooter should be lying flat on the ground with chest slightly elevated, legs straight and spread apart, creating a 30-40-degree angle, and feet with toes pointed to the sides as flat as possible.

With the body in the proper position, the rifle is picked up by the right hand of the shooter, leveled and readied for firing. At the proper prone position, the right arm is placed on its elbow, but remains mobile to perform the loading and reloading operations.

The foxhole or shooting bench position is similar at the end, but with the main differences being on the approach. The shooter again approaches his or her spot with the AK held in the left hand by the hand guards. At the spot the shooter leans into the side of the foxhole (bench) and advances the rifle by extending the left hand over the edge of the foxhole. The rest is the same as the prone position, the gun is supported in place with the left arm that rests on its elbow.

All the controls and operations are performed by the right hand. Here I want to talk about the reloading or magazine change process while in prone or sitting at the bench (standing in foxhole).

Although in peacetime shooters at the range can take their time to reload their rifles, during a dire survival situation or gunfight there is no time to waste. Quick magazine changes are essential and as such, must be practiced over and over again.

The first and most important thing to remember when performing the magazine change is to get out of the line of fire. No matter how fast one can execute a mag change, there is still enough time to catch enemy fire. So for the operator engaging on the move, i.e. walking, he or she has to get behind cover if present, or simply make themselves as small as possible by kneeling or even lying down.

The principal of getting out of the line of fire also applies when firing from the stationary position. For both prone and foxhole positions the same reloading procedure is used. Upon firing a last round out of magazine, the shooter rolls slightly to his or her left in such a way that they rest on their lower part of the upper arm and side of the upper body. Meanwhile the hips and legs remain in place as before. This move would naturally rotate the AK rifle, exposing the mag well and charging handle for quick reloading.

For left-handed shooters there are few differences. They cannot just mirror the right-handed operation and roll to their right side. This will rotate the gun in the wrong direction, blocking the charging handle. The left-handed shooters should role to their left just like the righties. This again will expose the AK's controls, allowing the shooter to perform reloading with the right hand without taking the hand off the gun's pistol grip per Western standards.

However, there is a negative idiosyncrasy for left-handed AK operation: The AK rifles are muzzle-end heavy and as such it is hard to support the rifle by the pistol grip while reloading. Because of that, the shooters have a tendency to lift the muzzle to help to offset the weight and inadvertently telegraph their position while reloading. Otherwise, the muzzle of AK will most likely be dropped to the ground. No big deal if there is no mud, sludge or snow.

At this point, someone may ask why hold the gun by its hand guards with muzzle up instead of the way that Western doctrine teaches by the pistol grip muzzle down.

Not to discredit the Western way to run a carbine, which is very suitable for standing or kneeling and perhaps crouching positions, shooting a rifle or carbine in the prone or a foxhole dictates different handling technics directly tied to the lack of space directly in front of the shooter. While learning proper gun handling I would not recommend for anyone to approach an intended firing position with a gun held straight up by the shoulder. This would also give up the shooters position.

The other two popular shooting positions are standing and kneeling. The standing position is widely taught at most of the tactical carbine courses through the USA today. The standing shooting is taught with several variations, depending on the instructor and purpose of the course. But the basic standing shooting position remains the same and is geared toward reliably striking targets and advancing movement, although there is no base to provide support of a rifle, the basic marksmanship principles still are applied for the standing shooting position.

In the old days when rifles were long and heavy, the use of a shoulder sling was taught and practiced by all shooters. Today most of the rifles are of carbine size and weight and do not require the additional support that slings provide

To be honest I am a big fan of slings for long and precise shots.

But in a dynamic fight the sling wrapped around your arm is a hindrance, to say the least. The stance has also changed. In the old days, shooters were taught to face the target with their side, with the weight distributed over both legs evenly and support arm bent at the elbow and resting on the hip. This shooting stance is still widely employed by the competition shooter at the Olympic-style events like biathlon.

The modern fighting carbine stance is drastically different. It is more frontal with the shooter facing the target. Feet are spread apart with left foot slightly ahead of the right and knees bent in a universal athletic stance with the body leaning forward.

Once the rifle is shouldered the elbows of both arms are pointed down and slightly apart. The right cheek rests on the comb of the rifle's stock with the neck slightly extended forward.

Unlike the "Olympic" style standing shooting position, the modern stance is geared more toward gun fighting and more conducive to transition to movement or position change.

This stance allows the shooter to fire his or her rifle with relative accuracy at shorter distances, easily switch between targets, and move freely. To shoot in this standing position, the shooter approaches a firing line carrying the rifle with both hands on the gun and muzzle pointed down and slightly forward. Once at the line the rifle is shouldered with the stock placed at the shoulder and then leveled.

Kneeling is another dynamic shooting position that easily transitions to and from standing. The basic kneeling firing position is designed to fire from temporary cover. This position is a hybrid between the prone and standing stance. Raising or lowering the hips by means of adjusting the angle of the right knee works as an elevation adjustment of sorts and allows one to shoot either down or uphill. Having the foot on its toes also allows for quick transitioning if there is a need to move or change positions.

Depending on who you ask, there are several ways to reload an AK while in stand-ing (walking) or kneeling position. As I've mentioned before, no matter what position is selected for firing, the first thing to do when you are out of ammo is to get out of the direct line of fire, and only then perform a magazine change.

Some instructors would disagree with me and that is fine. I won't argue against their methods, but the idea of standing upright in the gunfight without returning fire even for just three seconds is ludicrous to me, to put it politely.

In a SWAT situation where the SWAT officers usually grossly outnumber their opponents, if one team member runs out ammo there are other officers firing, laying down suppressive fire, and providing a window of time to reload.

In military operations, however, the ranges are longer, the opponents are more evenly matched, with both sides using snipers in gunfight, and the "take cover live longer" principle applies. Whatever method is chosen, it must be practiced over and over.

Kneeling is the second-best shooting position to the prone. It makes the shooter "smaller" and provides enough support for more accurate fire.

Magazine changes should be practiced with either hand if the spare mags are distributed all around a shooter's body.

As they say, the simplest is usually the best. Recharging an AK after a magazine swap is done more reliably with the right hand. However, the over-the-top left hand method also has merit.

Shooting from a foxhole is one of the positions taught by the Soviet and later Russian Army.

While standing or walking, the side and hand with which the AK is reloaded is determined by the combat load or where the magazines are. Simply put - if the mags are on the right the reloading is done with the right hand; if the mags are on the left, reloading is done with the left hand.

In both cases, the nose-heavy AK has to remain leveled and if possible loosely shouldered, allowing a small rotation of the rifle along its longitudinal axis to assist with reloading.

In the case of reloading with the left hand for right-handed shooter, the magazine change is easy and straightforward. The question arises how to charge the gun with the bolt handle on the right and out of im-mediate reach by the left hand. I am going to stop being polite and simply say: To cycle an AK with the left hand while holding it by the right on the pistol grip under the magazine is not only awkward, but stupid. Anyone who thinks otherwise needs to try to perform it while prone, sitting at the shooting bench, or standing in a foxhole.

The much better and by far more practi-cal and safe way to do it is to rotate the rifle in the opposite direction until the charging handle can be seen and then using the left hand over the top of the gun, cycle the bolt handle back. The same principles apply to the kneeling positions.

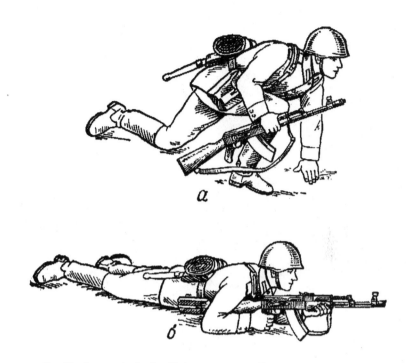

a

б

Transition to prone is also taught, to ensure proper rifle handling and positioning.

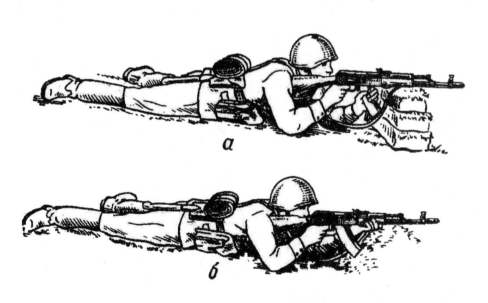

a

б

While prone, shooter can use a natural feature, his or her gear or just elbows for support.

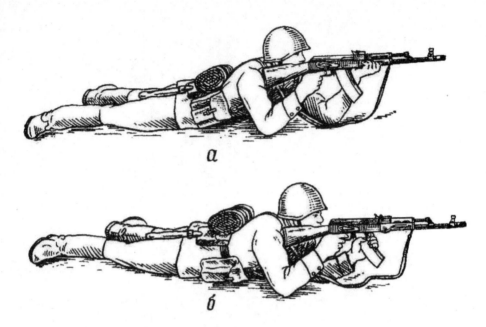

In prone position, shooter can have different grips on his or her AK rifle. Holding it by the magazine would allow change elevation of aim.

The most important thing to remember while reloading is to get off a direct line of fire.

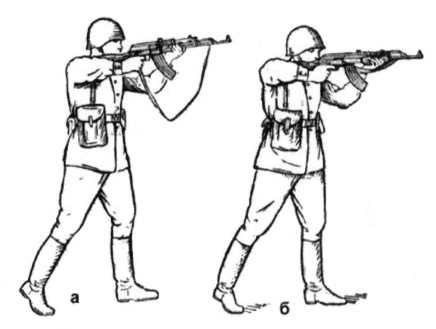

Shooting while walking or on the run is also taught by the military.
Since the soldier operates within a unit, precautions are taken in the way of various formations.

Moving and shooting is inherently dangerous activity. It is best to be familiar with the surroundings and a path ahead.

CHAPTER NINE

AK LOAD-BEARING GEAR AND SLINGS

When shooting the AK at the range, all you need is a rifle, a couple of magazines and an ample supply of ammo. However, when someone decides to take a carbine course or any other shooting or tactical course the need arises for load-bearing gear. Usually AKs are issued to soldiers with four magazines and a belt pouch to hold them.

All the 7.62X39mm models, from the AK-47 to the AKM, were issued with a three-cell belt pouch, and AK-74 rifles with four-cell.

Most of the Soviet satellite countries followed suite. The fourth cell in the AK-74 pouch was designated for ammunition on stripper clips. Obviously, soldiers in the field would source a fourth extra mag and stick it in the pouch instead of stripper-clipped ammo. All of the "minor" wars and conflicts

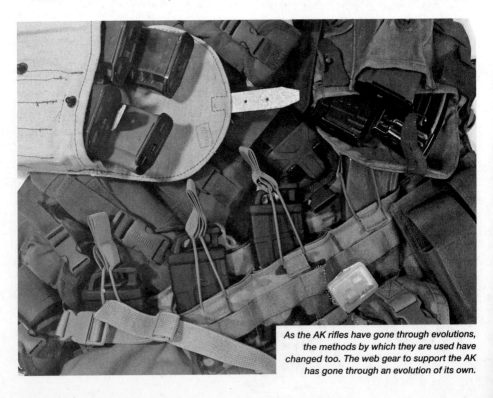

As the AK rifles have gone through evolutions, the methods by which they are used have changed too. The web gear to support the AK has gone through an evolution of its own.

Originally the three-cell pouch was issued with AKM rifles. With introduction of the AK-74, a four-cell model replaced the old one. Though it had four cells, it still was meant to hold only three magazines, reserving the fourth cell for ammunition on stripper clips. The sense of it escapes me to this day.

in Asia in during 60's and 70s saw advancement in combat load-carrying gear.

It is hard to say now what military or paramilitary group first introduced the chest rig (pouch) for AK magazines, but it laid a foundation for further development of ingenious ways to carry magazines. Nowadays, only lazy gear companies don't make them,

no matter what gun it is for. Nevertheless, there are many different types of load-bearing rigs and systems one can choose from.

When choosing AK load-bearing gear one must take a few things into consideration. First, and most importantly – is the shooter left or right-handed? This will determine with which hand all of the AK reloading is done, and therefore where on the body to place the magazines.

The next consideration is where to position the load in such a way that it will not interfere with any movement or shooting position, and be readily accessible for fast reloads.

My personal recommendations are for stationary positions, either prone, sitting, or foxhole, where the shooter can and should take several magazines out of the whatever rig he or she is using and place them within easy reach of their reloading hand.

For standing (walking), and kneeling positions, additional magazines should be placed on the body in such a way so that they can be readily accessible for reload-

The first Soviet-made chest pouch modeled after the captured Chinese or Pakistani rigs appeared in the mid 80's.

The chest pouch or any load-bearing equipment must accommodate shooter methods and habits. The rig should be chosen based on a shooter's way of running a particular gun.

I have tried and worked with many AK-designated load-bearing rigs. My personal favorite is this BCS AK chest pouch that I bought from Beez Combat Systems.

ing and within reach of the reloading hand.

However, additional magazines should not be placed around the waist or across the abdomen. This will interfere with going prone if the need arises. They should also not be "hang-ing" off the sides below the waist belt line. This will prevent a shooter from performing any rolls, getting in and out of vehicles, or going through structures.

In other words, all of the additional magazines should be carried up high on the chest (hence the chest rig and not a belly rig) and/or on the sides on the body above the waist line. In real combat situations this also may help with shrapnel from explosive ordinance.

CARRYING THE AK, AND SLINGS

A sling for a rifle is like a holster for a handgun. As such, it is very important. In the old days, slings were an inseparable part of the gun and specifically designed to assist a rifleman not only with carrying the gun,

but also with precise shooting. Those days have come and gone, however.

Today the use of the sling is rare for most shooters, and can be seen only at competitions or historical rifle matches. The design of the sling has gone through several evolutionary stages based on material and functionality requirements.

The AK sling however, has seen little change from its beginning. The thick, 1¾-inch wide canvas sling is designed to thread through the sling ring on the buttstock, through its buckle and then attach to the front of the AK rifle by means of the steel carabiner.

It is simple and practical, as well as easy and cheap to produce. It can easily be adjusted for length, and lasts a long time.

The original AK canvas sling appears pretty simple and straightforward. It loops around the rear sling attachment and attaches to the front attachment by its karabiner.

Some industrious marksmen even found a way to use it for additional stability when shooting unsupported.

With the introduction of the folding stock it even became tactical. The traditional AK sling is what is described as two-point sling. That means it has two points of attachment to the gun. It is designed for carrying an AK on the march, sentry duty, and in combat.

On march or sentry duty, the AK is carried muzzle-up, slung over the right shoulder flat against the back, with magazine facing out to the right at elbow height. The right arm is bent at the elbow with hand wrapped around the sling, applying tension and securing the gun.

During a parade presentation, the AK is placed diagonally on the chest with the muzzle of the gun pointed high and to the left and its sling is slung over the right arm and head. The right hand of the soldier grips the neck of the buttstock and the left hand is wrapped around the front hand guard. This has nothing to do with practicality and has a pageantry

The original canvas sling is issued with modern Russian rifles today. It is used with two-point attachment for garrison duty service.

When outside of the garrison confines and/or in a forward area, the AK is usually slung over a right shoulder with muzzle down.

When on patrol, the rifle is "cradled" in front with operating hand on the pistol grip and rifle resting across the opposite forearm with sling usually slung just over a head.

The original AK sling can be used as a one-point-of-attachment sling when carried in combat. The sling is slung over a head and right arm. Opposite for the left-handed shooters (left).

purpose with its roots going way back to when the bayonet charges were normal.

In combat, there were two ways to carry an AK: alert and relaxed. The alert way places the gun across the chest gripped with both hands at all times, or with the right hand on the pistol grip and with the front hand guard resting on the left forearm. In both cases, the rifle is either completely unslung or slung around the neck only.

The relaxed way to carry an AK is to have it slung over the right shoulder with muzzle pointed down and forward. This way the rifle could be quickly grabbed and rotated forward with the right hand and made ready for combat within a moment's notice.

The same basic principal applies for the folding stock AK models during peacetime. The main difference is the way the sling is used in combat. The rear sling attachment (ring) is located at the front of the stock or on the butt of the receiver, making it an almost perfect spot for a single-point sling, which is when the sling's both ends attach to the same attachment.

The stock AK sling with its front carabiner attachment makes it easy to transition between a two-point sling for garrison duty and single-point for combat. By disconnecting a front carabiner from the front of the gun and clipping it to the rear sling ring, the sling creates a loop.

There are two schools of thought for using a single-point sling or how the shooter slings it. The traditional or Western way is to

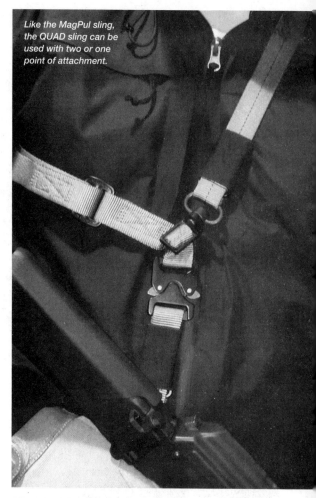

Like the MagPul sling, the QUAD sling can be used with two or one point of attachment.

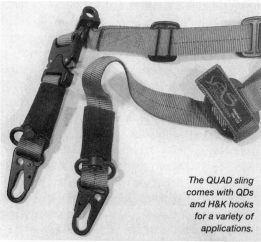

The QUAD sling comes with QDs and H&K hooks for a variety of applications.

Often the rifle is slung in the ready position.

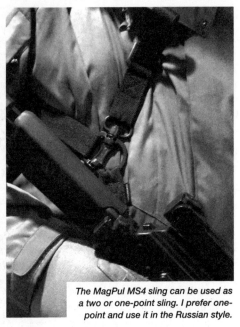

The MagPul MS4 sling can be used as a two or one-point sling. I prefer one-point and use it in the Russian style.

have a sling slung over the head and left arm with the gun flat against the chest, with muzzle pointed to the left and pistol grip down and ready for the right hand. Remember, the left-handed shooters must mirror my writing to be able to achieve the same result.

This method is widely used here in the US and taught at almost every carbine course. The only problem with this method, and why the Russians did not adopt it, is that it creates a problem with the prone shooting position and when shooting around or over cover. Additionally, the buttstock of the rifle "hanging" in front of the shooter's face would most likely cause an injury to the shooter when mounting or dismounting an armored vehicle or during a sudden change of position.

The method the Russian Armed Forces adapted for a combat carry for their AKS, AKS-74, AK-74M and 100 Series rifles is to sling the gun over the head and the right arm of the operator. For lefties, it is opposite. This way the rifle hangs straight down in the shooter's front and to the right side with its

stock even with the right armpit.

The gun then can be moved out of the way and can be shouldered in a split second. Neither the sling nor the rifle interferes with rest of the combat load and works well with other equipment.

In fact, I have adapted this sling arrangement with my own rifle. On my "work" rifles, I use two slings that offer the same flexibility. One is the M53 from MagPul, which is very reasonably priced, and the other is the "Cadillac" of universal slings - the QUAD Sling from Savvy Sniper. Both of these slings can be used as two or single-point attachment slings, and offer quick length adjustment. Both of the slings also come with Quick Detach (QD) attachment for those shooters who "upgraded" their AK with modern furniture.

There are many slings on the market today. One can choose what he or she finds comfortable. However, one thing to remember is that a sling is a part of the, rifle and as such must be trained on.

CHAPTER TEN

REFLEX, COLLIMATOR, AND OPTICAL SIGHTS

The sighting system on the AK is pretty simple and practical for any combat scenario. Whether the shooter wants to hit a target at distance or at a close range, the AK rifle is set for either or. For close quarters, the AK's front sight is practically a black dot with point and shoot capability. Just placing the front sight post with the hood over a human-size target at ranges up to 200 yards would be sufficient to strike that target. And when there is a need to reach out and touch someone or something, one can use the AK's front and rear sights.

However, the human eye has limitations and sometimes requires help. We can only see so far and to aim the gun precisely at distances where the front sight post covers the target is nearly impossible. We also do not see well at night.

To overcome our limitations scientists and engineers have come up with implements we call scopes.

SOVIET, RUSSIAN AND BELORUSSIAN OPTICS

The Soviet engineers utilizing their vast experience with gun-mounted telescoping sights during WWII, came up with a very good scope mounting solution on AK rifles in the 50's.

It was not easy to mount anything on the AK simply because it did not have a solid and sufficiently rigid surface on the top of the gun to support any type of scope to provide the required stability for returning zero, especially when the AK was fired in fully automatic mode, because the rifle flexed so much.

The solution came in the way of the side-mounted rail. The dovetail rail was permanently riveted to the lower backside of the receiver on the left of the gun. This gave the AK the flexibility of using several optical and NV sights available at that time.

The late 70's and the 80's saw the most development in Soviet combat optics, con-

For quick target acquisition in CQB scenario, the AK front sight is a rudimentary black dot that can be deployed with success.

From early on, the Soviet Armed Forces' reconnaissance units were expected to use their AK rifle at low light conditions. The side rail optics mounting system has been developed for mounting night optics.

ventional and NV. Apart from standard-issue NSPU starlight NV scope, the AKs with rail could be equipped with a variety of scopes that were removed from other weapon systems, including sniper rifles, grenade launchers, and machine guns.

It was not until the 90's that Russian and other former Soviet optic plants started to produce AK-designated scopes and 'Red Dot', "Black Dot" collimator and reflex sights.

The most popular optical 4X scope that was adapted for AKs by Russian troops and later sold to the American civilian market was the original PSO-1.

Originally designed for use with an SVD sniper rifle and made by the Novosibirsk Optical Plant (NPZ) in Novosibirsk, Russia, the PSO-1 and its more modern version the PSO-1M2 was a natural choice, maybe because there really was no other choice. The PSO-1 scope was the only scope that would fit side rail.

These were also mass-produced and supplied to the US in the 90's by the BelOMO

One of the most popular early optics that was used on the AK is the SVD PSO-1 scope.

Optics plan in Belarus. The scope had everything going for it: the military look, pretty good lenses, an advanced reticle with built in BDC (Bullet Drop Compensator), optical range finder to 1000 meters, lighted reticle, and some even had an IR detection capability.

The fact that this scope was designed for a sniper rifle firing a cartridge with completely different ballistic characteristics from the AK, so the the BDC and elevation adjustment turrets' scale on the scope would not correspond with the trajectory of the 7.62X39mm round, did not bother anyone. It looked cool mounted on the AK and it could be made to work with some modifications and a set of the shooter's own "dope" (table of hold-over adjustments).

The other scope that would also be adapted for use with an AK was the PSO-1's cousin, the POSP that was originally designed for use with the permanently suppressed VSK-94 and VSS "Vintorez" special sniper rifles chambered for the 9X39mm subsonic cartridge.

The POSP looked identical to the PSO-1 scope with the only differences being the reticle designed for use with 9X39mm subsonic ammo, the range finder only to 40 meters, and the elevation turret scale would only match bullet drop for 9X39mm round. Both of these models could be sighted in and made to work with AKs by the experienced shooter. I even hunted with an AK-103 clone rifle equipped with the POSP scope, taking several deer in central Alabama.

At that time, the American market viewed anything Russian with fair amount of skepticism. Therefore, the prices of these scopes hovered around $150 for quite some time. I personally bought several of these scopes back then.

As time progressed, so did the Russian and Byelorussian manufacturers driven by the increasing demand for more powerful and modern scopes for military use, mirrored by the civilian market. Eventually several varieties of POSP models with several levels of magnification and even variable power were introduced. The US AK enthusiasts now had a choice, and as demand grew so did the price.

Today a variety of PSO-1M2 and POSP scopes produced for the civilian market can be easily purchased from several distributors such as Kalinka Optics and Optics Planet or on the secondary market, but the time when one could get one of these for $150

has come and long gone.

The Soviets also had developed a somewhat decent collimator sight in the late 80's, but the real growth in development of this type of sight happened after the dissolution of the Soviet Union.

The 90s saw a number of collimator, both projection and reflex sights, from several older and established military optics manufacturers as well some newcomers hoping for new Russian military contracts.

As the new Russian Armed Forces were financially pressed in the early 90's and struggling to maintain their aging equipment, there were no plans to purchase newly developed sights for the troops in mass. The manufacturers had to turn to the commercial civilian market that was ready and willing to buy military-grade sights from Russia.

The first such sight that started to arrive stateside was the NPZ-manufactured 1P29 (UPO-1 civilian designation). It was essentially a copy of the British Trilux/SUIT scope with a few important improvements. The scope had a reticle calibrated for the 5.45X39mm cartridge, a range finder, and tritium reticle illumination. Once on the rifle, the 1P29 sits a bit high for my taste,

The 1P29 sight was a well-built Russian copy of the British Trilux sight.

The Obzor sight, among others, is issued to the Russian Armed Forces today.

but is still very useful for quick target acquisition. The price for the 1P29 was an arm and a leg then and it still is now.

Based on that initial success, the NPZ plant has come up with several other models that are available to the US AK shooter. These are the 1P63 "Obzor", 1P78 "Kashtan", NIT-A and PO1X20A "Rakurs". All these scopes have been developed for and used by the Russian Armed Forces. I have tested all of them. Some I like better than the others based on strictly personal preferences, but all of these are good to go for any AK enthusiast.

A more popular and widely available AK-specific scope is the 1S-03 "Kobra" collimator sight. Driven by the potential commercial reward, a less established "Axiom" company out of Izhevsk, Russian came up with this laser projection universal sight. Although never officially adopted, the "Kobra" sight immediately became popular with Russian

The 1S-03 Kobra projection-type collimator sight is probably the best-known AK sight in the US.

troops fighting in Chechnya in the 90's. The sight's popularity has spilled over to the US AK market.

The "Kobra" sight is loaded with features. Shooters can select between four different reticles and several brightness settings, all easily accessible. Perhaps the best feature of this sight is that it is not tied to any particular caliber and can be used with any caliber AK rifle.

To this day, "Kobra" collimator sight remains probably the best option for an AK, apart from the modern Western collimator sights. In the 90's AK shooters could find a deal on these sights. Today, however, although they are widely available from several distributers, one should expect to pay close to $400 for one.

One more entry that I've selected for this section is the Belorussian PK-AS. This is perhaps the best Red Dot/Black Dot scope for the AK rifle to come out of the former Soviet Union. It sits low enough on the gun and does not require an additional cheek piece to ensure a good cheek rest. It is a true 1X that provides for easy use of both eyes. The reticle is easy to use with a circle and a center 1.5 MOA dot that are both etched. The center dot is illuminated with several levels of intensity. This scope is designed for the 5.45X39mm caliber rifle but could be sighted for other calibers.

The PK-AS features external elevation and windage adjustments, with a specialty tool that is provided with the scope. Once sighted in the external elevation drop compensation adjustment is easily accessible. This feature, coupled with the 1.5 MOA reticle, will allow more precise hits at distance. Other AK scopes produced by the BelOMO plant in Belarus such as PK-A and PK-1 are also viable options for an AK shooter, based on personal preference.

As I have said earlier, the scope manufacturers in the former Soviet Union continue to develop and build sights for the AK. Lucky for us here in the US, most of the models are freely available. Though the prices have gone up dramatically, these scopes and sights for AK rifles are still more reasonably priced than their Western counterparts. The only monkey wrenches in this mix are the newly-developed and updated sights from China, which are still cheap, and of decent quality.

Today any AK enthusiast can easily find the sights I've described above and others from many dealers and on the secondary market on the Internet.

MODERN WESTERN SIGHTS, SCOPES AND MOUNTS

Mounts

Manufacturers of sighting systems have made a quantum leap in developmental achievements since the time of my service in Afghanistan nearly 30 years ago. Red dots, reflex sights, and collimators are more efficient and reliable now than when they started appearing in the 1970s.

The PK-AS sight mounts on the AK using the rifle's side mount and sits nice and low on the gun.

Midwest Industries' Quad Rail AK Hand Guard is probably the most popular aluminum mount for modern sights on AKs.

Modern optical and collimator sights require a modern way to be mounted on the AK. There are several ways to mount any desired modern sight on your AK rifle.

We all know of the battle-proven optics that have been available on the American commercial market for many years - Aimpoint, EOTech, Leupold, Meprolight, Trijicon. Most of those brands will do the job required of them just fine, and some do it perfectly. All of them are designed to assist a shooter in achieving a quick and positive target acquisition. Unlike the AK-specific sights and scopes, none of the modern Western optics comes with side mounts to fit the AK mounting rail.

All of the modern sights are designed to fit a MIL-STD-1913 rail, AKA the Picatinny rail mounting system that is usually positioned on the top of the gun. In order to use one of these sights on AK rifles, the transitional side or top mount had to be devised.

Luckily for the AK enthusiast, the spirit of innovation coupled with entrepreneurial drive spurred the development and introduction of several viable mounting systems.

There are really three types of the new AK mount to accommodate modern optics. The first is a front hand guard replacement that offers a quad rail mounting solution.

The second is the modification to the AK top cover with an installation of the 1913 (Picatinny) rail, and third is a separate side mount that is optics-specific or provides

One of the details that separates Midwest Industries from the rest is their optic-specific upper hand guard replacement. The drive behind the optic-specific upper mount was to be able to co-witness with irons sights. Midwest Industries makes several versions of their upper mounts to accommodate the most popular sights on the market.

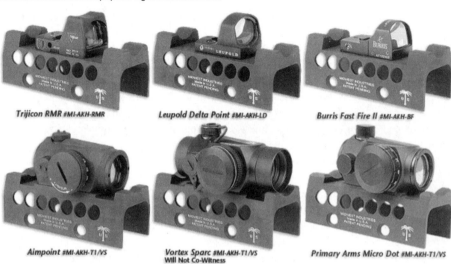

Trijicon RMR #MI-AKH-RMR   Leupold Delta Point #MI-AKH-LD   Burris Fast Fire II #MI-AKH-BF

Aimpoint #MI-AKH-T1/VS   Vortex Sparc #MI-AKH-T1/VS Will Not Co-Witness   Primary Arms Micro Dot #MI-AKH-T1/VS

Krebs Custom's aluminum Quad-Rail Fore-End also provides a solid top mount for any collimator sight.

scope rings or Picatinny rail.

The AK front hand guardrail mounting solution is one of total replacement of the original hand guards. It can be made of plastic, aluminum or even steel. Because of the original design, the AK hand guards are not positively retained, and subject to movement. Both the upper and lower hand guards are subject to movement. Therefore, the plastic replacement hand guards with mounting rail on them cannot be considered for mounting any optics, or any sights for that matter.

The plastic rails on the hand guards should only be used for mounting non-essential accessories such as flashlights, vertical grips, etc. There are other types of replacement hand guards that are made of aluminum and mount on the gun and secured in place with a series of positive mounts to avoid any movement.

Midwest Industries Inc. of Waukesha, WI makes several models of their AK47/AK74 Universal Hand Guards in Quadrail, SS, KeyMod or M-LOK™ versions.

The Midwest Industries lower hand guard hard mounts on the barrel close to the front trunnion block with a couple of setscrews resting against the gas tube for positioning and additional rigidity. The upper hand guard with a four-inch rail bolts to the lower independent of the gas tube. This mounting solution is rigid enough for collimator red dot or reflex-type sights.

Midwest also makes optic-specific upper hand guards to accommodate the most popular Western sights. This move was made to provide a low enough mount for co-witnessing in case of the electronic sight failure and lack of QD mount.

Co-witnessing on a firearm is the ability to see both rear and front iron sights through the scope or any other optical or collimator sight. In case of electronic component failure, the shooter can still aim his or her rifle with iron or open sights that are visible through the scope or collimator sight.

Krebs Custom, Inc. from Wauconda, IL offers its own version of the AK hand guards mounting solution. Their Quad-Rail fore-end for standard AK rifles is similar to the Midwest Industries one in the way that it has four permanent 1913 rails, but the retention of the hand guard is different. Instead of mounting the lower hand guard on the barrel, it is slotted into the receiver and retained in with the original AK lower hand guard retainer.

To provide the necessary rigidity the hand guard is secured with the additional bolt through the cleaning rod hole in the retainer. The upper hand guard with 4" rail mounts to the positively-installed lower hand guard.

The latest introduction from Krebs is their AK-U.F.M. hand guards with Key-Mod mounting system on the side and the bottom and 4" rail on the top. This hand guard system is secured in place similarly to their quad-rail hand guard but offers a much smoother modern and slick design with the option of mounting different-length individual rails on bases.

The biggest problem with using Westerns-type sights on AK rifles is the co-witness issue with sights that do not have the quick-detach ability, so the sight cannot be removed in case of its failure.

One solution to this problem is the Ulti-MAK AK-47 Optics Mount from UltiMAK, Inc. of -fittingly so - Moscow, Idaho. The UltiMAK Optics Mount is essentially a replacement for an original AK gas tube. The UltiMAK tube is installed in the place of the gas tube and secured in place by two "U" shaped yokes wrapped around the gun's barrel. This mount sits low enough to provide co-witnessing for just about any low-mounted modern sight. This tube type mounting system can be used with the rifle's original lower hand guard. However, it would also

The UltiMAK AK-47 Optics Mount replaces the original AK gas tube and is easy to install.

In my opinion, this type of optics mounting system can be used on AK rifles only if others are not available, and for mounting small red dot-type sights only, as it would sit away from the shooters eye.

The idea of placing a sight near the gas exhaust system and on the top of the heat-generating portion of the gun is not very attractive to me. Even though I have used this type of mount for my work AK's I have dismissed it on account of this arrangement adding additional weight to the already front-heavy AK, and too-high positioning when used with quick detach clamps. Additionally, the metal hand guards will get hot especially during a rapid session. Therefore, I would strongly recommend using a vertical front grip with these products.

expose the shooter's hand to the extremely hot metal parts of the gun by removing the original upper hand guard.

A similar gas tube mount comes from Troy Industries and their AK-47 Top Rail. The idea behind is the same as the Ulti-MAK's: to make a mount low enough for a smaller collimator sight to be able to co-witness with iron sights. However, that is where the similarities end.

Whereas the UltiMAK AK-47 Optics Mount is shorter than the actual AK gas tube and is secured to the gun by the "U" shaped yokes, the Troy Industries Top Rail installs into the gas tube slot in the rear sight block and fits over the gas block the same way the original tube would.

To take any movement, the front part of the Top Rail then torques, spreading the Top Rail between mounting points to provide a solid mounting base. Because of the "spreading" feature the Troy Industries' railed gas tube can fit most of the AK carbine models. And due to the fact that it installs into the original gas tube place it can be removed for cleaning and reinstalled again without any special tools.

I guess now would be a good time to mentioned that in this section of the book I have purposefully selected the mounting systems for the AK that do not require any permanent modifications to the rifle. Some manufactures that I've mentioned here make products that offer more mounting options, but with "deeper" and permanent modification to the rifle. I will cover them in the Accessories Section.

The top cover mounts can be two types as well: those that attached to the top cover or its integral part, and those that go over the top rail and are secured to the gun independently.

After years of personal testing and thousands of rounds fired, I have pretty much dismissed any half-ass attempts to just rivet or bolt a Picatinny rail section to the AK top cover as outright impractical and wasteful of everyone's time and money. This led me to select three mounts in this category that have worked for me in the past: the Parabellum Armament Groups AKARS rail (AK Adaptive Rail System), Texas Weapon Systems Dog Leg Scope Rail Mount, and

Krebs Custom's AK RSRS (Rear Sight Rail System).

All three "top cover" mounting systems rely on a hinge attachment to the AK's rear sight mount, with removal of the sight itself.

Two of them, the TWS Dogleg and Parabellum AKARS systems, are actually attached to or are an integral part of the rifle's top cover. Only one, the RSRS rail from Krebs, is independent of the top cover and mounted over the top of the gun to the rigid mounting points. This type of mounting of the optics rail between two rigid points of the AK rifle provides enough rigidity and stability to reliably support not only collimator or reflex sights, but also a multi-power scope. That is why I would start with it.

Krebs' Custom's Rear Sight Rail System, or RSRS for short, is made out of a solid piece of aluminum with an integral nine-inch Picatinny rail. The front part of the RSRS mount that is attached to the mounting rail itself via a hinge is installed into the ears of the rear sight leaf on the rear block of the AK rifle. It is secured in place with a set-screw and creates positive and solid mount. The rail is placed over the top of the gun and attached to a "doll head" pin that replaces the original AK's stock mounting screw.

Note that the RSRS rail will only work with fixed stock model AK's and those that have been converted to folders by replacing a fixed stock only. Under-folding models and Russian or Bulgarian AKS-74, AK-74M or 100 Series rifles will not accept this rail on account of lacking the stock mounting rear trunnion tang.

The Krebs RSRS rail-mounting system is not attached to the parts that flex most during firing, instead they are secured between the rear sight and rear trunnion block. The flexing of the receiver and top cover do not affect the position of the rail. Therefore, the RSRS ensures the scope's zero reliably.

Since the RSRS rail sits over the top cover of the AK, it is in the way of gaining access to the rifle's internal components. In this case the front hinge is provided. For cleaning or repair, the RSRS rail is detached from the rear trunnion by disengaging the pin and simply hinging it away from the gun.

After the gun is reassembled the rifle is hinged back and pinned in place. Because the rail is returned to the same place every time, it does not negatively impact the optical sight's zero. As I've mentioned before, because the original AK rear sight has to be removed to be able to install this rail system, the Krebs' RSRS rail comes with M-16 style aperture sight with windage adjustment.

Another top cover optics mounting system is the Dog Leg Scope Rail Mount from Texas Weapon System, Inc (TWS). The Dog Leg rail provides a full-length Picatinny rail on the top cover of the AK rifle for a number of mounting options.

The Dog Leg Scope Rail Mount is made out of a solid piece of aluminum together with an integral top cover to replace the gun's original stamped steel cover. It is hinged at the rear sight block with a single finger hinge placed between the rear sight mounting ears and attached with the provided rail system hinge pin that is threaded through the mounting ears and rail itself.

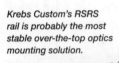

Krebs Custom's RSRS rail is probably the most stable over-the-top optics mounting solution.

The TWS Dog Leg Scope Rail Mount installs in place of the AK's rear sight and hinges away to gain access to the rifle's internal components.

This allows the top cover to be lifted for clearing and maintenance and to be returned to relative zero every time. Once on the gun, the TWS Dog Leg Scope Rail Mount sits pretty solidly, aided by the specifically designed tension feature at the back of the cover and a return spring guide and wedge shaped spring retainer tang. This replacement spring guide is also provided with the Dog Leg installation kit. Again, since the TWS Dog Leg rail uses the mount for the rifle's original rear sight it comes standard with a non-adjustable aperture sight.

Just like the TWS Dogleg rail, the AKARS mounting system from Parabellum Armament Group is installed into the AK's rear sight mounting ears. The hinge part of the rail is placed into the rear sight block and threaded through with a hinge pin that is provided with the installation kit. The pin itself is secured with a setscrew in the rail. Because the AKARS' hinge is a three-finger

type and thus more rigid when installed, the 7½' 1913 rail itself is separate from the rifle's top cover.

Though it comes in the installation kit, the AKARS top cover is the standard AK top cover with rail mounting block installed at the back. After the rail is installed on the rifle, it slides into the guide pins of the top cover mounted block. The top cover is then installed very much the same way as a standard AK cover, i.e., placed into a top cover slot in the rear sight block and snapped in place over the main spring retainer tang.

The rail is designed so that it isn't required to be affixed to the top cover, but instead remains loosely attached to allow the top cover to be installed. Once on the gun it is solidly locked to the rifle. Like the Dog Leg rail, it swings away from the gun for cleaning and maintenance. Unlike the TWS rail where the rear sight leaf spring must be removed for the Dog Leg installation, with

AKARS the spring remains in place and by applying tension on the rail provides additional stability.

The other difference from the TWS Dog Leg mounting rail is that the AKARS has a machined-in "U" type nonadjustable rear sight. The new Gen 3 AKARS comes from Parabellum Armament Group with standard aperture rear sight.

I have used both of these rails extensively. They work great. I would not hesitate to use them for 4-6 MOA Red Dots. I will, however, remain skeptical about mounting a multi-power scope for precision shooting on either of them.

To get a stable enough mount for an optical sight on the AK, one has to use the originally designed side rail and a good mount.

Lucky for the AK enthusiast, there are many options. I think that the side-mounting rail on the AK rifle is the best option not because it was designed by a team of PhDs, or tested by the Soviet military research specialists, or because it has proven itself over and over in various conflicts, but because it offers an AK shooter options and flexibility

Perhaps the most reliable mounting system for collimator as well as optical sight on the AK is a side rail attached mount, like this picatinny rail side mount from Russia.

without any modifications to the gun, and by design any sighting system can be quickly removed from the rifle.

I personally prefer the AK's side rail also because the engineer in me sees that it is simply mounted in the most rigid part of the AK rifle and thus would doubtless offer return to zero every time, as has been proven with a similar setup on the Dragunov sniper rifle or the SVD.

Not all AK's come with a side rail and installing it in the garage or basement is not easy unless you are a gunsmith and your

Just like the Dog Leg, the AKARS installs in the place of the AK rear sight and hinges away for maintenance and cleaning.

shop is in the garage or a basement. Nevertheless, the side rails are available from any company that specializes in AK parts and accessories and just about any AK smith would be happy to install it. In any case, most of the guns sold today have the rails.

There are two types of side-mounted optics mounts for AK rifles: optic-specific or with scope rings that are an integral part of the mount itself, and the side mount with universal 1913 Rail that is positioned over the top cover of the AK rifle when installed. The latter offers a flexibility to use different optics, but at the same time tends to be a little heavier when compared to the optic-specific mounts.

The first examples of the AK side mount with Picatinny-style rail came from Russia and Belarus back the early 90's. Some of these are still floating around and can be found for sale on the Internet.

These early mounts had several flaws. They were heavy on account of heavy steel parts usage, and generally these mounts sat way too high over the top of the gun, making the use of a scope very awkward to say the least.

The idea of the high position of the side mount was that it would not obstruct the removal of the AK's top cover. That reason is far from valid, because even with the top cover removed, the scope still impedes any proper maintenance on the gun, and the quick detach mechanism on all of the side mounts makes removal of the scope a matter of a split second.

The majority of the good Russian side rail mounts were hard to get. What trickled in through the grey market were models that had many shortcomings; too large an offset toward the back, making proper eye relief a problem; too high a mount, making a proper cheek rest impossible; or a too-short a Picatinny rail, not allowing the flexibility of installing a variety of optical sights.

The real breakthrough happened when industrious American companies got involved. Based on years of research into the successes and shortcoming of Russian or East European mounts, several companies have come up with truly functional side mounts for side rail-equipped AK rifles.

Over the years I have possessed and/or tested several American-made side mounts for the AK. By trial and error, I wound up using mounts from only two American manufacturers.

I use this Midwest mount extensively on my work rifles with a variety of sights, including this ELCAN Specter DR.

The Midwest Industries' AK47/AK74 30 mm Side Scope Mount was designed with 30 mm tube fighting carbine scope in mind. The 30 mm Side Scope Mount would attach to any AK's side rail and provide solid enough platform for a multi-power telescopic sight. The Midwest's 30 mm scope mount allows a scope to sit low enough to co-witness with iron sights.

Midwest Industries, Inc. makes not only AK mounts among its wide range of AK accessories, but also AR rifles and a full line of AR parts and accessories. RS Regulate is a much smaller company that concentrates on designing, developing, and manufacturing AK mounts and other accessories.

I currently own all three AK mounts made by Midwest Industries: The AK47/AK74 Side Rail Scope Mount with 7" of 1913 rail, the AK47/AK74 30mm Side Scope Mount, and the AK47/AK74 30mm Red Dot Side Mount.

All three side mounts are made out of solid aluminum with lightening hole and cutouts, and feature a proprietary locking mechanism that, unlike the original Russian mounts, positively lock from the bottom of the mount.

Both the red dot and scope mounts feature integrated 30mm rings and are designed to work with scopes with 30mm tubes. Today most modern carbine optics have 30mm tubes. The Red Dot Side Mount has only one ring and fits most of the red dot scopes on the market. The Scope Side Mount has two rings to accommodate the telescopic sight or scope. When installed on any AK both mounts sit low over the gun and do not require an ad-ditional cheek riser.

The universal Picatinny rail mount from Midwest Industries is one of the lightest AK side mounts, but also one of the most rigid, with a solid locking base connected to the seven-inch 1913 rail with three structural supports. Once on the rifle it locks solidly and places the mounting rail right over the centerline of the gun with less than ¼" clearance from the top cover.

RS Regulate is a much smaller company that dedicates itself to making high-quality AK mounts only. At least it was started as such. Today, however, it offers many variations of AK mounts, along with other accessories. What sets RS Regulate apart from the field is its innovative approach to AK mounts. All of its mounts were designed to be the lightest as well as to provide the stability needed for rifle sights.

The inherent flexibility built into RS Regulate scope mounts comes from splitting them into two parts: the base and the upper mount. The base is basically a Picatinny rail cut in half with a series of threaded holes. The upper mounts have slotted bottoms to

The RS Regulate's Universal 300 Series side mount base is truly unique. It is a light, strong and truly universal AK mounting solution for collimator sights. The 303 mount base can be fitted with an upper mount to accommodate any desired sight.

match the base and mounting bolt holes. This arrangement provides for unsurpassed flexibility for mounting any kind of optical sight on the same base. RS Regulate offers a number of upper mounts to accommodate any modern optical or collimator sight that AK shooters choose to use on their rifles.

Modern collimator and reflex sights

Many mounting options for AK rifles paved the way for use of any modern sight that American shooters know and love. All the usual suspects like Aimpoint, EOTech, Trijicon, Vortex, and others can now be installed on the AK. There are, however, limitations as to what sight can be installed where on the rifle.

Mini dots like the Aimpoint T-1 or T-2, Vortex SPARC II or Primary Arms Micro Dot or Advanced Micro Dot would fit just right on the upper hand guard or gas tube mount. When choosing mini dot-type optics for an AK one should consider either the quick disconnect mount or make sure the sight is co-witnessing with the gun's iron sights in case of electronic sight failure.

For co-witnessing, the Midwest Industries optic-specific upper hand guard that matches the quad rail hand guards or UltiMAK gas tube mount are low enough to allow the mini dot to have that ability. However, one must remember that any mini dot is a laser projection sight and a red dot that the shooter sees is projected onto the lens. The location of the small projection unit within the sight comes into play when the shooter is trying to achieve co-witnessing on the AK rifle. The mini dot sights with a projection unit on the bottom of the sight cylinder would impede the co-witnessing on the AK. The sights that have the laser projector moved to the side would be better suited for a use on the AK.

The reflex sights like the EOTech 500 Series or XPS and EXPS or Meprolight's M21 sights as well as larger red dot scopes

like the Aimpoint PRO or Vortex STRIKE-FIRE II would fit better on top of the gun toward the back for weight considerations and eye relief.

As I have mentioned before, the AKs are front-heavy and though one can install a larger sight on the top of the AK gas tube it would make the rifle unbalanced and therefore unstable. Adding some weight toward to back where the gun is positively fixed with a control hand and shoulder weld, would actually aid in balancing the rifle, and possibly even positively affect the accuracy of the shooter.

Top cover or side rail mounts allow the modern AK shooter to use just about any modern carbine aiming implement. As a matter of personal preference, I stay away from mounting any multi-power telescoping sights on the top cover mounts with the possible exception of the Krebs RSRS system. I find the side rail a better solution. I know that manufacturers of the top cover mounts

Modern "Western" optics have gained popularity with Russian troops today. Russian Spetsnaz GRU adapted EoTech collimator sights for their AKs.

A Mini Dot from various manufacturers is a natural option, as it is a simple collimator sight suitable for any rifle.

Larger collimator sights like the Aimpoint PRO can flawlessly function on any AK rifle.

as well as some of their customers would disagree with me. I totally respect their point of view and reiterate that I base my opinion strictly on personal preferences.

No matter what type of optics mounting system is chosen the AK enthusiasts can now shop in the same accessories store as their AR brethren.

Modern scopes for AK

I too have my favorite Western optics that I use on my rifles. When selecting what really works for the AK I set a criteria that the modern optical sight should fit.

Though it was designed as a main battlefield rifle, the AK is truly a fighting carbine, in the scope of modern combat. That means it is expected to engage targets from 0-800 meter ranges, i.e., the operator should be able to clear buildings, engage in urban combat, and hit targets in the open at long ranges using one rifle.

The idea of having to switch between types of guns to address threats positioned at different ranges is not practical, especially when the gun is capable and the only limitation is the shooter's eyesight.

The scoped carbine is the solution, and the AK, with its size-enabling CQB long-range capability, is perfect for modern warfare. This is why a practical optic chosen for the AK should have 1-4X power adjustment, an illuminated reticle for close-range shooting in different lighting conditions, and a BDC-type reticle, preferably with a built-in range finder.

Ranging in price between $300 and nearly $2,000, here are three optic alternatives to the better-known brands that I have extensively tested and would feel comfortable in personally recommending.

I have chosen these scopes based on what I said above and their ability to go from 1X to 4X and back relatively quickly. Quickly is a relative term, as there are only two ways to change the magnification a scope: by "flipping" a lever and thus switching between optical elements, or the more conventional rotating a ring, thus changing the distance between lenses.

The Specter DR's reticle is simple and easy to use. Range, position and shoot. It can be illuminated entirely for low light long-range engagement, or the center dot only illuminates for use as a Red Dot sight on 1X power.

Unlike the ELCAN scope that had to be adapted to work with the 5.45X39 mm AK, the Hi-Lux's CMR 4-AK762 scope was designed for an 7.62X39 mm chambered AK.

One of my absolute favorite carbine scopes is the ELCAN Specter DR 1-4X.

The first scope that would meet my expectations is the Elcan SpecterDR 1-4X. It has everything: instant switch from 1X to 4X and back, illuminated tactical universal reticle with BDC for 5.56X45 NATO cartridge for carbine or MG and range finder, quick detach ARMS mount and even backup irons on the top.

The Elcan SpectreDR 1-4X is not a stranger to the US Armed Forces. In fact it comes mounted on most M249s as standard equipment. It is in the commercial carbine market where this scope may lack the same notoriety. It is not the lightest scope and will add some weight to your carbine, but considering the red dot and magnifier needed to achieve the same effect the SpecterDR provides, it is a wash.

When I first laid my eyes and hands on this scope I was immediately drawn to the size of the tube and ocular and objective lenses, which are large enough to be able to use the SpecterDR as a reflex sight on the 1X setting.

Though the 1X power is not a true 1X, more like 1.5X, the SpecterDR was a breeze to run my carbine with both eyes open at all times. The scope's overall small size (5¾" length) did not caused the "tube" effect, and blocked very little of my inside peripheral vision. On 4X setting it behaved just like any 4X scope. The large objective lens drew a sufficient amount of light in low light condition that I was able to shoot my Bravo Company USA BCM-4 carbine well into twilight and after sunset.

I must comment on the reticle itself. Having good glass is only one necessary trait of any scope. Having the right reticle makes the scope. In my opinion having a well designed, nicely laid out and simple reticle that is easy to learn and even easier to use is essential for any carbine shooter. A reticle that gives you the ability to use the scope to the fullest of its potential is priceless. The SpecterDR 1-4X has one.

As I've mentioned before the Specter's reticle is designed for the 5.56X45 NATO (.223) cartridge with BDC already built in. It made a very easy job for me to work my targets over out to 600 meters. It was literally like point and shoot. Just place the hash mark with corresponding number over the center mass on the target, take wind into account, and pull the trigger. It's that simple. Although I already knew all the ranges, one can estimate a rage to the target rather quickly and easily using the provided "choke" type range finder.

To assist with low light conditions the SpecterDR's reticle is illuminated and has two modes of illumination: the simple 6 MOA center red dot for CQB and the entire reticle for longer ranges. I found them both simple and useful as intended.

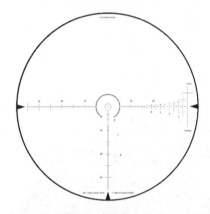

Although the CMR's reticle appears complicated, it is not. Once learned, is quite simple to use. It has a range finder and built-in BDC for 7.62X39 mm round fired out of 16" barrel. All critical components of this reticle are illuminated.

The CMR 4-AK762 scope has traits of classic variable power high-end scopes. The change between magnification settings is achieved by rotating a ring at the ocular end of the scope. This scope also has protected tactical turrets and is built on a 30mm tube.

Using a side scope mount specifically designed by Midwest Industries, the CMR 4-AK762 sits low on the gun allowing co-witnessing with iron sights.

With the next scope I went from one end of the spectrum to the other, from the most expensive option to the most economical. Enter the Hi-Lux CMR1-4X24, what I consider one the best fighting carbine scopes for the money.

The CMR1-4X24 has the appearance of the conventional scope that we all know and love. It has tactical elevation and windage turrets. It sports a heavy-duty modern 30mm tube and measures 10" in length. It is relatively light but adding rings and/or a mount for use with side-railed AKs would make it on the par with Elcon's Specter.

Variable magnification is achieved by simply rotating the ring that is clearly marked with 0.5X increments and has a nub to aid rotation. The glass is exceptionally clear. Overall it has a look and a feel of high-quality European or high-end American optic. But what makes this scope is its

reticle. It is an illuminated quick-acquisition double horseshoe reticle with BDC suitable for .223 or 5.45X39mm calibers with windage scale.

It also has 13 levels of illumination, including a designated NV setting to illuminate the center dot and inner horseshoe. In 1X mode this makes this scope ideal for close contact target acquisition, with added precision to boot.

Though not apparently visible, the reticle has a built-in range finder based on the human body. Once learned it is easy to use. Perhaps the best feature of this scope that is accountable for its commercial success is its $300 price tag.

Hi-Lux now also offers several CMR scope models that are caliber-specific. Their recently released CMR 4-AK762-R has a 7.62X39mm caliber-designated reticle with a modified horseshoe design, as well as a built-in BDC and separate "Cross" choke type rangefinder, all of with are illuminated with 10 levels of intensity, including 3 levels for NV.

This next feature is especially appealing to the AK shooter: The windage turret has been relocated to the left side to get out of the way of ejected casings. It is all in the details, I say.

There are many mounting options for these scopes. Being of traditional configuration, the Hi-Lux CMR scopes could be mounted with regular 30mm rings of your choice. For AK shooters using the side mount, Midwest Industries Inc. has designed a designated 30mm Scope Mount for the CMR.

Another sight is worth mentioning is the newer EOTech introduction. Based on their highly successful XPS Series sights, EOTech recently released a .300 Blackout model. Though it is not a multi-power scope, but rather a projection collimator sight, it is designed to work with the popular .300 Blackout caliber.

The Primary Arms fixed 4-power Compact Prism Scope with the Patented 7.62X39/300BO ACOG-like reticle is another AK-specific scope on the market.

The EOTech XPS and its new version 300 Blackout is another sight that can be used on 7.62X39 mm AK, with or without magnifier.

The sight itself looks and operates the same way as any other EOTech XPS collimator sight, but with one difference: The new reticle has a second "lower" center dot. When the upper center dot is sighted in for 100 yards, the second or lower is automatically sighted for 300. By its design the .300 Blackout cartridge is a clever merger of 7.62X39 mm and 5.56 NATO rounds. The initial trajectories of the .300 Blackout and 7.62X39mm rounds are very similar. The major deviation occurs past 300 yards. That makes the new EOTech sight almost uniquely suited for use on an AK.

Although the 300 Blackout sight is just a collimator and not a telescopic sight it could be used in tandem with a magnifier such as

EOTech's model G33 or Vortex's VMX-3T, or any other magnifier that matches sight quality. When mounted on a flip mount the magnifier gives a shooter the capability to turn a 1X collimator sight to a 3X scope for more precise shot placement. Unfortunately, this feature is limited and would not perform the same as a fully functional telescopic sight.

Often overlooked, and undeservingly so, Primary Arms is one company that actually makes AK-specific optical sights. One is the fixed 4-power Compact Prism Scope with the patented 7.62X39/300BO ACOG-like reticle designed for the 7.62X39 mm round ballistics. The other is 1-6 variable power, with 7.62X39 mm-specific reticle.

Talking to the company's management, I've naturally asked why only 7.62 and not my personal favorite 5.45. The answer was simple and I already knew it. The ballistic deviations between 5.45X39 mm cartridge and 5.56X45 are minimal, if any, throughout the engagement range within fighting carbine capabilities and do not warrant the special reticle.

Primary Arms' 4X Compact Prism Scope

The Compact Prism scope from Primary Arms is a fixed 4X power scope that can turn your AK into DMR with reliable accuracy.

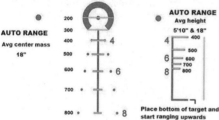

The Compact Prism scope's reticle is of the "Range, Point and Shoot" type. It is easy to use and illuminates for low light conditions.

The Primary Arms Prism Scope comes with base mount, and when attached to a side rail mount may appear too high for some shooters. There are several mounting options available from RS Regulate.

is a short fighting rifle scope. It falls into the same category as Trijicon's ACOG.

Similar to the ACOG, it features the patented 7.62X39 mm round ACSS reticle, providing quick ranging with built-in optical range finder, BDC, wind holdovers and moving target leads for 7.62X39 mm round in an easy to use sighting system at fixed 4X power. The etched reticle requires no illumination, but it is for low light conditions. It has 12 brightness settings and is powered by a CR2032 battery.

The scope is extremely durable, designed to handle heavy recoil and extreme weather conditions, with a one-year warranty. A 1913 (Picatinny) rail mount is included, but his versatile optic is also able to accept ACOG, quick detach, and standard bases. The low price of $256 does not match the quality and execution of this scope.

The Primary Arms' 1-6x24 SFP scope with 7.62x39 reticle is designed for CQB and medium range shooting. Just like the Hi-Lux CMR, this scope is variable power that is changed by rotating a ring near the ocular lens.

The other AK scope from Primary Arms is the variable power 1-6x24 SFP scope with 7.62x39 reticle.

Just like the Hi-Lux CMR scope, the Primary Arms SFR uses a classical variable power scope configuration where the magnification settings are adjusted by rotation. It displays hi-end scope traits with great glass and modern 30 mm tube.

USE 50 YARD ZERO

The SFR scope's patented ACSS reticle is very simple to use. It comes with range finder and built-in BDC for 7.62X39 mm cartridge. The center chevron is illuminated for CQB capabilities on 1X power.

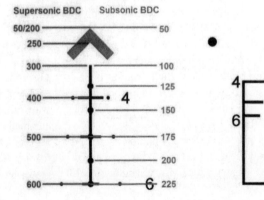

Supersonic BDC   Subsonic BDC

50/200 —————— 50
250 ——
300 ——————— 100
——————— 125
400 —————— • 4 — 150
500 —————— 175
—————— 200
600 —————— 6 — 225

The SFR scope goes to 6X magnification that helps shooters engage targets at extended ranges with relative ease and accuracy. The ACSS reticle has the BDC and optical range finder that take the guesswork out of the equation.

The center upside-down chevron of

The Primary Arms' 1-6x24 SFP scope sits comfortably low on my gun using low rings and Midwest Industries' side mount. It cannot co-witness with the AK's iron sights because its objective passes past the rear sight of the gun. However, using QD rings and/or QD side mount it could be easily removed in a nick of time.

ACSS reticle is illuminated and has 12 brightness settings. Illuminating just a center chevron turns this scope a CQB fighting Red Dot sight when set on 1X. The ACSS reticle provides quick ranging, wind holds and moving target leads for 7.62X39 mm round, in an easy-to-use sighting system at 6X power.

The Primary Arms' 1-6x24 SFP scope is well done and has the appearance of a very expensive optic implement. It is tough, waterproof, fog resistant, and covered by a three-year factory warranty. At less than $270, it won't break the bank, but it will fit your AK rifle beautifully and will serve you for a long time. It even comes with set of flip-up caps.

I have tested both of Primary Arms' scopes and they held up beautifully. The ranging and POA adjustments were a breeze. How will they hold up in the future? Time will tell. So far, so good.

Today, pretty much any AK rifle can be equipped with modern optical or collimator sights placing it more in line of the modern fighting rifles.

Just as a point of interest to AK shooters, there is another fixed power ELCAN scope that can easily be used with on any 5.45X39 mm chambered AK/RPK. The ELCAN Specter OS4x fixed 4X power optical sight with its built-in range finder and 5.56 NATO BDC will suite sub caliber AK just fine.

CHAPTER ELEVEN

AK ACCESSORIES

BUTTSTOCKS

The main argument in the never-ending AR vs. AK battle lies in the modularity of the rifles. Although the AK has been produced with a side rail mount since the 50's, the main purpose of the side rail was to mount night vision or a limited assortment of optical sights.

The real breakthrough in accessorizing the battle rifle came with the introduction of the "flat" top AR model in the 90's. The MIL-STD-1913 Rail, or as it is widely known, the Picatinny rail, is a variation of the Weaver rail mount adopted as the standard rifle mounting system for the US Armed Forces.

The adoption of the Picatinny rail led to a surge in development of mounting solutions not only for optics or other sighting implements, but also for other rifle accessories, essentially making a battle rifle modular and ready to be configured for each soldier individually, depending on his or her mission requirements.

Converting the gun's fore-end or hand guards into a quad rail system provided a very flexible mounting platform for a variety of combat accessories such as laser designators, Infra Red (IR) illuminators, flashlights, etc.

In this regard, the AR took a giant lead over the AK in the battle of the "Black Rifles". However, the gap was narrowed rather quickly with efforts from both sides of the "pond". Before long the AK rifles could be upgraded to compete with their American counterparts. It started slowly at first with the introduction of quad rail hand guards,

followed by the Picatinny rail on the side mount, and spilling over into the fixed stock AK conversions.

Today the AK accessory market is so wide and diverse that one can take any model of AK with milled or stamped receivers and turn it into a modern modular fighting platform that will accept the same combat implements as the AR.

When talking about the AK accessories, I did not want to start in chronological order, but rather by the ease of installation and the greatest impact on the rifle's performance from a shooter ergonomics point of view.

The "hanging" accessories" can come and go depending on what the shooter is trying to do with the rifle, but some of the semi-permanent or permanent modifications to the rifle itself will improve the gun's performance and operator expectations no matter what accessory is hung on the gun.

I also decided to concentrate on improvements to the AK that can be reversed and will not require the permanent modification of the gun. Nothing cut off, milled, or filed away. However, I will talk about the accessories that are available from several manufacturers that when installed by modifying the AK rifle would also offer additional benefits mainly associated with mounting solutions.

First, the AK stock. Personally, I like the AK stock in its classic form and length, which has come to be known as "Warsaw Pact" length in the US AK world. Some may argue about the shortness of it, but as soon as a heavy winter coat or body armor or both

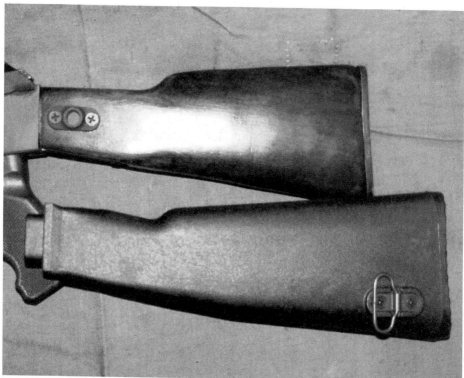

The AK stock length is considered somewhat short by the American shooters. The longer stockd are available as a replacement.

are put on, that argument is gone out the window.

The Soviets came up with the AK buttstock length not out of economy of wood (God knows there is no shortage of that in Russia), but because of the six months of winter fighting they had to do in defense of their Motherland.

Today with wide use of body armor, the AK stock length has become more relevant. Not ideal, but relevant nonetheless. The differences in AK stocks are attributed to the various models and their further development.

From the initial introduction of the AK as a main battle rifle for the Soviet armed forces there was a need for a model for the airborne troops that would have a shorter length, allowing it to be placed on the soldier while parachuting. Hence the folding stock model, the AKS-47 or AKS for short.

The original design was directly "borrowed" from the German MP-38 and MP-40 sub-machine guns and encompassed a steel folding stock that folded under the gun with a hinged buttplate resting under the lower hand guard. The stock made it possible for the AK rifle to be secured in the paratrooper rigging and allowed the gun to fire with the stock folded. The AKS stock was folded or unfolded by simply pressing a button on the side of its hinge.

Though initially loved by the troops for making the gun compact and offering carrying flexibility, the under-folding stock had its shortcomings. It was longer than its fixed cousin. It had to be longer in order to

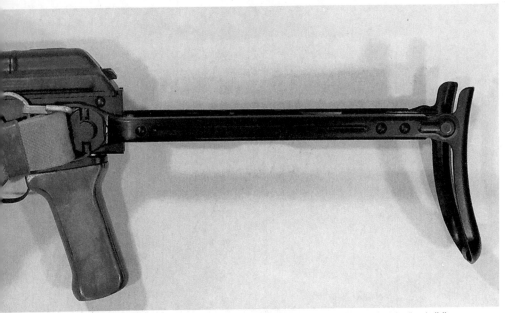

Because the AK under-folding stock has to clear the magazine it is much longer than its fixed sibling.

clear the AKs magazine. The cheek weld was questionable at best. In Afghanistan, Soviet troops would use a trauma pack and a rubber tourniquet wrapped around it for additional comfort. This "modification" would of course render the rifle's folding capabilities useless, which was a moot point in-theatre where there were no parachute drops anyway.

Meanwhile, the fixed AK stock has also gone through an evolution of sorts. The original AK-47 stock was made of hardwood and, in its contour and placement in relation to the rifle's bore, followed the conventional lines of the battle rifles of the day, i.e., it had a six-degree downward angle slant from the bore centerline.

The idea was that during winter the heavy fur army winter clothing would provide enough padding to ensure a suitable cheek rest. With the introduction of AKM stamped receiver models and advances in laminate wood technology, the shape and positioning of the stock changed, as well as the material from which it was made. The six-degree slant was done away with and the new laminate wood buttstock had a better shape that was more conducive to the fighting carbine.

The stock retention or attachment to the gun also changed. Now the stock was tightly fitted into the receiver and the rear trunnion block of the rifle and secured with two self-threading screws through the trunnion block and its single tang, as opposed to the two tangs in the AK-47 models.

The AK stock kept its shape, material and attachment point to the rifle with several small changes all the way through the introduction of the AK-74 rifle in 1974. Several Soviet allied counties made folding-stock AKs for their airborne troops. China, Poland, and Yugoslavia opted for the under-folding stock. The others chose to modify their fixed stock model with folding stocks of their

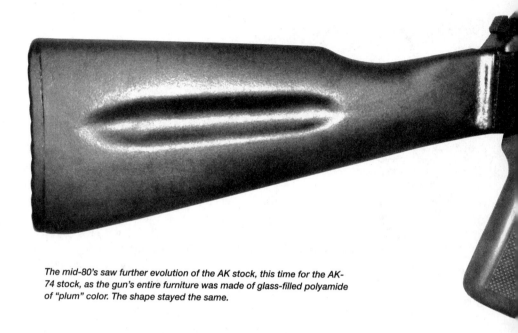

The mid-80's saw further evolution of the AK stock, this time for the AK-74 stock, as the gun's entire furniture was made of glass-filled polyamide of "plum" color. The shape stayed the same.

The Paratrooper folding model AKS-74 was now equipped with metal side-folding stock as opposed to the earlier under-folding. The side-folding stock was simple to operate and did not interfere with rifle operation when folded. It also easily cleared rifle's side rail.

The 90s saw additional improvement to the AK stock, with introduction of solid black polymer folding stock on AK-74M and 100-series rifles.

Most of the Warsaw Pact Soviet allies also adapted the 5.45X39mm AKs, but chose to equip their paratroopers with guns converted into the side-folding model using a universal wire side-folding stock.

design that would be a direct replacement of the gun's stock.

The adoption of the AK-74 platform by the Soviet military saw further modification to the AK stock. While the fixed stock had minimal changes mainly associated with its slimming and lightening grooves, the AK folding stock was dramatically changed. It was now made from stamped steel, mimicking the length and rudimentary shape of the fixed stock and folded to the left of the rifle out of the way of the gun's controls.

Because it was "skeletonized" it was slim and light and did not interfere with the AK's side rail. I still to this day think that AKS-74's side folding stock is perhaps the best folding stock solution that was ever made for a combat rifle. The only modification of this stock that actually improved it came with the introduction of the AK's plastic furniture in the late 80's. All of the new 100 Series AK's were now equipped with a solid polymer folding stock that used the AKS-74 folding mechanism, but by its shape resembled a conventional AK fixed stock.

The new stock offered better ergonomics and needed flexibility for a modern rifle. I still think that the 100 Series AK stock is very close to the ideal stock.

Close, but not perfect. One downside to the AK-74M or 100 Series solid polymer folding stock is that it cannot be replaced by

a better model. What I mean is it can't easily be replaced with some hard-to-get Russian stock that was made in some factory in very small batches, or a custom stock job. Not impossible, but in all cases it would involve a fair amount of professional gunsmithing to further "perfect" this already good stock.

Of course, perfection is very subjective. What's perfect for one may not be for the other. Many AK shooters addressed their ergonomic woes by simply replacing the fixed stocks on their rifles with longer plastic stocks. Although it is still the simplest and cheapest way to "improve" the ergonomics for some shooters, I've already mentioned what I think of installing a "longer" stock on the AK.

The real improvement came by way of replacing a fixed AK stock with an M-16/M-4 tube to allow the use of the telescopic AR-15/CAR-15-style stock. This modification is especially popular with American AK shooters who have made a transition from the AR to AK.

This mod has merit and addresses the variable length of the rifle depending on seasonal clothing or personal protection requirements. In addition, it offers the flexibility of using any collapsible AR stock that a particular shooter knows and loves. There is no shortage of AR buffer tubes for the AK on the market today. One can choose based

The most popular stock replacement for an AK rifle is the AR-style buffer tube telescopic stock.

on simplicity or price. There are as many or even more choices of the AR stocks that can be installed on the AK using the AR-style buffer tube.

I personally have used many AR stocks on my AK rifles, and based on years of experience with the buffer tube/stock combination I certainly have my favorite. When dealing with non-folding telescopic stocks I use the Vltor RE-47 AK Modstock adaptor because of its fit and overall quality, and the

fact it also serves as a storage container in combination with B5, MagPul CTR or MOE stocks. You just can beat the quality and weight coupled with the awesome value of these products.

But this is my personal opinion and should treated as such. Some AK shooters using the AR buffer tube conversion may have their own tested and proven preferences. The next step in the AR buffer tube/ stock combination modification for the AK

The AK shooter can choose from numerous replacement AR-style stock options with fixed or folding tubes.

Other than AR-style stocks, there are AK-specific folding stocks also available like this FAB Defense UAS-AK with "Galil" hinge.

rifle would be the conversion of a fixed stock model into the folder.

There are other options for converting an AK from fixed stock rifle to the folder using either available Romanian surplus folding "wire" stocks or newly manufactured stocks like Bonesteel, AK/Saiga Folding Galil style stock, or Mako's Tactical Side Folding Buttstock with Adjustable Cheek Rest, among others.

These folding stocks bolt in without any modifications to the gun. There is one particular stock in this category that deserves a separate mention in this book, which I will do later in this chapter.

The other way to convert a stamped receiver AK to a folding stock gun is to install the original Russian or Bulgarian AKS-74 or AK-74M folding mechanism and stock. This conversion would require a fair amount

of gunsmith work, preferably by a qualified gunsmith. However, the most popular fixed-to-folding AK stock conversion is the installation of an AR buffer tube with folding mechanism. This modification allows the use of an AR-style stock of the shooter's choice, offers telescopic feature, and folding stock capability.

There are a variety of folding AR-style buffer tubes on the market today, most of them using the Israeli Galil-style wedge lock folding mechanism. The AK enthusiast can also choose what material the tube and mechanism are made out of, steel or polymer, and to which side the stock folds.

Again, I have used this folding stock system on my numerous guns and have developed personal preferences. I would like the stock to fold to the right side of the gun so it will not interfere with a side-mounted optic. I also would prefer a steel mechanism over the plastic, due to rigidity and potential service life even though I give up some weight advantages.

My personal favorites are the Bonesteel AK/Saiga Folding stock or Mako's Folding Collapsible Buttstock Assembly with Metal Joint. I would, however, use these products in combination with MagPul CTR or MOE AR stocks due to their light weight and better dimensions. The MagPul stocks are slim and as a result fit nicely with this folding stock system on the AK rifle.

The Best AK stock

All of the buttstock options that I described above would work fine with pretty much any AK rifle. I simply described the available options for the AK shooters to go and explore and based on particular individual requirements and preferences to make a conversion decision with what option to go. Some of the stocks are better than others, all of the mentioned stock conversions have advantages and shortfalls.

One, however, stands as the all-around winner as the best folding stock for a fixed stock AK: the newest MagPul, the ZHUKOV-S AK folding stock.

The ZHUKOV-S stock is made entirely of hi-impact polymer that MagPul used for years on all their products, and it is known for its durability and light weight. The stock has an integrated folding mechanism that is activated by a pushbutton on the left side.

The stock's folding mechanism is not as "bulky" as some of its steel counterparts and folds the stock to the right of the gun and away from any interference with side-mounted optics. The folded stock still allows the rifle to be fired. It installs into the original fixed stock slot at the back of the receiver and is secured with a provided bolt and a bolt-driven wedge that also insures the proper alignment of the stock assembly. Because the rear trunnion block tang is not used, it is cleverly hidden.

The new stock is also telescopic and would accommodate any length-of-pull requirements for ergonomic reasons or

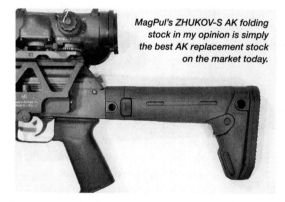

MagPul's ZHUKOV-S AK folding stock in my opinion is simply the best AK replacement stock on the market today.

The MagPul standard stock cheek risers fit on the new ZHUKOV-S™ AK folding stock.

The ZHUKOV-S stock folds to the right of the gun and thus does not interfere with side-mounted optics.

The new ZHUKOV-S™ stock is also telescopic and can be adjusted with the push of a button.

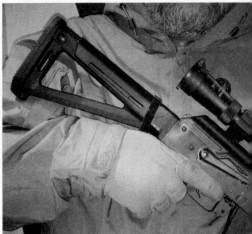
Another option from MagPul is their fixed MOE® AK stock. It is the lightest and most economically priced option for those who don't find a folding feature essential.

changes in seasonal clothing or body armor restrictions.

The ZHUKOV-S stock will also accept standard MagPul cheek rest risers depending on the type of sighting implement used. The new MagPul AK stock also has several QD sling attachment ports conducive to the use of tactical slings as I have described earlier.

When the newest Russian AK rifle, the AK-12, came out in 2012 the biggest improvement over the standard AK-74M was not the abundance of Picatinny rails, but the ergonomic buttstock.

The new Russian stock design has addressed all the so called "shortcomings" of the standard AK stock. The AK-12's stock is folding, it has an adjustable cheek riser and it is telescopic for adjustable length of pull.

I have attempted to build an AK-12 clone in my basement, and came close by adding accessories that mimic the AK-12 features on a standard I.O. Inc. AK-74.

One major thing that I could not clone was the stock. MagPul did it for me with their new ZHUKOV-S AK stock. Light, functional, and loaded with features, the ZHUKOV-S stock is, in my opinion, certainly one of the best, if not the best, stock for an AK rifle, period! But its best feature is the $99 sticker.

Among its new AK accessories line, MagPul also released their MOE AK Stock. Even lighter than the ZHUKOV, a slim fixed MOE stock that, at $49, can be another option for those AK enthusiasts who are not looking for a folder.

PISTOL GRIPS

Just like the buttstock, the AK pistol grip can easily be replaced by anyone with a flat-head screwdriver. The AK pistol grip is one of the features that will not change the gun's performance but could affect its ergonomics and the comfort level of the shooter. And, like a stock, it doesn't require irreversible modification to the gun.

In my opinion, there is nothing wrong with the AK original pistol grip. It fits my hand really well. Again, I must draw attention to the idea behind the AK design and the fact that Soviet troops wielding AKs in defense of their Motherland had to fight for six months in cold-weather conditions wearing proper clothing, including heavy gloves.

As such, the original AK pistol grip is rather slim and does not have finger grooves,

Just like the rest of AK furniture, the pistol grip has gone through an evolution. The laminate wood grip like this one has endured on the AK-47, AKM and RPK for a long time.

which as I've already said, is just fine for me. However, what's good for me is not automatically good for everyone. To address the difference in personal preferences, there are options available.

The original AK-47 pistol grip was a combination grip with steel frame and two Bakelite side plates. After switching to a milled receiver for the production model rifle the AK furniture received a face-lift and the pistol grip was replaced with a solid wood one that would be secured to the gun with one long bolt and "T" nut.

This simple pistol grip attachment survived the numerous grip design changes and it remains the way the pistol grip is attached to the most modern AK rifle models. With the introduction of laminate wood AK furniture, the AK pistol grip was also made out of laminate wood in line with the rest of the wood parts. The introduction of the lighter stamped receiver on the AKM rifle saw a new Bakelite pistol grip as a cost and weight cutting measure.

The switch to polyamide on the AK-74

rifles in the 1970s resulted in "Plum" color and later black plastic grips. And that is where the further development of the AK pistol grip in Russia stopped. The basic dimensions and form of the Bakelite AK grip have also survived until the recent introduc-

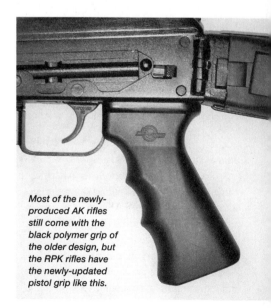

Most of the newly-produced AK rifles still come with the black polymer grip of the older design, but the RPK rifles have the newly-updated pistol grip like this.

With introduction of glass-filled polyamide, the material from which the AK pistol grips are made has changed. However, the shape and dimensions of it remained the same as those of Bakelite grip.

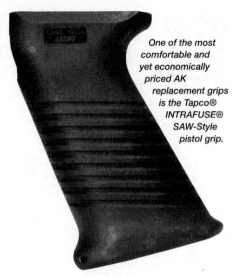

One of the most comfortable and yet economically priced AK replacement grips is the Tapco® INTRAFUSE® SAW-Style pistol grip.

One of my favorite AK replacement pistol grips is MagPul's MOE® AK grip. The MOE® grip is pretty slim and is very comfortable even for a gloved hand.

tion of Russia's new AK-12 rifle.

This lack of viable options for AK rifles in the pistol grip department had spurred many accessory companies to develop alternatives to the original 60-year old design. Today one can shop and choose an AK pistol grip that will fit his or her ergonomic preferences.

As I said, there are many options today, but replacing the AK pistol grip should not

be done simply for the sake of replacing; there must be some substantiated reasoning behind it. In most cases it would be to enhance the comfort level of the shooter.

In choosing a pistol grip for an AK, one must consider the thickness of the grip at the top, based on the size of the shooter's hand and length of his or her fingers.

One thing to remember: the AK grip is not just something by which to grip the gun while firing: it is also its primary carrying handle. Therefore, the rifle's pistol grip should aid and not impede the shooter when a heavy gun is carried.

The thickness of the gun's pistol grip should be such that it does not put a trigger finger too far away from the gun's controls (trigger, safety lever, etc.). It also should not change the shooter's grip or positioning when the rifle is operated with a gloved hand.

Most of the AK aftermarket grips are reasonably priced, so some AK shooter may go through several options before they settle on one particular model or design. I personally have my favorites.

Again, I base my opinion on years of experience with shooting AK's, but it is just

The U.S. Palm AK battle grip is my other favorite AK grip. The U.S. Palm AK grip narrows toward the top. This makes it exceptionally comfortable even when wearing gloves.

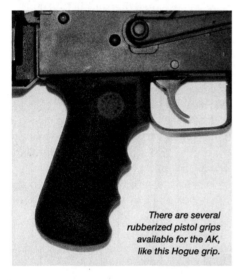

There are several rubberized pistol grips available for the AK, like this Hogue grip.

that - an opinion. Other than the AK's original polyamide grip, among my favorites are three models: the recently released MagPul MOE AK Grip and its rubberized mod the MOE AK+ Grip, the US Palm AK Battle Grip, and the Tapco INTRAFUSE SAW-Style Pistol Grip.

All three of these grips are made of polymer and offer a great degree of comfort, for me at least. The US Palm AK battle grip is an original, and MagPul's MOE AK grips are modeled after these companies' successful AR grips. The Tapco IN-TRAFUSE SAW-Style Pistol Grip's design follows the M249 Squad Automatic Weapon pistol grip, as the name suggests.

All three of these grips are slim at the top, allowing for a comfortable grip and perfect trigger finger placement. All three come with mounting hardware in place of an original AK grip bolt. The short mounting bolt allows using a hollow space inside the grip for storage. In the case of MagPul and Tapco grips, the trapdoor storage compartment is provided. All three grips install in place of the original grip as a direct replacement. The US Palm Battle and MagPul's MOE grips are priced around $25 and the Tapco SAW-Style Pistol Grip under $20.

The pistol grips above are my favorite to use on my personal rifles. They may work for some and may not for others. There are many other options when it comes to the AK aftermarket pistol grips. Some of the standouts that I have tested in the past are the Hogue OverMolded (rubberized) AK Pistol Grip, Command Arms (CAA) AK47 Pistol Grip and FAB Defense AK Pistol Grip, both of which come from Israel and are based on the Israeli Military design.

All of these grips offer some sort of advantage over the original factory grip with more ergonomic contour, finger rests, and some even have replaceable backstraps.

As I've said there are many options and one should choose which he or she more comfortable with. Quick and painless modification should add to the comfort level when shooting an AK rifle.

HAND GUARDS

I have said earlier that I did not have a problem with the AK's original stocks and pistol grips, not to the point where I absolutely have to replace them to improve performance of the gun or my comfort level. I cannot say the same for the AK's hand guards. Anyone who has had to use the AK extensively has burned their hands once or twice.

The size and design of the AK front hand guards are, in my opinion, not ideal. They are good enough and one can learn to work with them, but not ideal.

The evolution of the Kalashnikov rifle hand guards is in line with the rest of the gun's furniture, from hard wood to laminate wood and on to polyamide. One thing to notice is that the AK hand guards sit over the hottest area of the rifle. They "wrap" around the hottest part of the barrel and the gas tube.

As a result, the hand guards get very hot if the rifle is being fired at an intense rate of fire. The wood is a poor heat conductor, but works better than plastic.

The original AK-47 design hand guards had two heat venting ports on each side to help with heat dissipation. These ports remained on the AK's wood hand guards as the gun evolved into the AKM and later the AK-74.

However, later model AK-74 rifles' hand guard design did away with the ports due to a larger gap between the upper and lower hand guards. When the polyamide hand guards were introduced on the AK-74 rifles, designers took the heat into consideration and installed a heat shield into the lower hand guard. The heat shields on Soviet and later Russian-made plastic lower hand guards were polished almost to a mirror finish that set them apart from Bulgarian or US-made copies.

The shield would deflect the heat upward where it escapes through the gap between the upper and lower hand guards. This helped a bit, but still did little to help the gun move forward as a modern fighting carbine. Even the first attempts by the Russians to add some sort of mounting rails on lower hand guard offered no adequate mounting solutions for modern combat implements demanded by the modern military.

Again, the void was filled by the industrious American companies and later by Israeli and Russian manufacturers who had

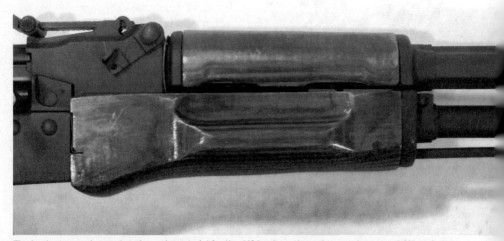

The laminate wood stayed as the main material for the AK furniture through several stages of AK evolution. The last laminate wood hand guards were made for the earlier AK-74 rifles.

followed suit. Today there are many options for AK aftermarket hand guards ranging in material, functionality, and even size.

The AK hand guards are also easy to replace and usually do not require special tools unless the new aftermarket hand guards require different mounting to the rifle. In this case most of the replacement hand guards come with necessary tools.

I have already touched on several hand guard options in the optical sight mounting solutions section of this book. But I will allow myself to be repetitive as these products are also used to mount other accessories.

The modern AK hand guard solutions usually come in two types: aluminum and plastic. The aluminum hand guards require a specific attachment method, unlike the plastic ones that use the original AK hand guard retention system on the rifle.

Plastic Hand Guards

Once again I will go from easiest to most complicated. Since the plastic hand guards are basically a direct swap with AK original parts, I will cover them first. As in the case with other AK accessories I have had the chance to test and use a variety of polymer or composite AK hand guards over the years.

The obvious choice for direct replacement would be the newly-produced Russian hand guards that the Russian armed forces adapted for the AK-74M modernization kit. These hand guards closely resemble the original non-railed hands guards of the AK-74M or 100 Series rifles and offer a four-inch bottom and two 1.5-inch integrated.

These are cool for those AK owners who would want to keep their rifles as close as possible to the original Russian-made models. However, it is not the most functional hand guard solution for a modern carbine.

Some other plastic hand guards like the CAA RS-47 and Mako's FAB Defense AK-47 Polymer Hand guard with Picatinny Rails offer slightly better flexibility for mounting various accessories, plus ease of installation where the lower part of the hand guard slides into the receiver of the rifles and then is secured in place with the hand guard retainer. The upper part is simply twisted into place like the original AK upper hand guard.

The same design black polymer hand guards were the standard issue with new Russian AK-74M and 100 Series rifles.

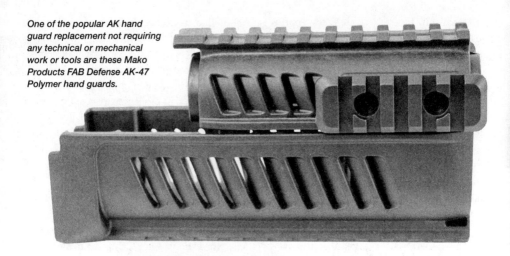

One of the popular AK hand guard replacement not requiring any technical or mechanical work or tools are these Mako Products FAB Defense AK-47 Polymer hand guards.

The Hogue 2-piece AK-47/AK-74 Rubber OverMolded Handguard represents different direct replacement AK hand guards option for those who like the rubberized feel.

However, these types of hand guards do not offer a rigid or reliable enough mount for an optical sight, or any kind of sight for that matter. They could however, be used for mounting a variety of other implements such as a vertical grip, combat light, or IR illuminator.

Mounting optics on the upper hand guard would require a mechanical fix that some other hand guard systems offer, such as the Mission First Tactical Tekko 2-Piece AK-47 Polymer Hand guard with Integrated Rail System.

This set of upper and lower hand guards has an upper guard with mounting rail that bolts to the lower. This provides for a better mounting option, but only for a collimator sight, and only for extremely close ranges. Just like the other plastic lower hand guards,

the Tekko guard installs directly as a replacement for the original AK part using the same retention.

As I've mentioned several times, it is not a solid or secure fix. Therefore, it is reasonable to expect a significant deviation of POI from POA. However, like the other plastic hand guard systems, this one is good to go for mounting non-essential (from the accuracy and marksmanship point of view) accessories.

Separately, I would like to mentioned the Hogue 2-Piece AK-47/AK-74 Rubber Over-Molded Hand guard. It is for those shooters who like the feel of a rubberized coating for extra grip.

The Hogue hand guards have a softer,

One of the better plastic AK hand guards is the MagPul MOE AK Hand Guard. Modularity is achieved through the use of the M-LOK mounting system.

smoother feel compare to the other composite hand guards. It is made of fiberglass with rubber overmold and installs the same way as the rest of the composite hand guards. As such it is susceptible to the same mounting woes as the rest of the field. The lower guard is contoured to follow the original AK hand guard design and therefore very comfortable until one installs the removable optional rail. All of the mounting rails on the Hogue 2-Piece AK-47/AK-74 Rubber OverMolded Hand guard are removable and offer some mounting flexibility.

Overall, I am not a fan of the plastic hand guards, at least not until I find something that is practical and useful. Despite the obvious weight reduction benefit, most of the AK aftermarket composite hand guards are suspect to me simply because of the fact that they are sitting over the hottest part of the gun. They may be OK while at the range shooting at paper, but when a greater intensity of fire is needed I would only trust the original factory composite guards with factory heat shield.

There is however, one AK composite product, or rather products, that I will not hesitate to use on my "work" gun. In fact, I would probably prefer it over the factory hand guard, the new MagPul MOE AK Hand Guard, MOE AKM Hand Guard, and ZHU-KOV Hand Guard.

When I first saw the MagPul AK hand guards, I already knew that I'd like them. The new MagPul AK hand guards look like they belong with the rest of the MagPul MOE family of products. The MagPul hand guards for ARs have been proven many times over on the battlefield. They have earned the status of being something to measure up to when it comes to rifle composite hand guards.

Using the M-LOK rail mounting system, the MagPul MOE hand guards offer vast mounting flexibility. The same unmistakable MOE pedigree has been built into the new AK hand guards. There are three MOE AK hand guards with two MOE guards designed to fit two different modification of the AK rifle without any permanent modification to the gun itself.

The third one, the ZHUKOV, is the longer hand guard that offers more mounting options and affords a shooter more gripping options for modern carbine handling or practical shooting. However, the installation of the ZHUKOV AK hand guards requires simple but permanent modification to the rifle, specifically removal of the front sling attachment from the hand guard retainer.

The new MagPul AK hand guards are longer that the original, offering better flexibility with gun handling. Note that all MagPul AK hand guards feature a simple replacement upper hand guard, but would work with any other upper guard mounting solution.

It can be done relatively simply with basic tools without any help from the gunsmith. Some shooters might shy away from permanently modifying their rifle and it is certainly understandable, but the potential benefit that the extended hand guard offers would most definitely outweigh any reason for keeping an ancient front sling attachment.

The MOE AKM Hand Guard is the shortest one of the three models and is a straightforward plastic hand guard that replaces the AK's original parts without any modifications to the gun. It utilizes the M-LOK mounting system for a variety of rails based on the shooter's requirements and offers more ergonomic hand placement and grip compared to the standard AK hand guard.

The MOE AK Hand Guard is designed to fit any stamped receiver AK rifle and installs in place of the original AK hand guard, with a small caveat: The MOE AK Hand Guard's lower guard is longer that the AKM model and as such covers the front retainer with standard sling attachment on most newer AK rifles. This would interfere with its installation. Because of this, removal of the sling attachment is required.

When I got this hand guard, I liked the length that provided extra space for accessories I was going to use on my gun. However, I was not keen on butchering my test rifle just yet. So instead of modifying the hand guard retainer on the rifle, I modified the lower hand guard itself using a simple Dremel tool. I've made two perpendicular cuts on the left side, removing the material slightly past the sling attachment, and the new lower hand guard fit like a glove.

The new MOE AK Hand Guard from MagPul obviously was designed to fit the Chinese Norinco Type 56 AK model without any modifications. However, with a miniscule amount of elbow grease it could fit on any stamped receiver AK rifle.

All three models of MagPul AK hand guards are made with proven high-impact composite material that is used on MagPul other products, and all three have an integrated heat-deflecting shield.

All three sets of MagPul AK hand guards come with the same small and light upper guard that slides on the gas tube in place of the original one. The MagPul designers did not have any illusions of optics on the flimsy AK gas tube, so they did not go for it. If there is a need for that mounting option, one should look into the UltiMAK or Troy Industries gas tube mounts that would work fine in combination with new MagPul hand guards.

Aluminum Hand Guards

Although the plastic hand guards with Picatinny rails would work fine on just about any AK rifle, the thing to remember is that plastic, like any material, is subject to fatigue and stress when under load. It will break, crack, melt, chip, or disintegrate at much less stress and load parameters than metal, including aluminum.

I have used the Midwest Industries AK47/AK74 Universal Handguards in Quadrail extensively. One of the options for any Midwest Industries AK hand guards is the flexibility of using an optic-specific upper mount.

The reason the original Russian polyamide hand guards could take more abuse is simply because they were steel-reinforced. For AK shooters who would like a more rigid mounting option that still involves the hand guards, there are several products made out of aluminum that offer just that.

Because the lack of elasticity in metal is simply the nature of the beast, almost all metal or aluminum AK hand guards require a mechanical mounting on the gun. They have to be securely bolted in place for a rigid installation because the upper part of the set that replaces the original AK upper hand guard is usually affixed to the lower hand guard with bolts. And since the lower hand guard is bolted to the gun, the aluminum hand guard system, as a general rule, offers a far better platform for mounting optical sights on the upper rail.

I have already highlighted several aluminum hand guard options in the "Mounts" section of this book, but I wanted to describe them in detail so that the reader gets a better idea how to install them and how they fit the AK rifle.

The first hand guard I would like to cover is Midwest Industries' AK47/AK74 Universal Hand guards in Quadrail. I have been using this rail and its variations for years now. It is a solid piece of equipment that once installed, will last for a long, long time.

The lower portion is rigidly attached to the barrel of the rifle and the upper part bolted to the lower. The beauty of the Midwest Industries AK hand guard system is that shooters can choose an optic specific upper instead of the 1913 rail. There are several variations to accommodate the most popular

Midwest Industries' AK47/AK74 Universal Handguard in Quadrail was probably one of the first viable aluminum AK hand guards that I encountered.

Midwest Industries also makes their hand guards to fit several popular AK variants like this Yugo M92 pistol.

optical or collimator sights and their copies. There are several variations of the original Quadrail hand guards now that the company released over the years. All had to do with different ways to install the "mission specific" 1913 rails instead of the integrated quad rail, thus reducing the weight and size of the hand guards.

There is an SS model that smaller two-inch rail sections can be attached to using screws. The SS model was followed by the more advanced KeyMod hand guard, and later an M-LOK version.

I have tested all of these and they are good-to-go no matter which one is chosen. They all attach the same way and accept the same top covers that are interchangeable. The Midwest Industries AK47/AK74 Universal hand guards do not require any irreversible modification to the gun and can be removed and replaced at will. The AK front sling ring stays untouched. However, most of the Midwest Industries AK hand guards come with built-in QD sling attachment.

The Midwest Industries' AK47/AK74

Universal Hand guards offer pretty good flexibility for mounting accessories on an AK. However, their longer AK47/AK74 Extended Hand guards offer even more.

Unlike the Universal hand guards the extended ones do require the permanent modification to the AK's lower hand guard retainer. Again, it has to do with the front sling attachment that must be removed. I said it before and I will say it again: the benefits far outweigh the small mod to remove a redundant part. Apart from the standard quad rail configuration, the extended hand guards come in SS and KeyMod versions.

In addition, Midwest Industries offers

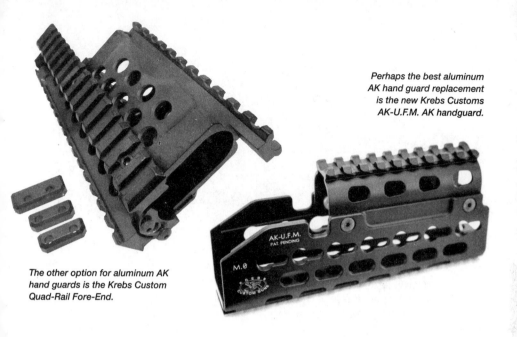

Perhaps the best aluminum AK hand guard replacement is the new Krebs Customs AK-U.F.M. AK handguard.

The other option for aluminum AK hand guards is the Krebs Custom Quad-Rail Fore-End.

several variations of their AK hand guards to fit just about any AK rifle model that is available on the market today. Having had a chance to work with these I would consider them to be second-to-none and among the absolute best AK accessories.

As I've mentioned before, Krebs Custom offers two types of their own AK hand guards. The Krebs Quad-Rail Fore-End for standard AK rifles is similar to aluminum hand guards with integrated Picatinny rails from other manufacturers, but with one exception: Krebs Custom has come up with a very solid attachment to the gun that does not involve the barrel.

The Krebs Quad-Rail hand guard is a very good option for an AK rifle. However, for those who don't like the "cheese grater" effect of the quad rail hand guard, Krebs Custom has released their latest AK-U.F.M. AK hand guards. These are perhaps one of the best aluminum AK aftermarket hand guards available today. The AK-U.F.M. hand guards install on the rifle similarly to the Quad-Rail and sits solidly on the rifle. The accessory rails attaches to the hand guards

with the KeyMod mounting system on the side and the bottom.

The top part of the hand guard, however, has a four-inch integrated 1913 rail. The new AK-U.F.M. AK hand guards from Krebs have rounded corners and feel just right in the shooter's hand. The smooth and slick form makes even an ancient AK rifle look like a modern fighting carbine. The hand guards' KeyMod system offers a necessary flexibility for mounting mission-specific accessories. The Krebs Custom's AK-U.F.M. hand guards are definitely one of the best aluminum AK hand guard solutions available on the market today.

The last option for an aftermarket AL aluminum hand guard replacement comes from Troy Industries with their AK47 Bottom Short Rail. Troy's rail is a one-piece replacement for a lower hand guard and works with either the AK's original upper hand guard or an aftermarket replacement.

I have already described Troy Industries' AK47 Top Rail as a replacement for the AK's gas tube in the "Mounts" section of this book. Together, the top and bottom rails

Midwest Industries also make the AK47/AK74 Extended Handguards in Quadrail version. However, permanent rifle modification is required by removing the hand guard retaining bracket.

make a complete and very flexible hand guard mounting solution for any AK.

The Troy AK47 Bottom Rail is made entirely from aluminum. It is long enough so when installed on the gun it goes from the front of the receiver all the way forward past the gas block covering it. With the added length, this hand guard not only provide an adequate space to mount any combination of tactical implements, but it also gives the shooter more gripping surface, which AKs usually lack to begin with.

The hand guard itself is rounded in its cross section, mimicking (to the point) the longer rounded AR hand guards. The shape and length of it is conducive to improved handling of the rifle, resulting from a better grip. The necessary rail-mounting holes are provided along the entire length of the hand guard. This allows any number of rail sections in different sizes to be installed if the need arises. Although this is a longer hand guard it does not require any permanent modifications to the rifle. It installs in minutes in place of the AK original lower hand guard using the same retention system. It comes with an Allen key wrench to tighten the tension on the hand guard retaining bracket. No other tools are necessary.

There are other options that come

from small and large manufacturers of AK accessories. The ones I have described above are the ones I have personal experience with. Whichever option is selected, the shooter must make sure that practicality is driving his or her decision on what accessory to use on the AK rifle.

MUZZLE DEVICES

With most of the important ergonomic and modularity enabling accessories covered, the only other important accessory left is the muzzle attachment. Though small, the

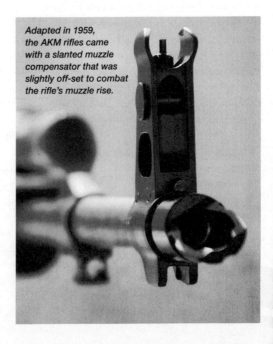

Adapted in 1959, the AKM rifles came with a slanted muzzle compensator that was slightly off-set to combat the rifle's muzzle rise.

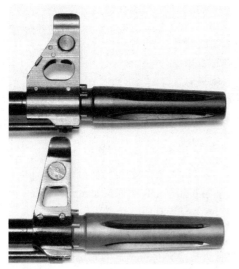

Some of the AKML rifles had a side-mounting rail for installing a night vision optical sights, and can be equipped with a very effective cage-type flash hider that was a part of the NSPU NV scope kit.

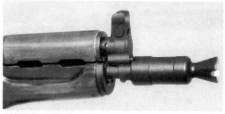

The AKS-74U shortened rifle was equipped with its own unique muzzle device. It was more of a compensator with flash reduction ability. It also had a wire-cutting feature.

muzzle attachment can impact the accuracy, recoil, and handling of the AK, or any rifle for that matter.

Originally the AK-47 main battle rifle that was adopted by the Soviet Armed Forces had a threaded barrel at the muzzle. However, no break or compensator was issued as standard equipment with the rifle. The threads were protected by a muzzle nut. The nut itself was kept from vibrating out by the spring-loaded detent pin. When the lighter

modernized version of the AK, the AKM, was introduced in 1959, a muzzle compensator was introduced with it to address the loss of stability due to a reduction in weight in the new rifle.

The new AK slanted compensator screwed on the existing muzzle threads asymmetrically and by 'catching" some powder gases, created a pressure opposite of the AK's natural muzzle climb, thus reducing the gun's muzzle jump during full automatic fire. This small compensator was surprisingly very effective and would remain on the rifle as standard equipment until the 70's, when the Soviets switched to the AK-74 family of rifles.

The only other standard AK muzzle attachments of that era were the PBS-1 (Device for Silent and Flameless Shooting) sound suppressor, and the cage-type universal flame suppressor that came as part of the newly introduced IR and Starlight Night Vision scope.

The AK-74 rifle muzzle break was a very effective device. But, it was not a flash hider. The sizeable muzzle flash was deflected to the sides and away from the shooter's line of sight.

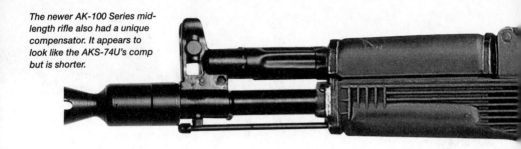

The introduction of the AK-74 family of rifles also saw the introduction of an ingenious muzzle brake device that also worked as a flash reducer/redirector. The AK-74 and paratrooper model AKS-74 had this muzzle device as standard equipment. The new AK-74 muzzle brake was far more complex than its predecessor, the slanted compensator. It had an expansion chamber to allow more time and space for powder gases to burn and reduce muzzle flash, a "pancake" muzzle brake to reduce recoil, and a built-in compensator to reduce muzzle rise.

The new AK-74 muzzle brake reduced muzzle flash significantly, but it did not eliminate it entirely; that is evident when the rifle is fired in low light conditions. But what it did is redirect the flash blast to the sides. This helped the shooter to not be temporarily blinded by the blast and allowed him or her to continue shooting the rifle. It also allowed the newer Starlight NV scopes to be use with the AK without having to replace the muzzle attachment.

This AK-74 muzzle brake was so effective in reducing recoil and increasing the rifle's accuracy significantly over its predecessors that all new Russian AK models, no matter the caliber, had this type of muzzle brake on them as standard equipment. Even the newest Izhmash offering, the AK-12, has a variation of this muzzle brake.

The other AK-74 family muzzle attachments came on the RPK-74 light machine gun and the AKS-74U, the shorted version of the AK-74 rifle.

The RPK-74 had a much longer and heavier barrel and bipod, so had no need for a recoil-reducing or stabilizing muzzle device. The longer barrel also offered more room and time for powder to burn, thus significantly reducing the muzzle flash. However, a small cage-type flash hider was installed on the gun as standard equipment. This small device worked like a charm and almost completely eliminated muzzle blast flash, thus eliminating the need to replace muzzle devices when using a NV scope.

The short AKS-74U device was an entirely different animal. The AKSU's 8" barrel provided no space for a finishing burn of the round's powder, and the resulting 10-foot fireball made the short gun a "flame thrower".

The new compensator/muzzle flash reducer had an expansion chamber and reversed cone compensator. Though muzzle flash was marginally reduced, this attachment significantly improved gun handling. The other interesting detail about the AKSU muzzle device is that it had two small notches at the coned compensator's tip. These notches were designed to shoot wire used in enemy fortifications by placing the notches on the wire and pulling a trigger.

The original AK muzzle attachments can be classified as compensators, flash hiders, muzzle brakes, and suppressors. There were attempts to make a combination muzzle

One of the most popular muzzle attachment replacements for the AK is the AR-style cage-type flash hider.

◀ The latest Russian development in the AK-74 muzzle break is its conversion to a flash hider.

brake/flash hider, but neither function worked perfectly.

There are many copies of the original AK muzzle attachments that are manufactured here in the States. It is illegal to import any "assault rifle" with a muzzle attachment that is considered a flash hider. The flash hiders are deemed an "evil" feature and are banned from importation. By the same token muzzle brakes are OK as long as they are permanently attached.

This also gave rise to the American-made AK muzzle devices as one of the six domestically produced parts to comply with BATFE 922r regulations when converting a sporting AK to more of the "military" configuration.

My philosophy on AK muzzle brakes is that they should only be replaced if the new device improves the rifle's performance. I personally absolutely love the original AK-74 style muzzle device. Therefore, I would not replace it on my AK-74 or AK-103 rifle with anything unless something better comes out.

So far, I do not think there is such a thing. However, gun development progress is not standing still and we may see something better in the future.

The cone baffle was added with cylindrical sleeve to contain and disperse muzzle flash.

Having said that about the AK-74-style break that comes standard on AK-74 and 100 Series rifles, I cannot say the same about the AKM-style slanted compensator. Although it works just fine, I think there is a lot of room for improvement in the muzzle brake and flash-reducing category. And that is where the US AK accessories manufacturers made huge strides.

Today there is a plethora of AK muzzle devices, with the lion's share being muzzle attachments to fit the left-handed 14mm AK muzzle threads. As I've said before, the AK muzzle device should only be replaced if it improves the performance and not the looks of the gun.

However, if the new device also looks cool, then it is an instant winner. On my personal AKM-style rifles I chose to go with muzzle flash-reducing attachment versus the muzzle brakes. However, it is just a matter of personal preference. When choosing a muzzle device for an AK, the shooter should consider what he or she is trying to achieve and start from there.

All of my work rifles are equipped with this simple and inexpensive accessory.

Most of the AK aftermarket muzzle attachments on the market today are reasonably priced so the shooter can easily choose a couple for different shooting conditions. In any case, American AK enthusiasts are lucky there is no shortage of various AK muzzle devices to choose from.

OTHER ATTACHMENTS

Front Grips

So far, I have covered the AK accessories that replace the AK original equipment. But what about the addition of non-standard accessories? One of the best-suited additions to any AK rifle is the front vertical grip, especially when the original hand guards are replaced and some other accessories are installed. The advantage of a front grip was recognized early on. Some of the Warsaw Pact countries, Hungary and Romania to be precise, even started equipping their versions of the AK rifles with front grips.

However, it wasn't until the wide use of the front vertical grips by the US Army on

its M4 carbines and USMC M16A4 rifle that the front grip was spread to the AK.

I personally went 180 degrees on the issue of front grip use on an AK. I was trained on and used a rifle that did not have front grip. Therefore, there was no need for it. Or so I thought. Old dog and new tricks I guess. But as soon as I installed a set of quad-rail hand guards with micro-dot sights on my AK rifle I realized the error of my ways. I could not handle the gun the same way I always did. The sheer size of the hand guard set up prevented me from gripping the rifle by its hand guards.

Enter the front vertical grip. I quickly became a convert to the concept of the vertical grip on the AK and now I use them on most of my "work" rifles. The advantages of a vertical front grip are obvious. It allows the operator to maintain a proper and positive grip on the front-heavy rifle; it make the gun more maneuverable especially in tight places; it provides support for the additional weight of the hand guard-mounted accessories; it protects the shooter's hand from burns if the hand guard gets too hot, and it provides for additional ways to carry an AK.

The MagPul RVG Grip (left) and TangoDown Vertical Stubby Fore Grip (right) are the two grips that I would select for use on my rifles. Their size allows me to install them closer to the receiver for better stability.

When choosing a front grip for an AK one must consider the way the magazine is inserted into the rifle. The front upper tip of the magazine is inserted first until it catches a trunnion block with its lip, then the magazine is rocked straight back until it locks in the gun. Because of the curvature of the AK magazine a vertical front grip may interfere with insertion of the magazine and its removal, so the length and placement of the front grip has to be considered.

For example, the shorter the grip the closer to the receiver it can be installed without interfering with a magazine change. The curvature of the magazine itself, which is dictated by the caliber of the AK, also impacts the location of the grip. The 7.62X39mm magazine has a smaller radius of curvature, or put simply, is more curved, and as such requires more clearance, forcing a shorter grip.

The 5.56 NATO (.223) magazine is the straightest out of all the AK mags, and as such would accept a longer or closer-mounted front grip. Krebs Custom for example went a different route and developed an offset front grip adapter that moves the front grip slightly off-center and to the side of the gun, and completely out of the way of the magazine. I have tried this set up and works great. However, I personally would prefer to have my grip directly under the centerline of the rifle. Again, it is a matter of personal preference.

The size and location of a vertical front grip on AK rifle is usually dictated by the curvature of the magazine and its unobstructed insertion.

Over the years, I have selected a couple of my favorite grips. However, readers of this book should not take it as a recommendation. This is simply what I found to work for my meaty paws. There are as many other opinions as there are front grips, most of them not without merit.

What I like and use on my personal guns are the MagPul RVG Grip for Picatinny rails, the MVG grip for M-LOK system, or the TangoDown Vertical Stubby Fore Grip QD or non-QD Stubby Fore Grip. The MagPul is a better value and the TangoDown QD grip offers better flexibility.

There are a few things to remember when choosing a vertical front grip for an AK. There is no such a thing as an AK-specific front grip. Any vertical grip that works on the AR or any other rifle will work on the AK.

Although some shooters would prefer a longer grip, I found it that the 3"-3½" grip works for best for me. This way it could be installed closer to the receiver without interfering with magazine changes and still provide adequate grip. It also would not throw off the gun's geometry too much when shooting from the rest. I also prefer the grip mounted on a quick detach mount, just in case I have to shoot off a sand bag and a pack for accuracy and for a long time.

In addition, I would also like to have the vertical grip installed as close to the receiver as possible to better support the heaviest part of the gun and not have the support arm extended too far forward. But my experience shows that the 3½" vertical grip should be placed right at the middle of the AK regular-size lower hand guard for the 5.45X39mm rifle and about one inch forward from the center of the hand guard for the 7.62X39mm gun. As I've said, the location may vary depending on the length of the grip. Also, the front grip should be located within the vicinity of other button-operated

implements such as a laser designator and/or tactical light.

Some may ask about the angled fore-grips instead of the full-blown vertical grip. While a solid product and a great fit for an AR carbine, the angled fore-grip is not a good solution for an AK, mainly because due to a possible interference with the magazine change. It can only be mounted toward the front of the hand guard, thus forcing the support arm to be extended too far. Another argument against it is that the AFG makes carrying an AK rifle by its hand guards problematic with providing an alternative as in the case with front grip. However, it is just an opinion and someone might find an AFG useful on their AK.

Other Great Accessories

Here are some smaller AK accessories that I think should be mentioned as an improvement to the gun's handling and performance.

Anyone who has handled an AK would know what the rifle's safety lever/fire mode selector look like. It operates simply by sliding down from the safe position: One click for full auto and two click for semi-automatic fire for select fire rifles and just one click all the way down for commercial sporting

Krebs Custom Mk VI Enhanced Safety can be operated by the trigger finger while maintaining a grip on the AK's PG.

guns, then back all the way up for safe.

The shape of the AK safety lever is to match the cutout on the rifle's top cover and to cover the opening for bolt carrier handle.

The usual operation of the AK safety lever is done by means of the right hand's thumb and index finger. This means the operator has to remove his or her hand from the pistol grip to perform safety lever manipulations. This is very un-Western like, although I personally do not have any problem with it and can perform this task quickly and efficiently.

However, for those who need to maintain a grip on the AK pistol grip there is a solution in the form of the Krebs Custom Mk VI Enhanced Safety. The lever has a small but important feature that significantly enhances its operation. Half way down the bottom of the Krebs Custom Mk VI Enhanced Safety lever there is an integrated lip that is within easy reach of the shooter's index finger.

When properly installed the Krebs safety lever can be operated by the trigger finger without releasing the pistol grip of the rifle.

The AK safety lever is under tension to prevent accidental movement. Its tip has a small detent that is stamped into it creating a small "bump" on the other side. The receiver has small dents corresponding with the mode of fire or "Safe" and "Fire" positions of the lever. The bump on the lever falls into these dents on the receiver making distinct clicks and securing the selector/safety lever in place.

Krebs Custom Mk VI Enhanced Safety is one of the accessories that would instantly improve your handling of an AK rifle.

Because the lever is under tension it rests in the chosen position rather reliably. However, too much tension on the lever makes it much harder to operate with the index finger alone. So a careful balance of tension and movement has to be achieved when installing the Krebs Custom Mk VI Enhanced Safety by slowly and carefully bending it away from the receiver. Any bending should be done in small increments until the desired tension is reached.

Another other small but important accessory is an ingenious replacement for the AK's original pin retaining clip, the infamous "paper clip."

We already know that AK is not the most sophisticated weapon. In fact, it is probably the simplest out of all the rifles on the modern battlefield. However, there is a certain degree of sophistication in Kalashnikov's rifle. After all, modern operating and manu-

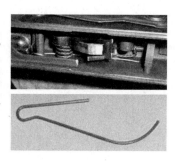

The incredibly simple axle pin retaining clip, aka the "paper" clip (Left) works fine, but the equally simple but much more practical and "modern" Krebs Custom Trigger Pin Retaining Plate is just better. Every AK rifle should have it.

facturing principals had to be employed to make this gun function, and for the most part it is very true.

Except, however, when it comes to the axle pin retaining clip. The clip itself is nothing more than a piece of steel wire that is bent to fit around the grooves on the axle pins. The clip is under tension and rests flat against the inner left side of the receiver while it is jammed into the pins' groove, preventing them from backing out of the gun.

It works just fine, but when the rifle is undergoing maintenance and the fire control group has to be removed and then re-installed again, it sometimes presents a challenge, especially for a less experienced shooter.

Again, the solution is simple, practical, and in my opinion the most useful internal AK parts improvement component: the Krebs Custom Trigger Pin Retaining Plate. The retaining plate simply drops in place and remains there secured by the safety/selector level. No tools of any kind are needed.

Once installed it can be removed and re-installed over and over again without worrying about losing tension and such. Install and forget. Both of these parts can be ordered from Krebs Custom, but I am sure there are other manufacturers who make

similar products. In any case, both are tested by me and are highly recommended.

For those AK shooters who do not like to venture too far away from keeping their rifles stock, but still want to modernize the way they are used, there is the Midwest Industries Rear Single Point Sling Adapter.

Unlike the folding-stock model AK rifles that have rear sling attachment at the folding stock hinge and thus allowing a use of single point sling, the fixed stock models have the sling attachment at the back of the buttstock.

The Midwest Industries MI Rear Single Point Sling Adaptor is one of those simple accessories that improves performance and/or handling of a rifle within minutes. It attaches to any wood or polymer AK stock.

The LINCH left hand integrated non-reciprocating charging handle is something I was asking for for years.

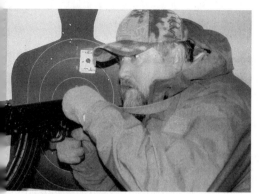

The LINCH charging handle makes it possible to complete reloading of the AK entirely with the left hand.

One can certainly attach the sling to it, but it would make it too cumbersome and not very practical.

The folks at the Midwest Industries came up with a nice little solution in the form of this sling adapter. This little gizmo is nothing more than a small base that attaches to the solid wood or plastic stock by two screws and a QD sling ring. This small accessory modernizes the fixed stock AK in minutes.

One more exciting AK accessory that I was begging numerous AK accessories manufacturers for years is finally here. The LINCH left hand intergrated non-reciprocating charging handle is designed as a drop-in application for AK rifles offered by Davis Tactical Solutions, LLC.

The LINCH charging handle resides on the regular AK top cover. It requires no modifications to the weapon system and installs in seconds by simply swapping the rifle's top cover. The LINCH charging handle delivers a primary and alternate means of operating the bolt carrier. The charging handle is non-reciprocating during firing. The handle itself is direct transfer from the FAL rifle. It can be folded out of the way when not in use. It

rides on the guide rails that are welded to the standard AK top cover. The inner tab of the LINCH charging handle "hooks" to the bolt carrier on the left by the front trunnion block and pulls the BC back to recycle the rifle after a mag change.

To summarize this chapter, I have to say that all of the accessories that I have described are what I have tested and liked. I continue to use several of these implements on my rifles today. However, as I've mentioned before, several times, what works for me may not work for someone else. The idea behind this chapter was to let the AK enthusiasts know that there is a good supply of the AK accessories out there to address any modification and/or improvements that they may want to make to their rifles.

One of the most important things to remember when modifying and accessorizing an AK is the additional weight. Excessive weight should always be considered when choosing an accessory. One should use plastic where possible, for example, when replacing the AK furniture. However, lightweight aluminum should be used for mounting critical attachments such as sights.

Always calculate the benefit of installing an accessory against the additional weight that it adds to the rifle, because the additional weight to the gun not only increases overall combat load (which is not important in peacetime), but also can throw off a gun's balance.

The LINCH left hand intergraded non-reciprocating charging handle simply added to the standard AK type cover. It also comes in several variations, like this one for the Yugo M92 pistol.

CHAPTER TWELVE

MY PERFECT AK

My perfect AK already exists, and the Russians have built it. It is their new AK-12. It has everything the modern AK shooter wants his rifle to have. Unfortunately, I don't think we will see a commercial version of this gun in the US anytime soon. All we can do is try to build a standard off-the-shelf AK rifle into something that would come close to it.

I have built many rifles that I've used one time or the other for work. I have tested many configurations employing many accessories from many manufacturers. I've rejected some and selected only the ones that worked perfectly for me based on functionality and practicality, and eventually wound up with what I consider a perfect fighting AK carbine.

I chose to build my perfect fighting

carbine from a normal, off-the-shelf I.O. Inc. fixed stock AK-74 rifle.

Why AK-74? If you have not shot one, shoot it. No additional explanation would be necessary. No appreciable recoil, accuracy, and the light weight of the gun and ammo should be enough for anyone to choose it as their favorite rifle.

The I.O. Inc. AK-74 rifle was built on I.O.'s own receiver with Russian (Bulgarian) parts and came dressed in Russian plum furniture. Since it was going to be a modern fighting carbine it had to be made relevant using modern accessories enabling the attachment of modern implements. I have already described the accessories that I personally prefer, so I would use those to configure my perfect AK rifle.

My "donor" rifle was the I.O. Inc AK-74 gun built on an I.O. receiver with Russian and Bulgarian parts. All the accessories that I chose for this project were "bolt-on" type.

There was no question what stock to put on my new work gun. MagPul's ZHUKOV folding stock easily was my one and only choice. Complementing the stock I chose the MagPul AK grip as one of my absolute favorites.

For hands guards I went with the smooth and refined Krebs U.F.M.-AK hand guards with the KeyMod attachment system.

STOCK

There is no other choice for me other than MagPul's ZHUKOV Stock. It fits right, and I can install a cheek riser to accommodate optics. There are three to choose from, with different heights. And it folds to the right so that I can use my side-mounted optics.

PISTOL GRIP

Again I went with MagPul's AK grip. I chose not to use their "+" rubberized model just because I like the feel of rough plastic better.

FRONT HAND GUARDS

It was a close toss-up between Midwest Industries and Krebs. I did not go with Mag-Pul's plastic MOE guards because I wanted a top rail just in case I wanted to use an NV illuminator in tandem with a micro-dot sight or laser target designator. The aluminum hand guards with their mechanical attachment to the gun provide good enough stability for that. So I went with Krebs' AK-U.F.M. hand guards because they are smoother, smaller in circumference, light and practical, similar to the original AK furniture.

MUZZLE DEVICE

I left the AK-74 muzzle device on the gun because it works great and there is no substitute for it yet.

That concludes the base for my perfect rifle. As for attachments here are a few:

MAGPUL RVG RAIL VERTICAL GRIP

Small, and as such allows me to place it as closer to the receiver.

LASERLYTE SMALL CENTER MASS SIGHT AND L3 INSIGHT ML1-AA COMBAT LIGHT.

Both of these were chosen on account of their extremely light weight.

ELCAN SPECTRE DR 1-4X SCOPE

This is the crowing centerpiece of my perfect fighting carbine. Some may say this optics option is overkill for an AK, at over four times the cost of the original rifle. There are other more economical options, but the Spectre DR in my opinion is the perfect fighting carbine scope, especially for AK-74 rifle.

Its 5.56 NATO reticle with built-in BDC corresponds perfectly to the 5.45X39mm cartridge trajectory out to 650 meters. I can't

The ELCAN Spectre DR 1-4 is my preferred scope/sight for a 5.45X39mm rifle as its 5.56X45mm NATO BDC reticle matches the AK-74 ballistics pretty closely to about 600 meters.

Using a 2" 1913 Rail section I hung the L3 INSIGHT ML1-AA combat light opposite a small LaserLyte designator. A stubby vertical grip completed the forend of the gun.

ask for a better match for the Elcan scope than the Midwest Industries' Side Rail Scope Mount, again, because it is light and yet offers a solid platform for multi-power scopes. I decided to use my rifle's side mounting rail instead of top cover mounts because I wanted to retain the flexibility of switching between optical options if the need arises.

And that's it. My newly-dressed perfect rifle was done, and after installing all the accessories, excluding the Spectre DR scope, I only added 0.7 lbs. over the stock gun.

As a side note, I have used a slightly different setup for my 7.62mm AK. Again, I went with MagPul products for the stock and pistol grip, but this time I also chose the MagPul MOE AK hand guard.

Although my I.O., Inc. AKM247C rifle was an essentially a close copy of the AKM, I went with the MOE AK rather than the AKM model. I had to slightly modify the lower hand guard to fit it to avoid the rifle's original sling attachment. However, the extra length of the AK model is worth a couple minutes with the Dremel tool.

Since the original AKM247C rifle came with the AKM standard slanted compensator, I wanted to add something that would improve the performance of the gun and installed the Midwest Industries AK Flash Hider.

Other additions naturally included the MagPul M-LOK MVG Vertical Grip, and Viridian X5L Light/Laser designator combination.

For the carbine sight, I chose the Hi-Lux 7.62X39 AK 1-4X24 CMR4-AK762-R scope mounted on the Midwest Industries AK 30mm Side Scope Mount. This rifle came out pretty light and functional with all modern implements, and I did not break the bank.

I often use the Midwest Industries Side Rail Scope Mount due to it being light and universal. It matches my ELCAN scope beautifully.

I also maintain a .30 caliber AKM rifle for some of the carbine courses I teach. I chose to dress my 7.62X39mm-chambered I.O., Inc AKM247 in MagPul livery as well.

For this setup, I chose to go with MagPul's MOE® AK hand guard. I had to modify it a bit to fit an AK-type rifle.

I used the Midwest Industries AK 30 mm Side Scope Mount, specifically designed for this scope, for my CMR sight.

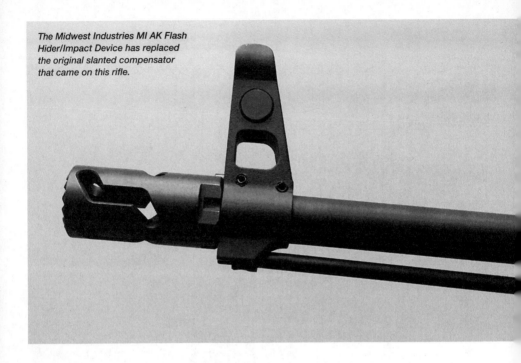

The Midwest Industries MI AK Flash Hider/Impact Device has replaced the original slanted compensator that came on this rifle.

SPARE PARTS

I should mention several places where any AK enthusiast can find spare parts and some of the original imported accessories. There are many companies that specialize in AK parts, but availability of these parts is unpredictable and spotty.

However there are companies that will have most AK parts and original accessories in stock at all times. Located in south Florida, Legion USA (legionusa.com) specializes in Russian-made AK parts and accessories. Some of the products they offer would make even a very picky AK collector drool.

K-Var Corp (k-varcorp.com) has been in the AK market for many years, supplying rare and hard-to-get Russian and Bulgarian parts and accessories. In addition to parts and accessories, K-Var carries a full line of Bulgarian and Russian AK rifles that have

been converted by the Arsenal USA facility in Las Vegas, NV.

One more source worth mentioning for AK parts is the AK Builder (ak-builder. com) web site. This resource is usually well stocked with many AK parts from various manufacturers, including complete parts kits.

Although these three companies are usually the most reliable sources for needed parts, they are not the cheapest, and they are not the only game in town. A quick search on the Web will produce many others, some even more economically priced.

The other source for AK parts is the secondary market from private individuals; auction sites or AK-themed forums such as akfiles.com or the AK section of ar15.com, among others. Between all these sources, if I need a part really badly I can find it within minutes with a few keystrokes.

CHAPTER THIRTEEN

RUSSIA'S AK MODERNIZATION PROGRAM

My efforts to build a modern fighting carbine out of "outdated" AK's were not that far off. As it turns out the Russians have come up with a modernization kit of their own.

Recently Kalashnikov Concern (formerly known as Izhmash) built - and Russian Armed Forces have adopted - a totally new Kalashnikov rifle, the AK-12.

The Russians took the proven AK-74 platform and incorporated the best ergonomic and operational features that AK shooters (mainly here in the US) have been using for years. These features were incorporated into the new gun not as add-ons, but rather designed into the rifle itself.

The new AK was "all that" with many features that enhanced its performance and handling, such as a bolt hold-open, a push-button mag release, ambidextrous thumb safety and charging handle, and an ample number and length of Picatinny rails all around, coupled with an ergonomic pistol grip and fully adjustable folding stock.

It also sported an improved two-chamber muzzle brake that, together with better

After the large-scale purchase of the AK-12 was rejected by Russia's top brass, Concern Kalashnikov came with an upgrade package for the large number of the AK rifles the Russian Armed Forces already possessed.

An ample number of 1913 rails were added for modularity.

The standard AK-74 muzzle break had an inner baffle and sleeve added to it to reduce muzzle flash signature.

weight distribution, improved accuracy of the AK rifle by 30 to 50 percent.

However, the introduction of the AK-12 to the Russian military was met with meager enthusiasm. The rifle's marginal performance improvements over its predecessor did not justify a huge and expensive re-armament program, especially considering the supposed 12 million AK-74 rifles still in the possession of the Russian Armed Forces, with the bulk of them still in factory grease, packed away in warehouses throughout the country.

This was a blow that could topple any manufacturer dependent on government orders to sustain its existence. However, the Russian top brass understood the need for the modernization of Russia's main battle rifle. The aging AK-74M gun was starting to show its age and no longer could fully satisfy the demands of modern combat.

Kalashnikov Concern and the Russian Armed Forces launched a modernization program that was unprecedented in its size. Two modernization kits were developed to bring the already-built rifles to the 21st Century, with one kit designed for installation by armorers at the bases, and the other developed for in-factory installation.

Overall, the new kit did not much improve the accuracy of the AK-74 rifle, as it already had pretty good inherent performance, well within the Russian military requirements. The only performance enhancement came in the way of a muzzle brake "shroud" that would install over the standard AK-74 muzzle brake to reduce its blast signature.

The other improvements addressed the

Ergonomic pistol grip and fully adjustable folding telescopic stock are the part of the Kalashnikov AK upgrade package.

handling and modularity of the rifle. Now all the fixed stock rifles were fitted with AR-style telescopic folding stocks that could fold left or right. The AKS model's folding stock was replaced with a new AR-style stock with an additional hinge that would also allow opposite-side folding. The lower hand guard had a bottom rail that the front vertical grip (also part of the new upgrade kit) could be attached to, and two smaller rail sections on both sides.

The upper hand guard was replaced with a 4.5-inch rail section in the same plane as the new hinged top cover with its own 7.5-inch Picatinny rail. The ergonomic pistol grip completed the upgrade kit. Basically, the Russians arrived with their own modernized fighting carbine on a mass production scale.

CHAPTER FOURTEEN

THE AK IN THE USA

The Chinese folding bayonet Type 56 AK variant was one of the first AK rifles imported into the US.

The largest AK commercial market is doubtless the United States. The history of the AK in the US is a tumultuous journey stretching from the very first Galil, Valmet, and Chinese Type 56 variants to today's smorgasbord, with a vast array of anything from truly collectable Tula and Izhevsk rifles to the US-made tactical carbines.

The US AK market has the characteristics of true capitalism: it addresses the demand with proper supply. The US AK market caters to all types of AK enthusiasts and shooters, from collectors who are sticklers for even the smallest details, to the everyday shooter who does not want to spend a fortune for the gun and ammunition. As such, there is a rather large price deviation.

What can one expect to encounter in the United States in the way of AKs? The answer is just about anything. What I mean by this is that there are rifles here from almost every manufacturer in the world, including Cuba and North Korea. There are many serious collectors who possess truly one-of-a-kind

original variants. How these rifles get here is as varied as the guns themselves, from mass importation to local production to battlefield pick up.

Like I said, there are AK enthusiasts who have been at the AK "game" for a long time and accumulated a large and historically correct collections. I personally possess several rifles that are truly collector's items. But an overwhelming majority of AK shooters would not care about a correct number of rivets and dimples on their AKs. They just want a gun that will shoot every time the trigger is pulled.

Most of today's AK owners get their rifles from commercially available stock imported or domestic. The modern AK has ceased to be an exotic rifle that has to be kept original and retain its distinct looks.

To today's modern shooter the AK is a platform on which to build a functioning and modular rifle, in much the same way that the AR is. So most of the AKs sold today wind up being built into something else by owners or professional gunsmiths. Don't get me wrong, the market is full of collector-grade AKs today, and there is a fair amount of trading going on in this particular area, usually involving much higher prices. But the $500-$600 rifle still holds a firm leading position when it comes to Kalashnikov rifle sales in the US.

The truth is we do need some way to separate and categorize all of the AK rifles available today. We have to, like they say in Russia, separate the flies from the meat, and create some categories for different types of AK rifles to better understand the market.

There are collectors AKs, imported AKs, domestically built AKs, domestically converted AKs from imported guns, sporting AK-based rifles, and parts kit rifles. A separate category for AK guns would be guns specifically designed and developed by gunsmiths or gun manufacturers, like tactical AK rifles.

COLLECTORS

The collectors AK's are the rifles that at one point have been imported into the United States years ago and have since gotten banned from further importation. Some of the kit guns built by reputable gunsmiths are also collectable based on the origin and value of the kit.

A good representative in this category would be Chinese-made Norinco Type 56 (AKS47S) and its variants. The Polytec Legend is the closest thing to the original Soviet milled receiver AK-47 model, and the early-import Egyptian MAADI rifle is the closest copy to the original Soviet AKM rifle.

There are of course thousands of rifles that have been built by premier gunsmiths like Marc Krebs, Richard Parker, or Ted Marshall to mimic the original Soviet rifle using original Soviet parts kits that were available at one time from several companies. One can still find these kits floating around in cyberspace and have someone build an exact copy of the Soviet AK with all the right marking and correct coating and finish. Expect to drop close to a couple thousand dollars for one of these.

IMPORTS

The imported AK category deals with complete imported AK rifles from various countries. The country of origin, models, configuration and quality of these rifles has always fluctuated. One constant was (and is) the low price compared to specialty-built rifles. Though some of the serious AK aficionados would thumb their noses at the economically priced imported AKs, these rifles gained their immense popularity with shooters because of their availability and low price.

One could walk into any sporting goods store and walk away with a Romanian WASR-10 or Egyptian MAADI. The quality of finish and coating on these guns was not on par with what you would expect from a new, out-of-the-box rifle. However, the $300-$500 price tag and ability to modify the rifle overcame the small little imperfections.

Today, the imported guns are of much better quality and finish.

Most of the rifles that come in the States must be compliant with the firearms importation regulation and in most cases have to be "finished" or turned into a more sellable condition by an American importer here in compliance with the BATFE 922r regulation. The rifles that have been imported at one time or the other and/or are still being imported and available on the US market today are listed below.

Chinese MAK-90

Probably the first mass imported "economically" priced AK that hit these shores after the 1989 "assault rifle" import restrictions were introduced. The MAK-90 was essentially a civilian version of the famous

Polytec Legend (Top) and Norinco Type 56 were the main representatives of the AK family rifles here in the states for quite a while.

The commercial version of Chinese Type 56, the MAK-90 equipped to comply with assault rifle import restrictions was one of the most popular imported AKs at one point.

Chinese Type 56 rifle with several "evil" features removed.

The model designation MAK-90 stands for Modified AK-1990. This rifle lacked muzzle threads and a bayonet lug, it was semi-automatic only, and came with an elaborate, thumbhole sporterized stock.

Other than that, the MAK-90 was a Chinese factory-built AK exported from China in 1990-94 by Norinco and PolyTech. MAK-90s were mainly chambered in 7.62X39mm with a fair number of rifles imported in.223.

At that time the MAK-90 rifle could be had for under $200. Since these rifle are no longer imported or will never be imported today if one is lucky to find a MAK-90 on the Web he or she should expect to pay several times that.

Egyptian MAADI

Not to be mistaken for the early import rifles: These rifles came in a sporting configuration with thumbhole stock, machined-off bayonet lug and non-threaded barrel. The

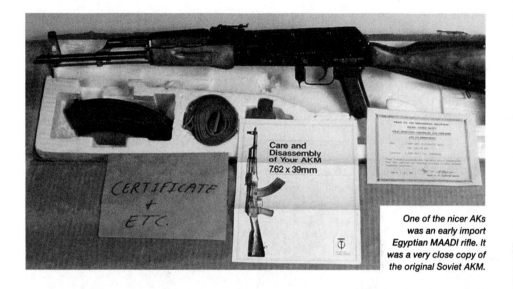

One of the nicer AKs was an early import Egyptian MAADI rifle. It was a very close copy of the original Soviet AKM.

Romanian Romak 1 in 7.62X39 mm and Romak 2 in 5.45X39 mm calibers were widely available in just about every gun store.

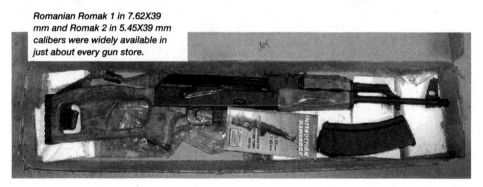

overall quality of these rifles was not on par with their early import MAADI siblings. There are no more AK rifles imported from Egypt.

Romanian Romak 1 and 2 Series

These rifles were imported during the Clinton-era Assault Rifle Ban of 1994. Like the MAK-90 and MAADI rifles, the Romak guns were based on Romanian military AKM-style stamped receiver rifles and were stripped of all the 'evil" features such as full automatic rate of fire and bayonet lug.

Additional not-so-evil items have also been installed, like a welded-in-place muzzle

nut to hide the threads and a very elaborate thumbhole sporting stock.

Overall the Romak series rifles had a very nice finish and beautiful light laminate wood furniture. The sporting stock was reminiscent of the Soviet Dragunov sniper rifle, the infamous SVD. The same stocks were installed on the Romanian version of the sniper rifles, the Romak 3 aka FPK, or later PSL.

The Romak rifles came chambered in the two main AK calibers. The Romak 1 was chambered in 7.62X39mm and the Romak 2 in 5,45X39mm. There were a couple of subtle differences between the two guns.

The Romak rifle gave way to the other Romanian mass import, the GP WASR-10 that is still a very popular rifle today.

Other than the pre-ban FEG SA-85M import from Hungary, the AMD-65 was the coveted and perhaps the most unique AK variant. It can easily be recognized by its metal lower hand guard, lack of upper and "crotch" folding stock. Note the 20-round magazine.

The Romak 2 had a very distinct bulky front sight block and elongated bolt carrier charging handle. At that time there was a plethora of the Romak rifles in every sporting goods store and they could be had for under $300.

Hungarian AKM-63

First produced in 1963, the AKM-63 is a full-size rifle with a wood stock and a metal fore-end with a vertical wood foregrip to help control recoil during automatic fire. There is no upper hand guard. Only about 1,100 of these were imported, so they are one of the rarest AK variants on the U.S. market.

Hungarian AMD-65

Chambered in 7.62x39mm, this short, 12.6-inch-barrel rifle has the same foregrip as the AKM-63. A side-folding wire stock is fitted to make it more maneuverable in confined spaces such as armored vehicles and tanks. The shorter sight radius and barrel make this a less accurate rifle than the AKM-63, but the overall handiness offsets the loss in accuracy. Note the 20-round magazine.

Polish Tantal

Based on the Polish Military Tantal WZ88 rifle chambered in 5.45x39mm, the commercial or civilian version of the Tantal rifle has been imported by Century Arms in the past. The Tantal is a slight departure from the traditional looks and function of the Soviet AK-74 gun.

The military Tantal is distinctive in that it features a three-round-burst capability in addition to the usual semi-automatic, single

Polish AKM (Bottom)
and AKMS (Top) rifles
are considered to be
the closest copies of the
original Soviet AKM rifle.

The Polish Tantal rifle is Poland's take
on the 5.45X39-chambered AK. The
Tantal rifle is a departure from the
traditional Soviet copies.

shot, and full auto capabilities. The commercial version that was imported into the US obviously lacked the full auto and three-round burst feature.

The Tantal rifle had a unique selector switch on the left side of the receiver that could be operated by the shooter's thumb. Most of the US models had a wire folding stock that bolted to the rear trunnion in place of the standard fixed one. It was fitted with a distinctive muzzle brake with a grenade-launcher capability. The Tantal rifle also came with a clip-on bipod. A specific saddle for it was pressed on the barrel. It also had Bakelite hand guards. The supply of these has gone dry, although there are some Tantal rifles for sale floating around cyberspace.

Romanian WASR or Wassenaar Arrangement Semiautomatic Rifles

These rifles are sportorized versions of the Romanian Military PM model 1963 rifle that were built with export in mind. The PM model 63 itself is a close copy of the Soviet AKM. These rifles have been imported into the US for quite some time and are still being imported by Century Arms today.

The WASR series rifles can be easily identified from the earlier imported Romak or SAR guns by lack of "dimples" on the stamped receiver at the magazine well, which were dropped in favor of internal guides for ease and lower cost of production.

The imported versions of the WASR are intended to accept single-stack magazines. The rifles feature hard chrome-lined barrels, side-mount scope rail and non-laminate wood furniture with laminate wood stocks. Before WASRs hit the store shelves Century modifies these rifles to appeal to potential AK buyers. All of the modifications have to comply with Title 18, Chapter 44, Section 922(r) of the United States Code. The mods include installation of the US-made gas pistons, fire control groups, pistol grips, and stock.

Serbian Zastava PAP

This rifle is based on the M70 Yugoslavian Kalashnikov variant. Today Century Arms imports the sporterized version of the Serbian M70 rifle that has been reconfigured to comply with the US firearms import laws. The new N-PAP M70 rifle that is sold by Century saw several "shooter friendly" modifications compared to its military sibling. The new gun is built on a lighter straight-cut 1mm receiver, double-stack bolt, AKM-type trunnion, and side optic mounting rail.

Although the gun retains the look of the Yugoslavian M70 rifle, it has been brought closer to the typical AKM variant.

The new N-PAP M70 is a much nicer rifle in comparison to the WASR guns. No crudeness and the finish is smooth but not shiny, with light-finished solid wood furniture. The PAP M70 is easily distinguished from other AK rifles by the three cooling slots on the hand guards, the light-colored teak furniture, different fixed stock attachment with black rubber buttplate, and AK-47-style front sight.

Likewise, the barrel is not chrome-lined, making it more accurate than a standard AKM, but at the cost of increased susceptibility to corrosion. Century Arms performs all the necessary modifications to their PAP rifles that are required by the US Government before the rifles are sold. All of the N-PAP rifles are chambered in good ole 7.62X39 mm caliber. The under-folding stock model M70 AB is also offered by Century.

Polish Radom 47

This is a commercial version of the Polish Military PMKM rifle and imported into the US by I.O. Inc. It is chambered in 7.62x39mm and based on the gun that is the closest copy of the Soviet AKM rifle. It has a stamped-steel receiver and comes with either a laminated wood or synthetic stock set and a slanted compensator. It is the highest-quality imported AK one can get today. Just like Century with its guns, I.O. Inc. converts the Radom 47s into military configuration at their new factory in Palm Bay, FL. At $500 the Radom 47 is a bargain.

Polish "Beryl" Archer

This rifle is a commercial version of the current Polish military Beryl rifle. This highly sought-after rifle is now imported by I.O. Inc. It is made in Radom, Poland and features a hammer-forged barrel and the integrated bold-hold-open thumb safety lever on the left side of the receiver. It is chambered in the 5.56 NATO round and comes with fixed polymer stock that can be swapped for the original Polish telescopic

The most interesting AK variant imported today is the commercial version of the current Polish Armed Forces Beryl rifle, the Archer.

stock that is included in the package. Also included is the removable top rail for installing optical sights. Just like the Radom 47, I.O., Inc. converts these to be fully 922r compliant. Naturally, it is fair to expect a slightly higher price compared to other mass imported rifles.

Bulgarian SAM7 Series

These rifles are built by the famed Arsenal factory in Bulgaria and imported into the US by Arsenal USA. The SAM7 rifle represents a merger between the milled receiver AK-47 and the more modern AK-100 series of the guns. A robust milled receiver guarantees the legendary AK-47 reliability and the factory chrome-lined barrel assures the rifle's high pedigree. The rest of the components directly borrowed from the Russian-designed AK-100 series, with 90-degree gas block and AK-74-style muzzle brake. These rifles are finished at Arsenal USA's factory in Las Vegas and come in several configurations with fixed, side-folding and under-folding stocks. As a rule SAM7 rifles come with polymer furniture in several colours, but the customer can also get a quad-rail hand

guard. All SAM7 rifles come chambered in the original 7.62X39mm caliber.

Bulgarian SLR Series

These rifles are based on the AK-74 family and AK-100 Series rifles and may be the closest variant to the Russian military AK rifles. Built on stamped receivers, these rifles come with chrome-lined barrels. Once again, the finishing is done at the Arsenal USA facility. The SLR rifles also come in a variety of configurations with a choice of different furniture and stock options. They also come in all three calibers. The SLR-107 is chambered in 7.62X39mm, the SLR-104 in 5.45X39mm, and SLR-106 in 5.56X45mm NATO. The finish of the SLR rifles is the typical Russian modern military rifle hard enamel. It gives the gun a smooth and finished look and feel. Unlike the PAPs and WASRs, AK enthusiasts would be expected to pay more for both the SAM7 and SLR rifles. However, considering the quality of these rifles and overall finish of the product ,the higher price is justified in my opinion.

The rarest and probably the nicest AK-74 variant rifle is the East German MPi-AK-74N.

DOMESTICALLY CONVERTED AKS FROM IMPORTED SPORTING AK-BASED RIFLES

Until recently Kalashnikov Concern, through its intermediary, Kalashnikov USA, imported around 200,000 of their sporting/hunting Saiga carbines stateside. The trade sanctions imposed by the US Administration in 2014 as a reaction to Russia's supposed role in the event in Crimea and Eastern Ukraine put an end to any further imports to the US from Kalashnikov Concern.

The other Russian arsenal "Molot" also produced its own line of sporting rifles based on the famed Kalashnikov RPK machine gun. These rifles are called "Vepr" and still are imported into the USA by Sporting Supply International (SSI) and others.

These rifles come into the US in their "sporting" configuration with hunting "Monte Carlo" or thumbhole stocks and sporterized furniture. They lack any of the features that would consider them an "assault rifle" by US firearms laws. Although both the Saiga and Vepr are semi-automatic rifles, they can only accept a special hunting five or 10-round magazine on the account of the missing bullet ramp.

One positive feature that the Saiga and Vepr rifles came in with were military-grade chrome-lined barrels, unlike the same model designated for Europe where the laws require the barrel of a hunting rifle to have a different twist rate to drastically reduce the gun's range.

Several companies in the past would take these rifles and convert them to the military configuration. One of the first companies to do so was Krebs Custom.

Krebs would take a stock Saiga sporting rifles and turn them into close copies of original Russian AK-74s or AK-103s.

In fact, that is what the Krebs model designation was for the Krebs Custom AK-103, with a slightly shorter version called the AK-103K.

The quality of Krebs' AK rifles was impeccable. The finish was as close as you're going to get to the original factory finish. They looked and worked great.

Krebs Custom has since stopped making these AK clone conversions in favor of more drastically modified rifles of their own design. I assume there are some floating out there on the Internet and can be bought at the premium. I certainly will not sell mine any time soon.

Krebs also converted Saiga rifles into slightly shorter versions of the AK-103K

Arsenal USA also converted Russian Saiga rifles into at one time very popular SGL rifles.

Arsenal's SGL31 rifles were close copies of the Russian AK-103 chambered in 7.62X39 mm caliber. All of the SGL rifles came with several furniture and configuration options.

Another company that converts the sporting Saiga rifles into military configuration is Arsenal USA. They will continue to do so until the supply of Saiga rifle dries up. Arsenal makes two main models, the SGL21 chambered in 7.62X39mm and SGL31 in 5,45X39mm. Both models have several versions with side folding stocks. The SGL guns are the closest one can get to the original Russian built AK-74 or AK-74M and AK-103.

All Arsenal SGL rifles come out looking like the original Russian guns. Finish is spot-on. The overall quality is better than just good. They are not quite as refined as the Krebs rifles, but certainly better than most.

One can still order an SGL from Arsenal USA or their distributer K-Var Corp., but the supplies will not last for long, as Kalashnikov Concern was barred from importing its products to the USA in 2014. As such, get them while they last or pay a premium later.

As a collector, I had to have these converted rifles for my collection because they were the closest things to the original AK to come out of Russia. There is definite value in that. But as a shooter I also appreciate the smoothness of operation of these guns and the grace with which they fire every round.

DOMESTIC-BUILT AKS

Rising demand, constant disruption in the supply of imported guns, and the simplicity of the AK design led to several companies launching domestic production of the AK here in the US. It was a baby-step process at first, with some locally-built parts and some still sourced from overseas.

Ultimately, however, the appropriate investments were made in castings, and the end result is the American-built AK.

Now there are many companies that build AKs here in the US. The introduction of a locally made stamped receiver followed by a milled one made it possible.

NoDak Spud is the company that took the lead in making AK receivers, and putting many firearm manufacturers large and small into the AK-making business.

Although many companies claim to be building American AK rifles, oftentimes the gun's receiver and barrel are the only two American-built parts, and the rest are from somewhere else. The availability of parts kits following a significant influx of them a few years back, and general widespread availability of AK parts makes it possible to launch into AK assembling business. Therefore, there are many AKs out there built on Bulgarian, Romanian, Polish, Hungarian ,and even Russian part kits that were available at one time or the other.

Parts kits are still available from several companies on the Web. Although the prices obviously have gone up, they still hover about $400 for a complete kit. Add your own receiver and a barrel for an additional $200, plus gunsmith labor, and you may wind up with a Polish, Romanian, Bulgarian or Hungarian domestically-built AK clone for about $1000. Or you can let the firearm manufacturers to do all the sourcing, making, building, and assembling, and get an all-American-built AK rifle.

Two companies that build their AKs from "scratch" are Century Arms and I.O. Inc. Both companies have been in business a long time, with Century being the oldest. Both companies are also importers of AKs and all things firearm-related to the US, so there is no shortage in parts supply from their partners overseas. However, both

Century Arms' C39 Centurion is all American-made milled receiver AK rifle. It is slightly on the heavy side, but a extremely nice-shooting gun.

companies decided to go a different route and started building their own AKs here in the US.

Several years ago Century came up with their first all-American built AK rifle, the Centurion C39. I had a chance to work with this gun. Unlike most of the domestic AK builders, Century chose to go with a milled receiver instead of the stamped one, for added robustness and supposed reliability. They made the rest of the components in-house, either directly copying the original 7.62X39mm AK-47 design or modifying it to improve it.

The Centurion had several practical features added to it. One was the lightening cuts in the bolt carrier to soften the impact from recoil. A second was the proprietary chevron-style muzzle brake that also seemingly reduced the gun's recoil. A new set of polymer furniture with longer buttstock concluded the configuration of the new gun.

Since the initial success of the Centurion C39 rifle, Century has come up with the C39v2 and several variations. For under $800 Century's Centurion C39 all-American built AK rifle is a bargain.

From its beginning in 1995, I.O. Inc. was always one of the larger suppliers of AKs to the American shooters. I.O. started producing AK rifles at its facility in Charlotte, NC. In the beginning the guns built by the company were hybrid AKs with US receivers and barrels and the rest of the parts coming from Romania.

The overall quality of their rifles was, as one would expect from a low-end AK, hit or miss. The guns worked fine and maybe needed some finishing touches here and there, but the one thing that made them stand out was the lifetime transferable warranty.

I.O. would take the gun back and fix or replace it at no additional cost to the customer. Well, that wasn't good enough for the owners of the company and in 2013 they relocated the plant to a state-of-the-art facility in Palm Bay, FL.

Hiring quality personnel gave the company and the products it made the quality boost they needed. I.O. invested heavily in casting and CNC machines and now produces their AKs completely in house.

The all-American AK rifles that I.O. produces can be split in the two categories: the classic and the tactical. The classic category is represented by the AKM247, AKM247C, AKM247CUF, and the AKM247UF.

The AKM247 is a very close copy of the fixed-stock Soviet AKM rifle based on Polish drawings. The rifle comes dressed in either the American-made black polymer or laminate wood furniture, mimicking the original Soviet furniture by shape and color for the C variant. The AKM247CUF and AKM247UF are the under-folding stock models. All the AKM247 rifles are cham-

I.O., Inc.'s line of all American-made AK rifles are based on original Polish drawings. Not a prom queen, but a solid performer.

bered in the original 7.62X39mm caliber and have the slanted compensator on the threaded muzzle.

The I.O. "tactical" line of AK's is represented by the M214 rifles and their several modifications. The main difference between AKM247 and M214 rifle is that the M214 has a gas block/front sight combination as opposed to two separate components on the original AKs. Other differences include a tactical full-length quad-rail fore-end and a polymer stock patterned after an East German design. All of I.O. Inc.'s AK rifles come with nitrate-treated barrels and the ever-present lifetime transferable warranty. All that for less than $800.

One more I.O. Inc. AK that the AK enthusiasts may run into is the AK-74. This gun is the Bulgarian kit-built rifle that I.O. sells based on availability.

I have tested and worked with all of the American-built AK rifles I've covered in this section. They have worked as they should.

I have liked some features on some rifles more than on others, and I was able to work around the small things that I did not like.

All in all, having these American-built AKs available to the American shooters from the American manufacturers is a comforting thought. In case the supply of imported guns suddenly dries up, we would still have a source for our beloved rifles. But in actuality, it is more than that. We now have a choice how to spend our hard-earned money.

AK-BASED MODERN RIFLES

A separate category for AK guns would be those guns specifically designed and developed by gunsmiths or gun manufacturers to be tactical AK rifles. Often built on Russian sporting Saiga or Vepr rifles, these guns are something beyond just changing a gun's furniture and attaching few accessories. I am talking about a complete redesign of the core gun to produce something that is modular, handy, and corresponds with the demands

Krebs Custom's drive to produce better AKs resulted in creation of the KTR series of rifles. Earlier KTR rifles like this one still looked like an AK.

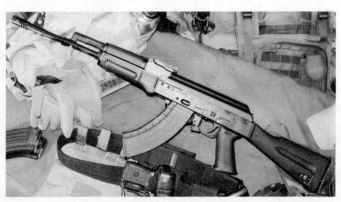

As Krebs continued to improve on the original design of factory AKs and introduce proprietary parts and accessories, the KTR rifle continue to improve.

laid forth by the modern gun operator.

I've mentioned that Russian hunting/ sporting Saiga and Vepr rifles are often used as a core guns for their quality and military grade barrels, but other rifles are also used.

My introduction to the specialty build AK rifles by the American companies came many years ago with Krebs Custom KTR rifle.

Krebs has built a fair amount of these in various modifications, all featuring accessories and improvements of their own design.

All of the Krebs KTR rifles were built on the original Russian Saiga barreled action, which also sported original front sights and gas blocks with no bayonet or accessory lugs. The KTR usually was dressed in stand- ard AK-100 Series black plastic furniture except for its ergonomic SAW-type pistol grip. KTR rifles also could have a variety of muzzle devices. Some rifles were equipped a speed loader device. No matter the modification, all KTR rifles were de-horned with a smooth finish and exceptional paint job. These guns are still around and can be purchased from private individuals only. One should expect to pay extra for one of the Krebs Custom rifles.

Today Krebs Custom continue to build rifles of its own design based on Saiga and Vepr rifles. Two main production models Krebs builds are the AC-15 and its shortened version, the "Assneck".

Though one can easily recognize an AK in this Krebs KTR rifle, it has many Krebs-designed improvements like speed loader, safety, etc.

The next series of KTR rifles saw a departure from the traditionally configured AK. The KTR-09 has seen even more improvements, making it a truly new rifle.

Unlike the KTR-series rifles that had been converted from the Russian Saiga hunters, the KV guns like this KV-13 are based on the heavier duty RPK action.

Both rifles use the folding telescopic MagPul MOE stock and Krebs' own U.F.M. hand guards, with the AC-15 using the full length and "Assneck" using the shorter AK model. Both rifles equipped with a bunch of Krebs' improvements and carry Krebs' renowned quality, with a price to match. Both AC-15 and "Assneck" guns are available now and can be ordered from Krebs Custom directly or through distributers.

AK PISTOLS

One variation that needs a separate category due to the immense popularity of this type of AK is the AK pistol.

Ever since the short AKS-74U was introduced for service with the Soviet Armed Forces in 1974 as a part of AK-74 family of rifles, it instantly became popular on account of it being short, nifty, and "cool" looking.

Here in the US the short AK was an enigma until the first parts kits started to arrive stateside in the 90's. Everybody had to have one. The only problem was, and still is, that the short eight-inch-barreled AKSU rifle was subject to the National Firearm Act as an SBR (Short Barrel Rifle) and had certain amount of regulatory hassle attached to it.

The solution came in the way of a permanent barrel extension that is disguised as a sound suppressor, a longer barrel protruding past the front sight/gas block combo, or to have it as a pistol.

The first two options undermine the whole idea behind having a short AK. The pistol route appears more plausible for those who desire the compactness of the original AKSU shorty.

The AK pistol, like any rifle-based pistol, cannot have a stock nor in any way facilitate a stock installation, as it would immediately become an NFA-regulated SBR.

I should clarify that the AK pistol can

One of the most exciting and widely popular AKs is the AK pistol. These come in many forms and sizes, but are united by one thing – a short barrel.

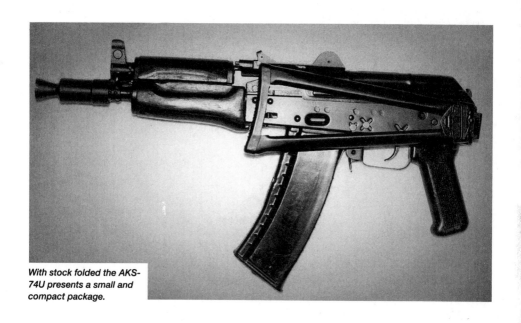

With stock folded the AKS-74U presents a small and compact package.

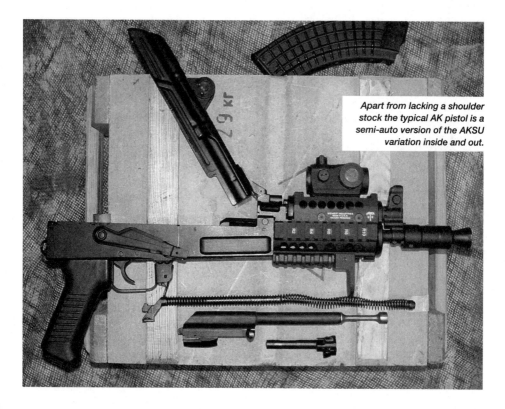

Apart from lacking a shoulder stock the typical AK pistol is a semi-auto version of the AKSU variation inside and out.

Century has been importing Romanian Draco pistols for years. Unlike most of the AK pistols on the market, Draco is not an AKSU-patterned gun, but rather a reduced version of the AKM-type rifle.

Even smaller, the Romanian Mini Draco takes the AK pistol idea a step further.

have a folding stock, but it has to be permanently pinned and welded in the folded position. Most of the AK pistols simply do not have it.

There are several manufacturers that make and/or import these awesome guns. Century Arms has offered imported AK pistols for years and recently added one of their own to the mix.

AK Draco Pistol

Romanian AK Draco Pistol in 7.62x39 caliber. It is only 21" long and comes with hardwood hand guards and polymer pistol grip. The 12¼" barrel has a combination gas block and front sight pressed on it and it's tipped with a muzzle nut. It comes in a matte black Parkerized finish. These AK pistols are made for Century Arms by the Romarm/Cugir plant in Romania.

Mini Draco AK Pistol

The Romanian AK Mini Draco pistol is also chambered in 7.62x39. The Mini Draco features a 7.5-inch chrome-lined barrel, AR-style birdcage flash hinder, synthetic pistol grip and hardwood hand guards. Its overall length is only 18⅜" making it one of the smallest AKs one can encounter. The Mini Draco is made for Century Arms by Romarm/Cugir.

Zastava PAP M85NP AK Pistol

The Serbian M85NP AK PAP pistol takes its roots from the Yugoslavian M70 short rifle patterned after the Soviet AKS-74U gun. This pistol is chambered for the 5.56x45 cartridge and has an adapted mag well to accept AR-15 magazines. It has a 10¼" barrel and is 21½" overall. It comes with the AKSU style hinged top cover with flip-up rear sight, standard front sight with auxiliary flip up white dot night front sight, black polymer Yugoslavian pistol grip, wood hand guards and removable AKSU pattern muzzle brake.

The PAP M85NP AK pistols are made for Century Arms in Serbia by Zastava.

Zastava PAP M92PV AK Pistol

The Serbian M92PV AK PAP pistol, like the M85NP gun, takes its roots from the Soviet AKSU, except this AK pistol is chambered in 7.62X39mm and accepts standard AK magazines. It has a 10¼" barrel and 19¾" overall length. Comes with the AKSU-style hinged top cover with flip-up rear sight, standard front sight with auxiliary flip up white dot night front sight, black polymer Yugoslavian pistol grip, wood hand guards. The threaded muzzle is covered by the muzzle nut. The PAP M92PV AK pistols are also made for Century Arms in Serbia by Zastava.

All of Century's imported AK pistols are sold around $480 and widely available from numerous distributors.

Centurion C39 AK Style Pistol

Century Arms' all American-made Centurion C39 Sporter pistol is based on their successful in-house built Centurion C39 rifle, and like the rifle is chambered in 7.62X39mm. The Centurion pistol is 100 percent American made and the pistol features a milled receiver, adjustable post front sight integral to the gas block, birdcage flash hider, black synthetic ergonomic pistol grip, black synthetic upper and lower hand guards with Picatinny-style rails. It retails for around $1000. Considering the reliable and proven design and its American workmanship, a small price increase is rightfully justified.

Arsenal USA also offers a couple of AK pistols based on their line of Bulgarian AKS-74U variants. Compared to the Romanian and Serbian AK pistols, the Arsenal guns are more refined and may appeal more to the AK collector who is willing to spend a little more for the more authentic look. $480.

Another Century Arms import AK pistol is the Serbian Zastava N-PAP M85NP.

Another Century Arms entry into the AK pistol market is their RAS47 Pistol. Based on Century's best seller, this pistol has modern upgrades in the way of MagPul furniture.

SAM7K-01 AK Pistol

Arsenal's SAM7K-01 AK pistol is based on one of the best-selling rifles that Arsenal USA imports from Bulgaria. The SAM7K-01 pistol is built on a milled receiver and chambered in 7.62X39mm caliber. It has a 10½" chrome-lined hammer-forged barrel, scope mounting side rail. The AKSU pattern hinged top cover is equipped with an aperture sight. The SAM7 pistol has an ambidextrous safety lever that can be operated by a thumb. Total weight of this pistol is 6¼" Lbs. It is assembled and finished in Las Vegas at the Arsenal USA facility and contains US-made and imported parts. It is available from several distributers at an MSRP of $1300.

SLR106-58 AK Pistol

Arsenal's SLR106-58 AK pistol is based on another bestselling rifle, the Bulgarian-built SLR. The SLR106-58 pistol is built on a stamped receiver and chambered in the soft-shooting 5.56X45mm (.223 Rem.) caliber. It comes with an 8½" chrome-lined hammer-forged barrel that is tipped with a new-style muzzle brake. It also comes with a scope-mounting side rail. Its AKSU-pattern hinged top cover is equipped with an aperture sight. The SLR106-58 AK pistol only weights 5½" lbs. and is assembled and finished in Las Vegas at the Arsenal USA facility and contains US-made and imported parts. The SLR106-58 AK pistol is available from several distributers at an MSRP of $1250.

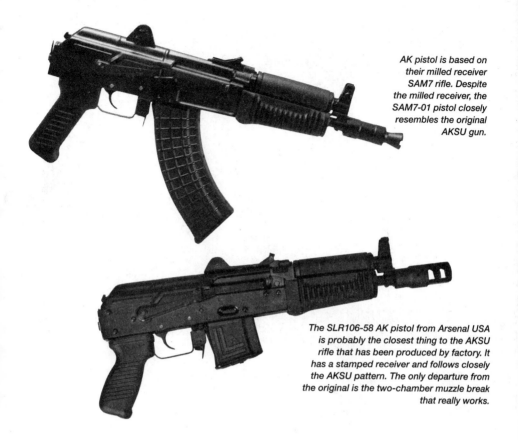

AK pistol is based on their milled receiver SAM7 rifle. Despite the milled receiver, the SAM7-01 pistol closely resembles the original AKSU gun.

The SLR106-58 AK pistol from Arsenal USA is probably the closest thing to the AKSU rifle that has been produced by factory. It has a stamped receiver and follows closely the AKSU pattern. The only departure from the original is the two-chamber muzzle break that really works.

I.O. Inc. has manufactured and imported AK rifles for years. It was only natural for them to jump into the AK pistol niche with offerings of their own.

M214 NANO

The I.O. M214 NANO is based on their all American-made M214 Series AK rifles. It is chambered in the popular 7.62X39mm AK caliber. The NANO pistol comes with quad-rail hand guards, a bolt hold-open safety lever, and accepts all standard AK high-capacity magazines. The M214 NANO pistol has a seven-inch barrel that is tipped with a compensator. It is one of the smallest functioning AK pistols on the market today and can be purchased for just over $600.

HELLPUP

Alongside their American built NANO AK pistol, I.O. also imports the HELLPUP Pistol from Poland. The HELLPUP is an intermediate-length AK pistol patterned closely after the Russian AK-105 intermediate-length rifle. This semi-automatic, long-stroke piston-operated pistol is chambered in the traditional 7.62X39mm caliber. The barrel is 9¼" long, and the pistol weighs in at only 5 lbs. The HELLPUP accepts all standard AK high-capacity magazines, has adjustable front and rear sights, and an AKSU-style muzzle device. Despite the HELLPUP's long-stroke piston it is still only 21" long. A compact package for less than $600 is not too bad.

Based on their M214 AK rifle, I.O., Inc. offers a M214 NANO pistol. One of the smallest AK pistols on the market, it comes with several cool features like quad rail short hand guards and Picatinny rail at the back of the receiver for attaching a sling of your choice.

The Polish-built Hellpup is an AK pistol based on the AKM with an intermediate-length barrel similar to that of Russian AK-104.

Due to the weight and lack of shoulder stock, aiming an AK pistol may be a challenge.

There are many other AK pistols that are made by smaller manufacturers or gunsmiths. I wanted to cover the models that are readily available to anyone who would like to take their AK hobby up a notch and have a load of undersized and compact fun.

On a practical note, aiming the AK pistol using open or collimator sights can be challenging, considering the pistol's weight. The law prohibits the use of a front vertical grip on this type of weapon. The wedge-like handgrip is also obsolete due to a lack of a buttstock. Use of a sling is recommended.

In either two or one-point attachment, the sling has to be slung around the head and left arm for right-handed shooters and the right arm for lefties. It should be adjusted in such a way that when the pistol is leveled and the sling is taut the butt of the gun's receiver is about 12" away from the shooter's shoulder. The pistol then needs to be pushed away from the body with tension on the sling, thus stabilizing the gun enough for consistent aiming.

Using a sling can greatly improve the accuracy of the AK pistol. By pushing the gun away from the body, shooter can use a taut sling as a cheek rest for consistent aim.

With practice one can achieve decent results. One thing to remember: the AK pistol is not a 100-yard weapon. However, what it loses in accuracy it compensates for with volume.

The other implement that would greatly improve accuracy of the AK pistol is the Red Dot sight.

The recent introduction of a stabilizing arm brace caused a rise in AK pistol popularity. It is easy to install on just about any AK pistol. Though the arm brace looks like a shoulder stock, it is not.

One of the coolest AK pistol accessories that came out recently is the stabilizing arm brace. It installs with a bracket that is held in place by the AK's pistol grip. It is designed to attach to the shooters forearm to enable one-hand shooting of the heavy AK pistol by countering its weight. The brace looks like a shoulder stock, but make no mistake about it, the arm brace is just that - a brace.

When this accessory was introduced, the BATFE issued a letter stating that the arm brace is not a shoulder stock and having it installed on the pistol does not turn that pistol into an NFA weapon (SBR).

However, the BATFE latter followed with an additional letter on the subject stating that although having the arm brace installed on the pistol is not illegal, having to shoulder it is. So make sure you are fully familiar with all federal, state or local laws before installing and/or using this and any accessory on your cool AK pistol.

OFF-THE-SHELF AKS

The times when you had to piece together a complete AK parts kit from parts found here and there and then have a gunsmith put it together are long gone. Today there are many choices of AK rifle available in the US. One can find whatever he or she wants when it comes to the type of rifle and size of budget.

There are still numerous reputable gunsmiths and custom shops that would gladly build a parts kit into a rifle. In this case, there is really no limit to how authentic the customer wants the rifle to be. Correct arsenal markings, Cyrillic engravings, proper furniture, all can be had for a price, and usually accompanied by a lengthy lead-time. This will, of course, pertain mostly to collector guns. I myself own several.

But what options are available for those who want to pick up a phone and purchase an AK with a reasonable delivery time, or just walk into a gun store and buy it outright?

In fact, there are many companies that import, convert or build and sell AKs. Several do a combination of all. Here are some (not all) of the AK rifles that are available, off-the-shelf, to everyone in the US.

IO, Inc.

Inter Ordnance, Inc (I.O., Inc.) has been involved in the US AK scene for years and is familiar to most US AK enthusiasts. I myself have owned several I.O. rifles and know of their performance firsthand.

I.O. has been around AKs for a while, as an importer at first, importing guns from Romania, Balkans and other countries to establish itself as a world-class importer. However, the inherent quality problems associated with East European manufacturers hindered the company's push for excellence. As a blessing in disguise I.O. was "forced" into becoming an AK rifle manufacturer. After acquiring the necessary machines and tooling and adapting technical documentation from actual translated Polish blueprints, I.O. never looked back. Today the company manufactures all American-built AKs in its new state-of-the-art facility in Palm Bay, Florida.

AKM247/AKM247C

Semi-automatic US-made AKM rifle per military specifications in black polymer. AKM247C comes dressed in laminate wood and equipped with side mounting rail. Rifle comes with one I.O., Inc. 30-round magazine and cleaning rod. Caliber: 7.62x39mm. Weight: 8lbs. Length: 35". Barrel Length: 16". Finish: Mil-spec Parkerized.

AKM247UF/AKM247CUF

Semi-automatic US-made AKMS rifle per military specifications with under-folding stock. AKM247C comes with laminate wood hand guards. Rifle comes with one I.O., Inc. 30-round magazine and cleaning

Unlike the AKM247 that is dressed in black polymer furniture, the AKM247C sports reddish laminate wood that is very close to the original.

The AKM247UF is the under-folding stock version of the AKM247. Note that the stock has been patterned after an older version AKS-47 variant.

rod. Caliber: 7.62x39mm. Weight: 8lbs. Length: 35". Folded Length: 24". Barrel Length: 16". Finish: Mil- spec Parkerized.

AKM247T

Semi-automatic US-made upgraded AK-type rifle, with tactical quad rail, phantom flash hider, and CNC-machined scope side-mounting rail. Comes equipped with black polymer East German style "clubfoot" stock and pistol grip. Rifle comes with one I.O., Inc. 30-round magazine and cleaning rod. Caliber: 7.62x39mm. Weight: 8lbs. Length: 35". Barrel Length: 16". Finish: Mil-spec Parkerized.

M214 and M214SF

Semi-automatic US-made upgraded AK-type rifle, with tactical full-length quad rail, phantom flash hider and CNC-machined scope side-mounting rail. Comes equipped with black polymer East German style "clubfoot" stock and pistol grip. M214SF comes with wire side folding stock. Rifle

The M214 NANO is one of the smallest production AK pistols on the market today.

comes with one I.O., Inc. 30-round magazine and cleaning rod. Caliber: 7.62x39mm. Weight: 9lbs. Length: 35". Barrel Length: 16". Finish: Mil-spec Parkerized.

M214 NANO

Semi-automatic US-made AK pistol. One of the smallest AK pistols made. Comes with tactical quad rail. Pistol comes with one I.O., Inc. 30-round magazine and cleaning rod. Caliber: 7.62x39mm. Weight: 5.5lbs. Length: 17". Barrel Length: 7". Finish: Mil-spec Parkerized.

The AKM247T is a slight departure from the traditionally configured AKM247. Although unmistakably AK, the AKM247T has few "tactical" features.

The M214 is a further development of the AKM247T rifle in an effort to modernize standard AK design.

Radom 47, Radom 47FS and RADOM W

Semi-automatic AKM rifle made in Poland to military specifications. RADOM 47FS comes with wire side-folding stock and Radom W comes dressed in laminate wood. Rifle comes with one I.O., Inc. 30-round magazine and cleaning rod. Caliber: 7.62x39mm. Weight: 8lbs. Length: 35". Folded Length: 24" (RADOM 47FS). Barrel Length: 16". Finish: Mil-spec Parkerized.

ARCHER (Beryl)

The legendary Polish Beryl assault rifle is now available in the United States in a civilian version, the Archer. This remarkable rifle is made in Radom, Poland by Fabryka Broni. The Archer features a hammer-forged, chrome-lined barrel. Collapsible stock, mil-spec receiver, tactical pistol grip, black polymer furniture, adjustable front and rear sights, and tactical sling swivels. This rifle comes with the matching Picatinny rail for an additional $100.00. All the 922r compli-

ance work had been done by I.O., Inc. at their facility. Includes a one-year warranty. Comes with one 30-round Pro Mag magazine. Caliber: 5.56X45 mm NATO (.223 Remington). Overall length: 36 inches. Weight: 7lbs. Barrel length: 16.25 in.Twist: 1:9 rh. Finish: standard Polish military finish.

The AK rifles made or imported by I.O., Inc. are available at most sporting goods stores or gun shops. They can also be ordered through I.O., Inc. on-line distributor, royaltigerimports.com. Most of the I.O., Inc. AKs with the exception of the imported from Poland "Beryl" Archer rifle that retails at $1380, sell for $570-$750 and are readily available.

Century

Century Arms, Inc. Company needs no introduction. It is safe to say that after 50 years importing and building various firearms for the US market, Century Arms, Inc. (formerly Century International Arms, Inc.) is one of North America's largest surplus and new gun suppliers today. When

Radom 47 can be ordered with laminate wood furniture as 47W model, and with side folding stock as a 47FS.

In order to comply with 922r regulations the Archer comes with the US-made "club foot" stock, but the original Beryl telescopic stock is part of the package.

The Romanian import GP WASR-10 may be the most popular economically priced AKM style rifle in recent years.

we are talking about AKs, Century offers a wide range of Kalashnikov rifle variants ranging from Yugoslavian M76 and Romanian PSL Snipers to Israeli Galani and their best-selling Romanian GP WASR-10s and Serbian N-PAP rifles. Century Arms also builds many rifles using surplus and newly-manufactured, US-made parts.

GP WASR-10

The Romanian WASR-10 rifles are semi-automatic versions of the Pistol Mitralieră model $^{1963}/_{1965}$ configured with a fixed wooden stock and hand guards. These rifles feature a hard chrome-lined hammer-forged barrel, side mount scope rail and accepts double-stack magazines. The WASR Rifle is a

perfect choice for hunters and recreational shooters. Comes with two 30-round, double-stack mags, side-mounted scope rail, classic slant brake, bayonet lug and a one-year manufacturer's warranty. Caliber: 7.62x39mm. Barrel: 16.25" with a 1:10 twist. Overall: 34.25". Weight: 7.5 lbs.

N-PAP

Semi-automatic rifle with military-style wood furniture. Made in the same factory that produced top-quality rifles for the former Yugoslavia like the M70B1 and M70AB2, the PAP rifles are the civilian version of the M70 series. These beauties are the latest imports from the world-famous Zastava factory. Century offers four styles

The Yugoslavian M70-based Serbian N-PAP rifle is one of the well regarded AK variants available today.

The N-PAP DF features the under-folding stock.

of the PAP rifles. Features a side rail and a hammer-forged barrel. Comes with two 30-round mags. Caliber 7.62x39mm. Barrel: 16.25" with a 1:10 twist. Overall: 37.25". Weight: 7.95 lbs.

AK74 M74 Sporter

The AK74 (M74) Semi-automatic Sporter rifle is chambered in 5.45x39mm cartridge and is dressed in original wood furniture. Comes configured with a side-mount rail, bayonet lug and two 30-round mags. Caliber: 5.45x39mm. Barrel: 16.25" with a 1:8 twist. Overall: 37". Weight: 7.6 lbs.

RAS (Red Army Standard) 47 Semi-automatic Rifle

Built entirely in the US on a stamped receiver. Chrome-moly 4150 nitride treated. Barrel 1:10 twist, 14x1 LH. $^{1}/_{16}$" stamped steel nitride treated receiver with RAK-1 Enhanced Trigger Group. Larger T-shaped magazine catch. Compatibility with AKM furniture. Side rail for optical sight. Retaining plate. Standard AKM sights. Bolt hold open safety. Slant brake. Bolt carrier heat-treated

to ensure maximum performance and life. Maple wood furniture. Comes with one 30-round Magpul mag. Caliber: 7.62x39mm. Capacity: 30 rds. Barrel: 16.5". Overall: 37.25". Weight: 7.55 lbs. The RAS47 rifle can be ordered with a set of MagPul furniture including the ZHUKOV stock and hand guards.

C39V2 (Centurion C39 Version 2)

Semi-automatic rifle build entirely in the US on robust milled receiver. American-made. Chrome moly 4140 nitride treated. Barrel 1:10 twist, concentric LH 14x1 metric thread and ready for a variety of muzzle attachments. Milled 4140 ordnance-quality steel receiver with RAK-1 Enhanced Trigger Group. Larger T-shaped magazine catch. Compatibility with AKM furniture. Standard AKM sights. Side rail for optical sight. Retaining plate. Bolt hold open safety. Proprietary Chevron muzzle brake. Bolt carrier heat-treated to ensure maximum performance and life. Walnut wood furniture. Comes with one 30-round Magpul mag. Caliber: 7.62x39mm. Capac-

The AK74 M74 Sporter is basically a copy of the legendary Soviet AK-74 rifle.

Unlike its all-American C39 Centurion rifle, Century's RAS47 is built in the US using a stamped receiver.

Building on the initial success of the C39 Centurion all American-built AK, Century Arms released its updated version, the C39V2.

Probably the coolest gun in Century's AK rifle lineup is the RAS47 SBR.

Milled receiver Bulgarian SAM7 is imported by Arsenal USA and represents a merger of old reliable milled receiver AK with modern AK rifle features.

ity: 30 rds. Barrel: 16.5". Overall: 37.25". Weight: 8.05 lbs.

The C39V2 rifle can be ordered with a set of MagPul furniture including the ZHUKOV stock and hand guards.

Century also offers both RAS47 and C39V2 rifles as cool SBR's dressed in MagPul furniture with ZHUKOV folding stocks or as the no-less-cool and widely-available pistol.

Most of the Century US-built or Imported AKs sell with an MSRP ranging from $670 to $1150 for the top-of-the-line model. Although availability of the imported rifles may vary based on foreign manufacturers' capabilities and capacity, one can always purchase the all American-built Century AK rifles from any sporting goods store or local gun shop or numerous distributers.

Arsenal USA

Arsenal, Inc., is a premier American importer and manufacturer of semi-auto rifles located in Las Vegas NV. Ever since Arsenal was established the company has concentrated on bringing AKs and other former Communist Bloc rifles, parts and accessories to the US firearms collectors and enthusiasts alike. Arsenal cut its teeth on Bulgarian rifles and parts, but now offers a wide variety of products ranging from the US-built AK parts to collector-grade rifles. However, what I wanted to cover are the current AK rifles that can be purchased today.

SAM7

SAM7 Series (7.62x39mm) rifles are top-notch Bulgarian-made milled receiver, semi-automatic modern sporting rifles remanufactured by Arsenal, Inc in Las Vegas, Nevada. All SAM7 rifles feature original Bulgarian-made milled and forged receivers,

The SAM7 rifle can be ordered in several configurations, including this side folder.

The SAM7 rifle can also be ordered with underfolding stock and in variety of polymer furniture of popular-for-AK colors.

The Bulgarian SLR series rifles are very close copies of the Russian AK 100 series rifles.

The SLR rifles can be ordered with original Russian designed AK-100 series side folding stock.

The SLR rifle comes in all three major calibers.

original Bulgarian chrome-lined hammer-forged barrels, US-made mil-spec polymer stock set with stainless steel heat shield, and 800-meter rear sight leaf. The SAM7R models come with a gas block with a bayonet lug, 14x1mm left-hand muzzle threads, muzzle brake, and black polymer furniture.

The SAM7UF comes with standard AKS under-folding stock. The SAM7SF model comes with right-hand folding tubular stock, 24x1.5mm right-hand threads, muzzle brake, bayonet and accessory lugs, ambidextrous safety, and in black, desert sand, OD green, or plum color furniture.

SAM7 Series features include: 100% new-production parts and components. Bulgarian hot-die hammer forged receiver, bolt, bolt carrier, and double-hook trigger. Cold hammer-forged 16.3" barrel from Arsenal's Bulgarian factory, built on Steyr manufacturing technology. Hard-chrome plated bore and chamber. Removable four-port muzzle brake with 14x1mm left-hand threads. AK scope rail. Intermediate length US-made 10" trapdoor buttstock. (Total length of pull 13.4".) Completely 922(r) compliant with US or imported magazines. Substantially extended service life over other types of assemblies.

Caliber: 7.62 x 39mm. Total Length: 927mm (36.5"). Barrel Length: 415 mm. Weight without Magazine: 3.67kg (8 lbs.). Muzzle Velocity: 710 m/s. Rate of Fire (practical): 40 rds/min. Twist Rate: 1 in 240 mm. Effective Range: 400m. Max Effective Range: 1350m.

SAM7SF series features include: One hundred percent new-production parts and components, including Bulgarian hot-die hammer-forged receiver, bolt, bolt carrier, and double-hook trigger, and a cold hammer-forged 16.3" barrel from Arsenal's Bulgarian factory, built on Steyr manufacturing technology. Hard-chrome plated bore and chamber. Removable muzzle brake with 24x1.5mm right hand threads. AK scope rail. 922(r) compliant with US or imported magazines. Substantially extended service life over other types of assemblies. Caliber: 7.62 x 39mm. Total Length: 970mm (38.2"). Folded length: 720mm (28.4"). Barrel Length: 415 mm (16.3"). Weight without Magazine: 3.85kg (8.5 lbs.). Muzzle Velocity: 710 m/s. Rate of Fire (practical): 40 rds/min. Twist Rate: 1 in 240 mm (9.45"). Effective Range: 400m. Max Effective Range: 1350m.

SLR-107, SLR-104 and SLR-106

SLR Series rifles are Bulgarian-made, stamped receiver, semi-automatic modern sporting rifles remanufactured by Arsenal. All SLR-rifles feature original Bulgarian-made 1mm stamped receiver, original Bulgarian chrome lined hammer forged barrel, US made anti-slap double stage trigger group, US made mil-spec polymer stock set with stainless steel heat shield, left-side folding solid polymer or metal buttstock, 1000-meter rear sight leaf, and trapdoor for cleaning kit.

The SLR FR models come with front sight block with bayonet lug and 24x1.5mm right-hand threads, gas block with bayonet lug, and removable muzzle brake. SLR UR models come with a AKS-74U front sight block / gas block combination and short gas system. The SLR FR and UR come with side mounted scope rails. All models are available in black, desert sand, or plum polymer stocks.

In a nutshell, the SLR Series Rifles are Bulgarian versions of the Russian AK-100 Series rifles. All of the SLR rifles can be

SLR-107	SLR-104	SLR-106
Caliber: 7.62 x 39 mm	**Caliber:** 5.45 x 39.5 mm	**Caliber:** 5.56 x 45 mm (.223 Rem.)
Total Length: 36 ⅞"	**Total Length:** 36 ⅞"	**Total Length:** 36 ⅞"
Folded Length (with muzzle brake): 27 ⅜"	**Folded Length (with Compensator):** 27 ⅜"	**Folded Length (with Compensator):** 27 ⅜"
Barrel Length: 16 ¼"	**Barrel Length:** 16 ¼"	**Barrel Length:** 16 ¼"
Rifling: 4 grooves	**Rifling:** 4 grooves	**Rifling:** 6 grooves
Twist Rate: 1 in 9.44"	**Twist Rate:** 1 in 7.87"	**Twist Rate:** 1 in 7 in"
Weight without Magazine: 7.3 lbs.	**Weight without Magazine:** 7.3 lbs.	**Weight without Magazine:** 7.3 lbs.
Muzzle Velocity: 2,329 fps	**Muzzle Velocity:** 2,953 fps	**Muzzle Velocity:** 2,985 fps
Effective Range: 550 yds	**Effective Range:** 684 yds	**Effective Range:** 550 yds
Maximum Range: 1,480 yds	**Maximum Range:** 1,480 yds	**Maximum Range:** 1,480 yds
Rear Sight: 800 m	**Rear Sight:** 1000 m	**Rear Sight:** 800 m

The SLR rifles are also offered in short AKSU configuration as SBRs.

One can also order the SLR in AKSU (Krinkov) configuration with long barrel to avoid any hassle associated with an SBR purchase and ownership.

ordered as an SBR in a very cool AKSU configuration. The SLR-107 can also be configured in an intermediate length like the Russian AK-105 (still an SBR).

Arsenal also offers a full line of SAM7 or SGL-based AK pistols. The finish on the Arsenal rifles is near perfect. With the Russian Saiga-based SGL rifles no longer available in any considerable mass quantities, the SLR rifles are perhaps the closest thing, apart from the custom built clone copies, to the original Russian-made AKs.

The Arsenal rifle prices are on the high side of the spectrum for a production model AK, hovering between $1017 and $1454 depending on options and configuration, and their cool SBR AKS-74U clone SLR models at $1699-$2169.

Krebs Custom, Inc.

When it comes to absolute AK quality, few will argue that Krebs Custom, Inc. (KCI) Company's rifles do not meet that description. Having owned and worked with Krebs' numerous rifles, I am here to substantiate the high praise for their quality. Krebs Custom, Inc. of Wauconda, IL has been producing quality AKs for over 10 years now.

The company was started by Master Gunsmith Marc Krebs, who first established himself as a top 1911 match handgun smith before moving on to Kalashnikov rifles. KCI started producing kit-built and converted AK's in the mid '90's with an idea to move toward production rifles and custom AK parts manufacturing.

Today Krebs Custom, Inc. offers a range

The Krebs Custom's AC-15 represents years of research and development and countless hours of trial and error before it became the coolest production AK-based rifle today.

of production rifles based on the Russian-built sporting Saiga rifles. Whereas Arsenal USA, along with most of the US manufacturers, converts their imported rifles to the original military-spec AK configuration, Krebs takes a different route and deconstructs the Saigas, stripping them down to barreled actions and then builds unique Krebs AK rifles using proprietary parts and know-how.

AC-15

The Krebs AC-15 long UFM variant is for customers who demand the ultimate in evolution from the AKM pattern rifle. The Krebs brand is synonymous with durability, quality, and battle-proven features. This version includes the Krebs Keymod U.F.M. hand guard for those who wish to extend their grip.

Chambered in 7.62 x39. Includes Krebs 4-prong flash suppressor with a ¾ removable birdcage compensator, which minimizes muzzle climb and flash. Muzzle device is permanently attached. Cold hammer-forged chrome-lined barrel shortened to 14.25", precision crowned and threaded. Krebs custom U.F.M. Rail fore-end. Rear sight support scope rail made from 4140 steel hardened to 40 Rockwell, which allows for co-witness using an electronic "dot" scope.

Trigger parts are machined and polished to Krebs Custom Specs. Action is tuned & bolt face polished for enhanced reliability and smoothness. Custom MK6 Enhanced safety allows shooter to manipulate safety without removing their hand from the pistol grip, and provides a MANUAL bolt-hold-open. Krebs Custom Trigger Pin Retaining Plate insures greater pin stability.

Trigger guard is polished and radiused to reduce stamped metal markings & insure shooter comfort. Magpul MOE pistol grip installed for improved ergonomic hold. Receiver cover is reinforced with a plate and wedge-lock recoil system to insure no movement of the receiver cover and return to "zero" when re-installed. Rear sight installed on receiver cover provides an increased sight radius and allows for a dual aperture sight picture. Iron sights and scope rails are laser bore-sighted

ACE side-folding mechanism. Magpul CTR buttstock provides adjustable length-of-pull. Rifle industrially tumbled and "dehorned" for fast painless operation. Rifle refinished with flat-black, baked-on, synthetic alkyd KrebsCoat finish.

Barrel Length: 14.25" with a permanently attached flash suppressor. Overall Length: (fully extended): 36.5". Weight: 7lbs.

Just like the AC-15 rifle, the "ASSNECK" SBR encompasses all the awesomeness that Krebs Custom could dish out.

ASSNECK

The Krebs ASSNECK SBR (short barreled rifle) is for customers who want the reliability of a Krebs rifle and the added maneuverability of a shorter gun. The ASSNEK also includes the Speed Load system. This system includes a mag well flange which helps guide the operator's magazine into the magwell. Additionally, it includes a magazine ejection spring and extended magazine release. This provides the user with the ability for a one-handed magazine ejection, while simultaneously speeding up the insertion of a full magazine. The Speed Load system is for users who require the ultimate in smooth and quick operation of their rifle.

Built on a Russian Saiga base rifle in 7.62x39. NFA Paperwork Required. Includes Krebs 4-prong flash suppressor with a ¾' removable birdcage compensator, which minimizes muzzle climb and flash. Muzzle device is torqued and pinned to Krebs specifications. cold hammer-forged chrome-lined barrel shortened to just under 9", precision crowned and threaded. Krebs custom UFM Rail fore-end.

Rear sight support scope rail made from 4140 steel hardened to 40 Rockwell, which allows for co-witness when using an electronic "dot" scope. Trigger parts are machined and polished to Krebs Custom

Specs. Action is tuned & bolt face polished for enhanced reliability and smoothness. Magazine ejection spring aids in clearing magazine from rifle

Custom MK6 Enhanced safety allows shooter to manipulate safety without removing their hand from the pistol grip, and provides a MANUAL bolt-hold-open. Krebs Custom Trigger Pin Retaining Plate insures greater pin stability. Trigger guard is polished and radiused to reduce stamped metal markings & insure shooter comfort. Magpul MOE pistol grip installed for improved ergonomic hold.

Both Krebs Custom production rifles are of impeccable quality. Once in your hands you would not want to put it down. All rifles that come out of Krebs' shop are industrially tumbled and "dehorned" and all of the internal parts are polished with the customer in mind. Should this attention to detail cost more? I think it should and it does. Buyers are expected to spend $2150 for an AC-15 rifle and $2630 for an "ASSNECK" SBR.

It is worth noting that most of the US manufacturers will accommodate their customers from more restricted states with the models that are made with those restrictions in mind. It is always a good practice to check the federal, state and local laws and regulations before purchasing a gun.

CHAPTER FIFTEEN

OTHER AKS

RPK

With the immense success of the Kalashnikov weapon operating system and configuration the Soviets wanted to capitalize on it and developed a family of AK-based weapons. The first representative of such guns was the Kalashnikov Light Machine Gun, the RPK.

The RPK is chambered for the 7.62x39mm cartridge. It is a light machine gun developed by Mikhail Kalashnikov in the late 1950's to accompany the newly-introduced stamped receiver AKM rifle. The RPK was a part of the new Soviet concept of adapting a family of battlefield weapons on common platform. The new machine gun used the same magazines that the main battle rifle AKM used, unlike the belt-fed RPD Dektyaryov machine gun it has replaced. The RPK operates identically to the AK-47 and uses the same 7.62X39mm ammunition. It has a similar design layout to the AKM and AK-47 series of rifles, with modifications to increase the RPK's effective range and accuracy and to enhance its sustained fire capability. To do so, designers equipped the RPK with a strengthened receiver and front trunnion, longer and heavier barrel, front mounted bipod, the "clubfoot" stock, and either a 40-round capacity magazine or 75-round drum.

The RPK's rear sight is elevation adjustable, and graduated for ranges of 100 to 1,000 meters, in 100-meter increments.

Apart from the conventional AK main battle rifle, there are other Kalashnikovs – the RPK light machineguns.

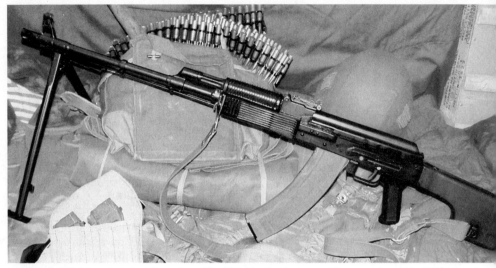

In 1974 the RPK-74 was introduced as a part of the AK-74 family of weapons. Once you shoot it the RPK-74 immediately becomes your favorite gun to shoot. In full auto the feeling is multiplied exponentially.

The rear sight leaf also features a windage adjustment knob, unique to the RPK series of rifles. The 5.45mm RPK-74 with fixed stock and RPKS-74 with side-folding stock paratrooper model light machine guns were adopted with the AK-74 family of assault rifles in1974.

The design differences from the AK-74 are similar to the differences of the RPK from the AKM, mainly the heavier-duty receiver, longer and heavier barrel, attached bipod and larger capacity magazine that is interchangeable with other guns of this family. The new components included a cage type short funnel flash hider and 45-round magazine.

The RPK-74 and its versions are still operational in Russia, the former Soviet republics and in a number of other countries. The RPKs or some versions thereof were also manufactured in Bulgaria, Poland, Yugoslavia, China, and Romania.

The most common RPK rifles in the US are the imported Chinese NHM-91, Romanian AES-10B, Yugoslavian M72, and gunsmith-built models derived from sporting Russian Vepr rifles. Recently a small number of Vepr-1Vs, which is essentially a factory-built RPK-74 in 5.56x45mm NATO caliber, were imported and converted per 922r regulation by the I.O. Inc.

Romanian AES-10B

The Romanian RPK AES-10B rifles are chambered in 7.62X39mm caliber. The rifle has a 23" long, heavy barrel with chrome-lined bore, removable muzzle brake, standard AK sights, bipod, and carry handle. Most of the recently sold AES-10B rifles were imported and converted per 922r regulations by Century Arms using both new US-made parts and original used surplus parts.

Yugoslavian Zastava M72

The original military Zastava M72 is a light machine gun developed and manufactured by then-Yugoslav Zastava Arms company. Its semi-automatic version has made its way to the States and had been sold here. The M72 rifle is a very close copy of the Soviet RPK chambered in 7.62X39mm caliber. The M72 rifles can be easily identified by the regular AK stock and lateral cooling ribs

The AES-10B is the Romanian version of the Soviet RPK. It is pretty much an exact copy of the original gun with exception of a carrying handle.

Just like the Soviet RPK and Romanian AES-10B, the M72 is the Yugoslavian (Serbian) squad automatic. It shares the heavier receiver with other Yugo AK rifles.

on the barrel toward the receiver of the gun. Versions of the Yugoslaviam M72 rifle have also been made in Iraq under the Tabuk name.

Chinese NHM-91

The NHM-91 is a semi-automatic commercial version of the Chinese Typa 56 rifle. It was imported into the U.S. by China Sports Inc. of Ontario, California in 1991, hence the "91" designation in its name. It was configured to comply with the 1989 Executive Order by President George H. W. Bush prohibiting importation of certain "assault rifles" in configurations of military-style semi-automatic rifles, such as the Norinco AKM/AK-47S. Modifications included a one-piece US-made thumbhole stock and a rivet on the receiver preventing the use of standard AK high-capacity magazines. This wasn't the most popular Chinese rifle at that time. However, after all Chinese made AK-type were banned under the 1994 Clinton administration, the NHM-91 became a hot commodity.

Vepr-1V

Recently imported in small numbers by I.O. Inc., the Russian Vepr-1V is the closest thing that anyone will come to getting a true Molot-built Russian RPK rifle. The Vepr-1V is chambered for the popular 5.56X45 mm NATO (.223 Remington) cartridge, but based in the standard Russian military RPK-74SN version. As such, it comes dressed in the RPK-74 dark plum color polyamide furniture, folding stock, and side-mounting rail. A small number of 45-round .223 magazines were also imported for this gun. It looks and feels like no other imported AK-type rifle. The Molot legendary quality transcends down to the last rivet. But the real beauty

The Chinese NHM-91 rifle that has been imported into the U.S. in the 90s is the Chinese take on the squad automatic, like the Soviet RPK.

One of my favorite recent imports is without a doubt is the Vepr-1V from legendary Molot Arsenal.

of this gun cannot be seen, it has to be felt. The Vepr-1V has to be one of the smoothest-shooting .223-caliber guns. It is truly a plinker. Only one other gun can rival the satisfaction from shooting the Vepr, and that is the RPK-74. If you never shot one, do it!

Today all of the above rifles are available on the secondary market. Arsenal sells the Bulgarian version of the Soviet RPK rifle. Several other distributors may have some Romanian and Serbian guns. There is also a chance that the Vepr-1V will be imported again. Nevertheless, the RPK rifles are here and can be found by those who look.

SNIPER RIFLES

We all know that the AK at the time of its inception was not meant to be a highly accurate weapon, so the idea that it could be a sniper rifle was absurd at best. The Soviets designed an entirely new rifle to fill a need for a highly-accurate battlefield sniper rifle and came up with highly-successful Dragunov sniper rifle, the SVD. The Soviets were not eager to share their wealth when it came down to the SVD licensing like they did with the AK rifles, so some of the Soviet Warsaw Pact partners and other AK manufacturing friendlies chose to explore the AK system's true potential, and created a couple

of AK-based sniper rifles. Lucky for the US AK enthusiasts these two rifles have been imported and sold here for some time.

Romanian PSL

The PSL is a Romanian military designated marksman rifle. It had been imported into the US by Century Arms International, Inter Ordnance, and Tennessee Gun Importers at one time or the other. The PSL rifles sold here were also called PSL-54C, Romak III, FPK, SSG-97, and Dragunov. Though similar in appearance, to a point, to the SVD Dragunov, the PSL rifle is actually based on the AK or rather the RPK action.

The PSL rifle's primary purpose is to be used by a platoon-level designated marksman to engage targets at ranges beyond the capabilities of the standard-issue AKM carbines. It is built around a stamped steel receiver similar to that of the RPK light machine gun; having a wider forward section enabling a strengthened, more substantial front trunnion. The PSL's operation is the same long-stroke piston action of the Kalashnikov family of weapons. The PSL is chambered for the same venerable 7.62x54R (rimmed) cartridge as the SVD, and feeds from a ten-round detachable box magazine.

Once the supply of the completely

The PSL is an outstanding rifle. Its scope is based on the famed SVD PSO-1 scope and thus easy to work with.

In good hands with a bit of practice the PSL is avery capable rifle, especially with quality ammo.

When Century imported the M76, the rifle came nicely equipped with a good compliment of original accessories.

Romanian-built rifle dried up, some of the companies started to offer a kit-built PSL rifles with US-made receivers. Examples of the commercial sporting version were also available (on a very limited production run) in the 7.62x51mm NATO (.308 Winchester) cartridge.

7.62x54R.Yugoslavian M76

The Zastava M76 sniper rifle was developed in the mid '70's by the Yugoslavian Crvena Zastava plant (today Zastava Arms), and was adapted for service with the Social Federal Republic of Yugoslavia army. Today, after Yugoslavia's demise the M76 rifles are in use by the armed forces of independent republics created after the split of united Yugoslavia. Apart from the "domestic" use the rifle was also exported.

The M76 sniper rifle is based on the design of the Kalashnikov Automatic Rifle (AK) and utilizes the much more powerful 7.92X57mm or 8mm Mauser rifle cartridge. Unlike the Romanian PSL rifle, the M76 receiver is milled and bolt-locking mechanism and gas system are basically identical to that of the AK. The trigger group is also

"borrowed directly from the Kalashnikov rifle, however the M76 lacks a full automatic capability.

The long, heavy barrel is tipped with cage-type flash suppressor. Standard night and optical sights can be mounted on a regular ComBlock style side rail. Similar to the PSL, the M76 rifle was issued with 4X Soviet PSO-style optical sight and could accept a variety of Warsaw Pact NV scopes. Though an entirely different rifle, one cannot help but compare it to the Soviet SVD Dragunov rifle. To avoid the weapon's balance shift from the movement of the heavy bolt carrier, the Dragunov adopted a short-stroke piston system for the SVD, whereas the 76 is chambered for one the oldest and most powerful cartridges, and yet utilizes the AK gas system.

In short the M76 is an AK with a longer and thicker barrel chambered in a more powerful caliber that ensures the improved accuracy that allows the use of the rifle as a sniper weapon. Century Arms imported these rifles at one time. I don't believe there are any more of them being imported from Serbia at the moment, but they are still

The Finnish Valmet M76 rifle was based on its military ancestor the R62.

The Valmet M76 rifle also came with its unique tubular stock that folded to the left.

available from several distributers and on secondary market.

Both the Romanian PSL and Yugoslavian M76 rifles do not come close to the optimum performance of the rifle they were supposed to copy. But that does not make them any less effective in the right hands. Both of them have seen their fair share of combat and continue to serve in various war zones. Since the Soviet or Russian SVD rifles are not available here and most likely will never be, both of these make a great alternative.

"IMPERIALISTIC" AKS

We are accustomed to the fact that the Soviets handed out licenses to build their AK rifles to their Warsaw Pact allies or friendly Communist or Socialist governments. But the Western and pro-Western countries also saw the advantages of using a reliable AK rifle. Two AK-based rifles were developed outside the scope of the Warsaw Pact, and both rifles were imported into the US at one time or the other.

One was Valmet, developed by the Valmet and Sako companies for the Finnish military, and the other was Israel's Galil rifle. Although there no more Valmet rifles being imported from Finland, they are still around and can be encountered on the secondary market. The Galil guns are still imported today by the IWI.

Valmet

The Finish Valmet or Rk 62 rifle was the standard issue weapon of the Finnish Defense Forces and was developed in 1962 and built by Valmet and Sako. Its design is closely based on the Soviet AK-47 Polish-licensed version design. The Valmet is chambered for standard AK-47 M43 7.62X39 mm cartridge.

Between 1965 and 1994 approximately 350,000 Valmet R62 rifles were produced jointly by Valmet and Sako. One of the most distinctive features of the Valmet rifles is its tubular fixed stock. The other is its open-ended, three prong flash suppressor with a bayonet lug on its lower side. Valmet's flash suppression was designed to cut wire by placing it on the wire and firing a round.

It is general consensus that the Valmet Rk 62 guns are some of the highest-quality AK rifles, designed to withstand the extreme environmental conditions of Nordic Europe.

The civilian version of the rifle is called M62S, and it is nearly identical in appearance to the Rk 62, except for the fire selector which lacks the automatic fire setting.

The RK 62 76, also known as the Valmet M76 is a modernized version of the old Rk 62 model.

The M76 rifle was in production from 1976 to 1986. Its receiver is made from stamped steel instead of the Rk 62's milled. There are eight variants of M76, four of which use 7.62X39 mm M43 ammunition, while the other four use 5.56X45mm NATO rounds. They use 15, 20, or 30-round magazines. Finland used the 7.62mm version, while Qatar and Indonesia use the 5.56mm version. All variants of the M76 are finished with an industrial-grade Parkerizing throughout. The Valmet M76 rifle is the one that we see here in the States. These rifles come with fixed and tubular folding stocks. If one is lucky enough to find one for sale he or she would be expected to pay a much higher price than that of the standard AK.

Galil

The Israeli Galil rifle was designed by Yisrael Galil and Yaacov Lior in the late 1960s and produced by Israel Military Industries Ltd (now Israel Weapon Industries Ltd) of Ramat HaSharon. The rifle design borrows heavily from the AK-47 and has a modified gas diversion system similar to the AK-47 to reduce the recoil of the rifle, making it easier to fire, especially in full-automatic mode. The Galil rifle is chambered in 5.56X45 mm NATO caliber. Several variations of Galil have been made to fire the 7.62X51 mm NATO rifle round. The Galil series of weapons is in use with military and police forces in over 25 countries.

During the Six Day War, the Israelis captured thousands of Egyptian AK-47 rifles and evaluated them. The rifle proved far more reliable and controllable than the standard Israeli Defense Force's issue FAL, and required maintenance was minimal so the conscripted troops would not need additional weapon maintenance training.

Because of this, the IDF began the process of procuring a new automatic rifle that would offer the same benefits of low-maintenance as the AK-47, but with the accuracy of the M16 and FAL. Several weapons were submitted. The US offered the M16A1 and Stoner 63 series, and Germany offered the HK 33.

The AK-47 design was also considered, but difficulty in procuring it made it difficult to adopt. The domestic design was offered by Yisrael Galil. His new rifle was based on the Finnish RK 62 Valmet rifle. It also should be noted that early Israeli-made Galil rifles were made on machinery and by documentation bought from Valmet. While the AK-47 and RK 62 fired the 7.62x39mm, Galili's rifle fired the smaller round. Galil was the standard service-rifle of Israel from the mid-1970's to the early 1990's. The Galil SAR was still kept in use by some rear-line services, including the Knesset Guard and the armored corps until the late 2000s.

A number of commercial civilian versions of Galil rifles have been imported into the US. A modernized and improved variant of it is imported today by IMI. Prices of these rifle are ranging from $1000 to $5000 depending on model, features and options.

HUNTING AND SPORTING AKS

In the early 1990's after the dissolution of the Soviet Union, Russia faced tough times. The economical decline forced most of the defense industry plants to look elsewhere for the customers willing to buy their wares.

Img 598 The Israeli Galil rifle was offered as an alternative to FAL rifles in service with the Israeli Defense Force.

Today IWI brings several variants of the Galil rifle to the US. These outstanding rifles are now widely available.

That included all of Russia's small firearm arsenals. Because of this conversion from strictly military products to the civilian commercial market we have Saiga and Vepr Kalashnikov rifles based on the AK and RPK respectively.

Saiga

The Saiga semi-automatic rifles are a family of Russian semi-automatic rifles manufactured by Kalashnikov Concern (formerly Izhmash), which also manufactures the original AK rifles, Saiga-12 shotguns, and Dragunov sniper rifles. Saiga rifles are a sport version of the AK series rifles, and are marketed for hunting and civilian use. In one form or the other the Saiga rifle have been imported to the US since the early 90's by various importers.

Named after the Saiga Antelope, the Saiga series of rifles is based on the AK weapon system originally designed by Mikhail Kalashnikov. Originally designed in the 1970s, the Saiga was reintroduced in the 1990s and was marketed as a rifle capable of

hunting medium-sized game. Improvements were made to the initial design from the 1970s which made the rifle capable of handling more powerful cartridges such as the .308 Winchester (7.62X51 mm) and the more prevalent .223 Remington (5.56X45 mm), 5.45X39mm, and 7.62X39mm calibers.

The modern Saiga rifles take many components directly from the AK-74 and AK-100 series rifles. It is built on a stamped receiver and it has a 90-degree gas block. The sporting Saiga rifle does not accept a standard AK magazine; physically the magazine catch will not allow a magazine to lock into place inside of the receiver. Even if the AK magazine is inserted the round will not feed because the Saiga's receiver lacks a bullet guide.

All of the Saiga rifles come with a "Monte Carlo" sporting stock and elongated hand guards. The trigger and trigger guard of most of the rifles in the US versions are placed farther back on the receiver than on a typical AK rifle.

Since the expiration of the 1994 Federal

Assault Weapons Ban in 2004, a wider range of semi-automatic rifles have become wildly popular with shooters in the United States. The Saiga rifle is no exception. Often, AK enthusiasts will "restore" a Saiga to the configuration of the modern AK-100 series rifles produced alongside the Saiga rifles at Kalashnikov Concern (formerly Izhmash).

To achieve this, permanent changes must be made to the rifle. The factory fire control assembly must be removed and replaced with a semiautomatic-only trigger group that fits in a standard Kalashnikov rifle.

The aforementioned absence of a bullet guide must also be dealt with. A hole must be drilled and tapped in the front trunnion of the rifle so that the bullet guide may be fastened in the receiver. Material must be removed from the magazine latch to allow a standard Kalashnikov magazine to be used. The factory butt stock is removed and replaced with a piece similar to that found on military-issue rifles. A pistol grip is installed. These are the basic steps needed to make the rifle consistent with most AK's in function.

Converted Saigas are notable for their "pedigree" among Kalashnikov collectors and enthusiasts. Value is given to the weapon based on the fact that it is made from brand-new parts, as opposed to many commercially-available AK pattern rifles, which are commonly built using an American-made receiver completed with surplus or retired parts kits from the rifles of the former Soviet Bloc. As a result, fit and finish on Saigas tends to fall into a higher category than the "de-milled" rifles of Romanian or Polish origin.

Rifles that have undergone more changes to resemble a military-issued weapon are often of a higher value than those that undergo a more simple conversion. These factors all enable converted Saigas to command high prices when sold relative to other Kalashnikov rifles. Such rifles may be sold at two to four times the value of a stock, non-converted factory Saiga.

Saigas are also considered to be "true" Kalashnikovs, since they are made in the same Izhmash Arsenal where the great designer worked.

However popular the Saiga rifles are here in the US, it seems that the further import of these guns has come to an end. Kalashnikov Concern is one of the companies on the list of US-sanctioned Russian entities. In 2014 the

Based on the Russian AK rifle, the sporting semi-automatic Saiga rifle has been imported to the U.S. in significant numbers.

An RPK descendant, the Vepr rifle was another Kalashnikov that made state-side in considerable numbers.

*Molot's ability to produce good quality barrels and the overall quality of
the Vepr rifle makes it easy to convert it to something more "sexy".*

Obama Administration imposed sanctions on several Russian companies and individuals in response to Russia's actions in Crimea.

Vepr

Another hunting/sporting rifle that is based on the Kalashnikov design is Molot Arsenal's Vepr. A series of semi-automatic rifles based on the RPK machine gun, these are manufactured by the Molot Arsenal in Vyatskiye Polyany, Russia. They are offered in several calibers, including: .223 Remington, 7.62X39mm, 5.45X39mm, 7.62X54R, .308 Winchester and recently, 6.5 Grendel. Another recent Vepr entry is a 12-gauge shotgun.

The hallmark of Vepr rifles is their heavy RPK receiver and barrel. The barrel, gas block, and bore are chrome lined throughout. They are intended for the civilian market, and are marketed as high quality hunting rifles. Due to this designation, they lack features seen on most AK type rifles.

Vepr rifles do not include a bayonet lug, integrated cleaning rods or tool kits, cannot accept standard AK magazines, and have wooden thumb-hole stocks. Some buy these rifles to "convert" into a traditional style AK rifle, installing new pistol-grip stocks and adding tactical accessories.

Early generations of the Vepr rifle were manufactured with slant-back receivers, making them incompatible with most AK furniture sets without a converter. The receivers were changed to straight-back in the second generation. Subsequent versions of the rifle reverted to slant-back.

With its inherited lineage from the RPK heavy receiver and barrel, the VEPR is a bit heavier than the standard AK. Even with the equivalent AK furniture, a VEPR weighs over a pound more than the Saiga.

One can easily tell a Vepr apart from other AK based sporting rifles. The front wider and heavier RPK style trunnion is machined rather than hot hammer forged, and the heavy barrel is cold hammer forged and heat treated for eight hours. It's then annealed and chromed under a vacuum, a

AK-based Russian Saiga shotguns have been imported to the U.S. for years in considerable numbers. The Saiga shotguns became very popular with American sportsmen.

The Saiga-12K is perhaps the most widely spread sporting configuration of the shotgun.

process that ensures high quality chrome lining. Each barrel is threaded to the Russian standard, 14x1 left hand. The muzzle nut is screwed on the threads of all sporting Vepr rifle and then welded in place.

The 1000-meter rear sight with windage adjustment is standard on all VEPR rifles. The VEPR has a forged steel bolt with a spring-loaded firing pin and two locking lugs. The VEPR in .308 Win. and 7.62X54R have three locking lugs for even more strength and accuracy. Each VEPR is hand-fitted and factory-tuned. Because of the generally high quality of production and better fitment and finish, Vepr rifle demand a higher price, Much higher than that of Saiga rifles. Currently Veprs are imported in to the US by SSI and several others and can purchased through numerous distributors.

AK SHOTGUNS

Because of the AK system's simplicity there were rifles build in larger calibers using the AK configuration. It was only natural

that this reliable gas-operated system would be employed for developing a shotgun.

It was Izhmash that developed first AK-based shotgun. It was named, like the other hunting Izhmash rifles, the Saiga. Today both main Russian Arsenals, Izhmash and Molot, make their respective Saiga and Vepr shotguns.

Saiga-12

The Saiga-12 is a 12-gauge shotgun based on the proven AK design and available in a wide range of configurations. Like the AK rifle, it is a rotating bolt, gas-operated gun that feeds from a box magazine. All Saiga-12 configurations are recognizable as Kalashnikov-pattern guns by the large lever-safety on the right side of the receiver, the optic mounting rail on the left side of the receiver and the large top-mounted dust cover held in place by the rear of the recoil spring assembly.

Izhmash also manufactures Saiga-20 and Saiga-410 in 20 gauge and .410 caliber.

The most desirable Saiga-12-030 that has a "tactical" undertone would have made it big if the import from Concern Kalashnikov would be allowed to continue.

Russia's Molot Arsenal's entry, the Vepr-12 shotgun has been configured in "tactical" guise from the factory.

The Saiga-12 incorporates an adjustable two-position gas system to be able to shoot different loads.

The Saiga shotguns have become immensely popular here in the States and were imported in great numbers. Prior to importation to the US, all Saiga shotguns are configured with a traditional fixed "hunting-style" rifle stock and 5-round magazine. Often gunsmiths would convert these hunting shotguns into more military configuration provided that federal and state laws permit.

The most recent addition to the Izhmash AK-based shotgun line was the Saiga 12K 030. This particular gun was a departure from traditional hunter-configured Saigas. This one was more "tactical". It features an extended magazine well, last round bolt hold open, hinged dust cover with Picatinny rail for mounting optics, Picatinny rail gas block, and a newly designed 8-round magazine.

A limited number of these shotguns made it here before the US sanctions were imposed on Kalashnikov Concern. Before that, when the supply of Saiga shotguns was a constant stream, one could pick up a regular sporting Saiga for well under $1000. Naturally, the tactical Saiga-12K 030 demanded a higher price. But this is in the past now and it expect prices for Saiga shotguns to rise dramatically.

Vepr-12

Like the Saiga-12 the Vepr-12 is a multi-purpose shotgun created and built by Molot-Oruzhie Ltd, and like Saiga-12, it is patterned after the original AK rifle.

However, since the Molot Arsenal is a builder of RPK machine guns, it was only natural that the new shotgun be built on the heavy RPK receiver.

From the get-go the Vepr-12 was built in a "military" or "tactical" configuration and resembled the Saiga-12K 030. That wasn't an accident. The Izhmash arsenal was or-

dered by the Russian government to "share" their new Saiga drawings and production data with Molot as a form of support for the floundering plant.

In the true spirit of friendly competition, not all drawings were shared and Molot was left to its own devices to finish the development of the shotgun. Though there are many similarities between the Saiga and Vepr shotguns, there are many differences that make Vepr slightly superior to the Saiga.

Like the Saiga, the Vepr-12 was designed to be a versatile weapons platform, capable of being used by hunters and professional shooters alike. With these considerations in mind, Molot introduced unique features, such as the ambidextrous safety selector and the bolt hold-open mechanism. A side folding stock is present on most models, however Vepr-12 shotguns are offered with fixed stocks as well.

Instead of the standard AK safety selector, the Vepr-12 has an ambidextrous safety that can be manipulated from either side of the rifle. The addition of a magwell, another unusual feature for an AK-type rifle, allows for "straight in" magazine insertion, as opposed to the "rock and lock" found on standard AK rifles.

The Vepr-12 is also chrome lined throughout, including the gas block, barrel, and chamber, affording the gun excellent corrosion resistance. Unlike the Saiga-12, the gas system on the Vepr-12 is self regulating, allowing it to shoot any commercially available 12-gauge load without risking damage to the gun.

The Vepr-12 lacks the normal AK side-mounting rail, instead using a Picatinny rail mounted to the dust cover for optic mounting. The dust cover is hinged, allowing the shooter to open and close the cover, without losing the zero of a mounted optic.

The Vepr-12 shotgun is imported into the United States by SSI and several other importers. The pricing of the Vepr-12, however, is subject to dramatic rises and falls. It has settled to around $1300. Having one of these myself, it is money well spent.

Chinese Catamount Fury

Nobody will outdo the Chinese. They wouldn't just stand aside and let others have all the glory. The new Chinese Catamount Fury AK-pattern semi-auto 12-gauge shotgun is now here. This shotgun is built on an AK-style receiver and uses AK-type gas operating system. The idea of a Chinese-built AK gun in the United States is an absurdity. After all, the importation of Chinese arms has been prohibited since 1993. However, they are still allowed to export sporting shotguns.

Century Arms currently offers two different models of the Catamount, the Fury and the Fury II. The Fury II is slanted more for 3-Gun type competition, with an AR style magazine well and SVD type stock. The standard Fury is configured with a sporting type butt and conventional magazine well. It is fitted with a 20" barrel chambered for 3"

magnums. The muzzle is threaded for choke tubes, but comes with only one in cylinder bore. The gas block is approximately 1.2" further forward than on a Russian Saiga. It features two gas settings and has a 2.3" modified Picatinny rail mounted at the bottom.

Unlike the Saiga, the Catamount Fury sports an upper hand guard similar to a standard AK. The gun's furniture is made from a black polymer. The butt features a rubber recoil pad ¾" thick and has a 14" length of pull.

Regarding the design itself, it is not simply an exact copy of the Saiga-12, although it is clearly where Chinese designers drew their inspiration. One cannot miss the obvious similarities. However, it is not an exact copy, and the Chinese designers did add some improvements of their own. The best feature of the Catamount Fury shotgun is that it is here and available at a much lower price that its Saiga or Vepr adversaries. It also continues to be imported by Century Arms in good numbers and distributed far and wide.

The only AK allowed to be imported from China is the AK-based Catamount Fury shotgun.

The catamount Fury shotgun may look much like the Russian Saiga-12, but there are many differences, cosmetic and functional.

AFTERWORD

When I embarked on the journey to write this book, my intent was not to rewrite yet another AK history book. God knows that the history of this infamous rifle has been written by many authors far better than myself. I wanted to write something that any Kalashnikov's rifle enthusiast, whether novice or a seasoned AK "veteran," would keep on his or her table as a reference. Not a precise reference, but a practical guide perhaps. I intended for this book to be helpful to all AK shooters no matter the experience level.

Often, when I am asked what type of rifle I prefer, I reply that a rifle is a tool, a tool for a specific job. As such, the tool has to be mastered. It does not matter if you use a Black & Decker or a Makita drill or saw. In the end, the right size holes have to drilled in the right places and cuts have to be made to correct measurements. The same goes for guns. They are just tools and have to be learned, practiced and mastered. So keep shooting, keep mastering the tools. And remember: The difference between a good and bad shot is the number of trigger pulls.